From

Th
124 Shore

CW00435609

steaming ahead

Léonie Caldecott and Stephanie Leland   Photo by Paula Allen

Léonie Caldecott is a freelance journalist and writer living in London.
Over the last few years her search for signs of hope in these dangerous
times has led her to become active in, as well as write about (though
the two are not *always* distinguishable!) broadly eco-feminist issues,
especially peace, the impact of technology on society, the cultural and
spiritual relevance of the women's movement. She has contributed to
several collections of writing, including *Keeping the Peace* (Women's
Press, 1983) and *Walking on the Water* (Virago, 1983).

Stephanie Leland is a committed feminist and envrionmentalist. She
is a founding member and national co-ordinator of Women for Life
on Earth as well as an active campaigner in the Green movement.
When she's not in vigil at her desk, her favourite pastimes include:
wine, women, children, playing the piano, and walking by the sea.

LÉONIE CALDECOTT
AND STEPHANIE LELAND
Editors

Reclaim the Earth
Women speak out for Life on Earth

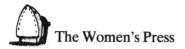 The Women's Press

First published by The Women's Press Limited 1983
A member of the Namara Group
124 Shoreditch High Street, London E1 6JE

Introduction and collection © copyright 1983 by
Léonie Caldecott and Stephanie Leland

The copyright in each of the articles and poems in this volume remains with
the original copyright holder. No part of any work in this collection may be
reproduced without permission first being obtained of the author in care of
the editors.

British Library Cataloguing in Publication Data

Reclaim the earth.
    1. Women—Social conditions
    I. Caldecott, Léonie   II. Leland, Stephanie
    301   HQ1154

    ISBN 0-7043-3908-0

Typeset by MC Typeset, Chatham, Kent
Printed by Nene Litho, Wellingborough, Northants
Bound by Woolnough Bookbinding, Wellingborough, Northants

Acknowledgements

If we were to thank, individually, all those whose help made this book possible, the list would take up a large proportion of the book itself. How do you thank a seemingly infinite network whose ideas, energy and vision fed into our work? Nonetheless, we should like to offer special thanks to Stephanie Dowrick and Ros de Lanerolle of the Women's Press, the former for her initial and continuing encouragement, and the latter for her patient guidance through the fraught process of putting the book together, as well as Christine Reason for her painstaking copy editing. Any flaws that remain are entirely our own responsibility. But most of all, we should like to thank the women who contributed material for the book, in many cases giving up a considerable amount of time and energy to do so. We should also like to thank those women whose work we were not able to include due to lack of space; it is to be hoped that this book will spawn others like it, since there is no shortage of ideas and writing from women engaged in the task of reclaiming this earth.

Finally, Stephanie would like to thank Chloe and Abigail, and Léonie would like to thank Strat, Moyra, Olly, Rachel and Serena, for surviving the experience of living with us – and continuing to love and support us – while we were putting the book together.

Grateful acknowledgement is made for permission to reprint the following:

'The Long Death', copyright Marge Piercy, from *Circles on the Water*, Selected Poems, Knopf, New York, 1982;

'Another Country', copyright Marge Piercy, from *The Moon is Always Female*, Knopf, New York, 1980;

'Greening the Desert', reprinted from *Earthwatch* no. 12, 1982, courtesy of the International Planned Parenthood Federation, 18–20 Lower Regent Street, London SW1Y 4PW,

'The Mothers do not Disappear', reprinted from the *Guardian*, 20 August 1982;

Contents

Foreword

Susan Griffin

When the rush of living stops, I confess to myself that a great change is coming. What the nature of this change will be I do not know. It is not a change that comes from the 'inevitability of history'. I do not believe that history is inevitable. Human beings make history through an infinite variety of choices. But this change reminds us of human limitation: we are flesh and blood and of this earth.

Enough bombs to destroy every American and Soviet city several times over. The shrinking of arable land and a widening circle of poverty. Our finite supply of fossil fuel, air, water diminishing. An epidemic of cancer from environmental pollution. But in the same quiet moment in which I consider these disasters, I feel another change too. The ground shifts and my old idea of economy or warfare, agriculture or technology is not the same. I see differently. I begin to look at this earth as my home, and myself as a part of everything here.

This book is a document of change. It is a cry of protest against the devastation of the earth. It gives evidence of a social movement whose size and depth we have only begun to imagine. It records a transformation in consciousness. And that this book has been edited and written by women is not irrelevant to this transformation. For women have long been associated with nature. And if this association has been the rationalisation of our oppression by a society which fears both woman and nature, it has also meant that those of us born female are often less severely alienated from nature than are most men.

What is this transformation? There is no single idea nor even event through which one can understand it. Like the earth itself, or the biosphere, or the spiralling strands of DNA which seem like a metaphor for a new way of thinking, this change does not move in a straight line but radiates out in widening circles, until many quite disparate thoughts and acts are connected.

As she stood on the deck of a sailing ship and watched the

1

uninhabited coastland of Denmark move past her, Mary Wollstonecraft had a clairvoyant vision of our future. She could see a time, she said, when all wilderness would be cultivated, and hence, famine would be universal and the world become 'a vast prison'. That, near the end of the eighteenth century, this great feminist theorist should have such a disturbingly accurate view of the future is no longer surprising to many of us. For now a large social movement exists which connects the devastation of the earth with the exploitation of women.

So many aspects of a woman's struggle for liberation lead her mind to the question of our survival as human beings on this planet. When a woman, for example, demands the right to seek an abortion, she begins to assert that she has a right to control her own body. She begins to question the doctors who treat her, and to examine the common medical practices to which her body is subjected. She discovers that birth control pills have caused blood clots, that oestrogen causes cancer, that DES, prescribed for infertility, has caused infertility and cancer in the next generation. She becomes critical of the medical establishment and discovers that this establishment harbours a distrust not only of the female body, but of the human body itself. And this finally leads her to the perception that not only Western medicine but Western science has as a fundamental bias a dangerous alienation from nature.

But there are so many starting points. A woman may, for another example, assert the right to be an artist. And when she begins to paint she may paint in a new way, as did Paula Modersohn Becker at the beginning of the twentieth century. Modersohn Becker was one of the first painters in the style we now know as German expressionism.

This manner of working depicts the inner feelings of the subject, and this emphasis is a radical departure from the old school which painted outward appearance. But because she was a woman, I believe, her paintings constitute an even more radical departure. For she chose as her subjects peasants, children and women and her own face and body. And when she looked on these subjects she painted their inner life, so that looking at her work one feels as a woman, a mother, a child, a peasant does. Perhaps the implication of this is not immediately clear, and yet it is as radical as a woman's demand to the right to abortion. For the old way of thinking, which exploits woman and nature, holds that woman and the natural world do not have souls and hence do not possess an inner life. But when women begin to paint and write we make this inner life visible.

And immediately another example comes to me. I think of the

2

philosopher Suzanne Langer and of her speculations about the nature of the human mind. Thought, she wrote in the middle of the twentieth century, cannot be separated from material. The human mind is physical. And even the language we use for thought is based on sensual perception. But what does such a perception do to the old notion that mind and body are separate? Or that matter is inert and without spirit? Or that spiritual man should dominate material woman, and culture should dominate nature? There are many starting points but all of them lead eventually to a fundamental change in consciousness.

Last year at dawn, in Berkeley, California, a group of men and women gathered to give their blessings to a woman's caravan which set out across the United States to protest against nuclear armaments. The artist, Helaine Aylon, working with the Women's Party for Survival, designed this event so that it could best express the feelings of the women she knew. We were invited to bring pillow cases and to write on these pillow cases what we wanted to say about war. She meant to say with these pillow cases, *we do not rest easy any more*. On my pillow case, I wrote, The Generations. And I thought of the pillow cases embroidered by my Great Aunt, and my Grandmother's mother, handed down so carefully from one child to another. This caravan went to Sac bases throughout the country, and there the women collected contaminated earth which they delivered by ambulance and by stretcher to the United Nations building in New York City.

And behind this is another story. As we stood outside the Lawrence Radiation Laboratory we learned that the widow of the Dr Lawrence after whom this laboratory was named, had requested that her husband's name be removed from this institution. He was a pacifist and would not have approved of the work they do there now, she said.

Then, last week, a woman from Maine, a poet, and a teacher, tells me that for her every moment she is laced with a concern for the survival of this planet. This is what she wants to capture in her poetry. Yes, I tell her. I too have the same preoccupation. And many of my students also.

You will not find these stories in this book. I tell them here only to let you know that a multitude of stories and moments from people's lives exist which are not in these pages. For the work you read here must be read as representative of a much larger movement of thought and action. And thus this book has a double life: the essays here are significant and vital in themselves, and they are also symbolic of a

3

significant and vital change in the world today.

If there is one idea that can be said to link together all that is said and reported here, this idea is also a feeling. It is a grief over the fate of the earth, that contains within it a joyful hope that we might reclaim this earth. Does this one idea answer all our questions? It is not meant to. It is meant to make us ask more questions. And it is not necessary that we agree on every point, for what we have in common is not small.

Berkeley, 1983

Introduction

Léonie Caldecott and Stephanie Leland

In many countries all over the world, women are taking an increasingly prominent role in political struggles: in the peace, anti-nuclear, health and ecology movements. Our traditional roles as mothers, nurses and guardians of home and community have placed us at the receiving end of an increasingly sophisticated technology, the implications of which have become alarming in the threat they pose to health and life on this planet. The time has come for women to take a leading role in rectifying the balance.

For a growing number of us, the women's movement has brought about a gradual release from the constraints of these traditional women's roles, thus enabling us to reclaim invaluable time and energy. This is a slow process, and by no means a universal one as yet. However, *within* this process, we are gaining a sense of our strength and worth as individuals and, in a collective sense, as women.

People are apt to talk of the women's liberation movement as though it were something new. Opponents of feminism all too often point to the seemingly destructive phenomena arising out of our efforts to liberate ourselves from the stranglehold of a society which constantly curtails our every gesture. It can be hard to tolerate anger in others, especially when that anger erupts with all the force of having been long repressed and bitten back. We for our part feel that the women's movement is not new, nor do we see it as having rigid ideological boundaries, with some women inside and some women outside. Whether we call ourselves socialist feminists, radical feminists, lesbian feminists, women for peace, workers, sisters or mothers, we have one thing in common: our debt to those who came before us and who struggled to make us both visible and audible in cultures which buried us under a mountain of male indifference.

All women, we have come to see, are connected both through history (aptly renamed herstory by many feminist writers) and through cultural differences. Our heritage is a long and rich one. Yet until recently it has been undervalued, and in many instances

5

blatantly suppressed. Woman as healer, wise counsellor, creator and innovator, respected in her community – all these images are being reclaimed as we grow in confidence and power.

The truth of the matter is that, even when we have very few resources at our disposal, women are often motivated to take practical action on behalf of the things we care about. For the two of us editing this book, each from a different background – one originally from the United States, a mother, living in the country, and the other from Britain, without children, living in the city – it was a common concern for life on earth, and a growing admiration for what women are doing towards creating an atmosphere in which this life can flourish, that prompted a pooling of our own scarce resources to create this book.

When we speak about life, we have in mind life in the fullest sense. It is neither the hand-to-mouth existence of the perpetually hungry and homeless, nor the nine-to-five grind towards a superficial material security. The growing Women for Life on Earth network through which the two of us have been working over the past few years springs, at least in part, from a recognition that human life and human culture are only a very small part of a larger ecosystem, stretching into realms that, even now, it is hard to imagine or understand.

It was the meltdown at Three-Mile Island that first prompted women in the United States to come together en masse to explore the connections between feminism, ecology and militarism and to share their visions for life on earth. This weekend meeting, on the 21 March 1980, attended by six hundred women, was called: 'Women and Life on Earth: A Conference on Eco-Feminism in the Eighties'. Ynestra King, an inspirational force behind the planning of the conference, expressed the spirit and politics of the gathering within her opening statement: 'We're here to say the word ECOLOGY and announce that for us as feminists it's a political word – that it stands against the economics of the destroyers and the pathology of racist hatred. It's a way of being, which understands that there are connections between all living things and that indeed we women are the fact and flesh of connectedness.'

This initial conference inspired the development of a broad eco-feminist network of women's groups and individuals in the northeast of America, as well as many women's actions and activities, among them the now historic Women's Pentagon Actions in November 1980 and 1981. A similar network began here in the UK in September 1980, first under the name Women and Life on Earth, and now

6

known as Women *for* Life on Earth, which was instrumental in organising the 12 December Action at Greenham Common in 1982.

We are in the process of creating a new vision for society. As Ynestra King says in this book: 'We see the devastation of the earth and her beings by the corporate warriors and the threat of nuclear annihilation by the military warriors as feminist concerns.' The life we envisage encompasses a different quality altogether from the one we are experiencing during this current climate of conflict and disruption. We envisage a life in harmony with the life on the planet as a whole, with the larger environment in which we find ourselves. As the Sicilian women in this book point out, the question of the *quality* of life is one which unifies many women who have struggled for a wide range of different goals down the years. Control over our own bodies, the right to choose our own sexual expression, health care which takes the whole person into account, technology on a human scale which works with, rather than against, the forces of nature are some of these goals. Others include the right of individuals to have a say in the decisions that affect them, coupled with respect for non-human life-forms, the growing attempts to find nonviolent ways of resolving conflict, and to educate ourselves and our children without suppressing individual identities. All these goals and more are part of a vision which women are articulating with increasing feeling and determination.

Nothing could be more timely. As the patriarchal structure threatens to destroy itself and life on earth with it, many of us have begun to apply our analysis and perspective as feminists not only towards issues which specifically concern women as a sex, but also towards the ills of the world as a whole. Rather than seeing the liberation of women in isolation, we conceive of our struggle in the larger context of human liberation and, furthermore, in the context of liberating the earth and all life upon it from the suffocating, annihilating grip of patriarchy.

This is obviously not a straightforward and easily accomplished task, but rather a challenge which requires the greatest number of resources that can be mustered. This means women with very different skills and perspectives working side by side in a lateral and flexible manner. What has been most inspiring for us in gathering these women together between the pages of one book is the diversity of approach they bring with them. To us it is a further illustration of our strength as women, a strength which comes from our growing ability to communicate with one another even across fairly deep-rooted differences of experience and opinion. It is very exciting to live

7

at a time when the various strands of the women's movement, and also the Green Movement, are beginning to be woven into one multi-coloured tapestry.

The very diversity of the contributions to *Reclaim the Earth* shows that this tapestry is not one in which we all subside into a uniform vision. Instead, women are expanding and evolving in a multiplicity of directions – a process which both takes us further than we have been before and connects us once more with each other. It is tempting to talk of a 'new wave' in feminism, in which the movement expands its base and expands its appeal to a wider constituency of women – and eventually men – who would not previously have associated themselves with its aims. But it is as well to remember that the new is only effective if it finds its roots in the old; each successive wave is only made possible by the waves that preceded it, creating the impetus on which we now ride.

In this context the usual disclaimer, that we as editors do not necessarily agree with every single view expressed by individual contributors, becomes a positive expression of the spirit that informs this book. Our concern has been to make connections that are not always made, to facilitate communication amongst women whose experience and concerns may differ considerably from that of other women with other backgrounds. We hope that by placing such different perspectives and approaches side by side we can make a first though by no means comprehensive step in this direction.

Whatever the differences between us, one thing is certain: we have gained, and continue to gain, an enormous sense of strength through working together in our struggle as women. Many of us are employing that strength in the world at large, creating conditions which ensure that we continue to be strong. We have discovered that there is another positive and meaningful definition to the word 'power'. Whereas in patriarchal terms it is concerned with domination and the exercise of control, many of us have experienced the sense of power we have as women through the regeneration of shared energy, the understanding that we are not alone, and the belief that together we have the power to act – to effect change. The perpetuation of patriarchy depends on a pervading sense of powerlessness. We hope that this collection of writings will serve to counteract that negative feeling of powerlessness. It is intended to reflect the positive process of change as initiated by women, encouraging and stimulating us to believe in our power to resist and create, and to act on our visions. This is the belief which empowers us when we say to one another: sisters, rise up, and reclaim the earth.

8

1

The Eco-feminist Imperative

Ynestra King

In March 1980, six hundred women met in Amherst, Massachussetts, USA, to explore the connections between militarism, feminism, healing and ecology. They called this conference Women and Life on Earth. There followed the development of a broad network of women's groups and individuals, out of which grew the Women's Pentagon Actions in November 1980 and 1981. In the following article, written in May 1981, Ynestra King, one of the founders of the movement, assesses the growth of eco-feminism in the USA.

In the one year since the Conference on Women and Life on Earth our movement has burgeoned. The Conference grew out of hope and fear – out of a fear for life and the awesome powers of destruction arrayed against it and out of a hope – a hope for women's power to resist and create. We came together following the meltdown at Three Mile Island. We talked of our sisters we knew by name and reputation through the mythology of our own movement and of what together we might be, and we decided to call sisters to a conference on Women and Life on Earth.

We are both a beginning and a continuation. We are a beginning for this decade but we continue the work of the many brave and visionary women who have gone before us. There was Ellen Swallow, the founder of ecological science. There was Rachel Carson, who wrote *Silent Spring* twenty years ago sounding a warning about chemicals and pesticides which was not heeded until many years later. There were the women of the Women's Strike for Peace and the Ban the Bomb movements of the fifties, mailing their babies' teeth to Congressmen as a reminder of future generations. And there are the brave women scientists who have spoken out more recently, and the women who have been at the forefront of anti-nuclear struggles, peace movements, struggles against toxic wastes and for occupational health and safety. There are those who have helped us to imagine the world as it could be: artists, poets, writers and dreamers who have given us new visions of culture, health, technology, community and politics. And there are our sisters the world over, with us in the creation of a planetary movement. We are shaking the world.

Over ten years ago this wave of the feminist movement began. We said then that 'the personal is political', that the denial of our selfhood was systemic and political, that masculine society even had a name: 'patriarchy'.

Many more women now see their oppression as political, not individual. Over the past ten years women have begun to rediscover our history, and to name and work to end violence against women in all its forms, demand equal rights, the right of every woman to decide when and if to bear children, and to express her sexuality freely.

But as we have gained in consciousness and numbers the devastation of the planet has accelerated. Every day brings new disasters, some irrevocable. The story of Love Canal where a school and homes were built on a hazardous waste site is a warning of things to come. Three to six nuclear bombs are produced each day. The Pentagon nuclear arsenal now numbers over 30,000 warheads and it is growing. There are thousands of toxic waste dumps around the country that will not be discovered until observant women notice a common birth defect or sickness in their neighbourhood. The coastlines are deteriorating, and the Amazon forest, the source of much of the earth's oxygen, is being rapidly defoliated. Each day a whole species of life becomes extinct, never to be seen again on this earth.

Eco-feminism is about connectedness and wholeness of theory and practice. It asserts the special strength and integrity of every living thing. For us, the snail darter is to be considered side by side with a community's need for water, the porpoise side by side with appetite for tuna, and the creatures it might fall on, over Skylab. We are a woman-identified movement, and we believe that we have special work to do in these imperilled times. We see the devastation of the earth and her beings by the corporate warriors, and the threat of nuclear annihilation by the military warriors, as feminist concerns. It is the same masculinist mentality which would deny us our right to our own bodies and our own sexuality, and which depends on multiple systems of dominance and state power to have its way.

At the same time as *we* have been making the connections between feminism, ecology, and militarism, *the New Right has been making those very same connections*. They are actively opposing women's reproductive freedom, attacking lesbians and gay men, undermining

10

battered women's shelters and efforts to introduce anti-sexist and anti-racist curricula in schools. The Family Protection Act, now being introduced in Congress piecemeal, is explicit about its intention to shore up patriarchal authority in every aspect of our lives. They want to be sure that strong, angry women do not stand in their way, as the carnivorous appetite of the military gobbles up food stamps, Aid for Dependent Children, medicaid, schools, legal aid and more. We are beginning to have an understanding for ourselves about how these concerns are intertwined and to act on them as we develop an imaginative, transformative women's movement.

Why women? Because our present patriarchy enshrines together the hatred of women and the hatred of nature. In defying this patriarchy we are loyal to future generations and to life and this planet itself. We have a deep and particular understanding of this both through our natures and through our life experience as women.

We have the wisdom to oppose experiments which could permanently alter the genetic materials of future generations. As feminists we believe that human reproduction should be controlled by women not by a male-dominated medical establishment. We insist on the absolute right of a woman to an abortion. We support the life-affirming right of women to choose when and if to bear children.

We oppose war and we recognise its terrible force when we see it, undeclared but all around us. For to us war is the violence against women in *all* its forms – rape, battering, economic exploitation and intimidation – and it is the racist violence against indigenous peoples here in the US and around the world, and it is the violence against the earth.

We recognise and respect the beauty of cultural diversity as we abhor racism. Racism divides us from our sisters, it lines the pockets of the exploiters and underlies the decimation of whole peoples and their homelands. The imperialism of white, male, western culture has been more destructive to other peoples and cultures than any imperialist power in the history of the world, just as it has brought us to the brink of ecological catastrophe.

We believe that a culture against nature is a culture against women. We know we must get out from under the feet of men as they go about their projects of violence. In pursuing these projects men deny and dominate both women and nature. It is time to reconstitute our culture in the name of that nature, and of peace and freedom, and it is women who can show the way. We have to be the voice of the invisible, of nature who cannot speak for herself in the political arenas of our society, of the children yet to be born and of the women

11

who are forcibly silenced in our mental institutions and prisons. We have been the keepers of the home, the children and the community. We learn early to observe, attend and nurture. And whether or not we become biological mothers, we use these nurturant powers daily as we go about our ordinary work. No one pays us to do this. If the children are born deformed or go hungry, if the people in homes built on a dumping site or near a nuclear weapons factory have terrible sicknesses, we are the ones who care for them, take them to the doctor, console survivors and soothe the terrified. And it is women who have begun to confront government agencies, politicians and corporations. As the deadly sludge of our political system encroaches on every aspect of our most intimate lives, all of us know that life cannot go on this way. The political and the personal are joined: the activities of women as feminists and anti-militarists, and the activities of women struggling in our neighbourhoods and communities for survival and dignity are the same struggle.

And with the same attentiveness we give consideration to the kinds of jobs people do. Many people in this society are compelled to accept jobs which contribute to the destruction of life. In the workplace women particularly are saddled with menial tasks and meaningless work. We oppose such 'jobs' and propose instead that work must involve free self expression and an execution which is playful, not drudgerous. Demands for full employment which ignore the ecological and social devastation daily wrought in the process of ordinary work are dangerously shortsighted. This technological society offers finally the possibility of a materially abundant society with meaningful work for everyone. It is this potential we must claim for ourselves – that these capacities be used for our needs and desires in an appropriately scaled, ecologically aware manner. To create such a web of life is a precondition for freedom. The creation of work that is not merely a job, or worse yet, a perpetuation of the kind of machines which daily destroy both the biosphere and the worker must be a feminist priority. To this end we propose that women begin to use the powers of imagination and creativity we possess as builders, engineers, scientist-alchemists and artists to develop the ways of livelihood and life which fulfil this promise.

In all our workings, we believe in the philosophy of nonviolence – that no person should be made into an 'other' to despise, dehumanise and exploit. As women we have been an 'other' but we are refusing to be the 'other' any longer and we will not make anyone else into an 'other'. Sexism, racism, class divisions, homophobia and the rape of nature depend on this process of objectification. Men's fear of female sexuality has led them to pile up institutions which limit women's options. These keep us obligated to man and unaware of alternatives to traditional women's roles and compulsory heterosexuality. It is in the interest of all women to support lesbian women. We oppose anything which prevents women from loving each other freely in whatever way we choose.

We are building a feminist resistance movement in the tradition of the militant suffragists of the last wave of feminism, from whom Gandhi and Martin Luther King drew their inspiration. We believe in and practise direct action. By direct action we do not mean activity which is necessarily either legal or illegal, but intentional activity which does not even recognise these governmental sanctions. We mean the creation of a tradition which demands that we act directly in all matters which concern us, that we do not recognise a higher authority whom we call upon to act for us. If we believe a parking lot should be a garden we might just dig it up and plant a garden. If we believe that there should be vigils of community women against militarism and violence . . . we go out and vigil. If we believe that there should be women's speakouts against violence in every community we will speak. If we believe that women should be safe walking the streets at night we will take back the night.

As eco-feminists the locus of our work is with women in our own communities, in small groups based on personal affinity, shared concerns and a sense of connectedness to our own landscape. But we are joining together regionally, nationally and internationally to confront systems of dominance that go beyond our communities and neighbourhoods. Women all over the world are engaging in imaginative direct action to stop the war machine, and to assert our right to our own bodies and our own sexuality and to a poison-free, fruitful earth. Our feminist embrace must come to enfold all these women struggling in our respective communities.

We are the repository of a sensibility which can make a future possible. Feminists must exemplify this in our ideas, our relationships to each other, our culture, politics and actions. It is by necessity that we are feminist utopians. We look backwards to woman-centered societies based on respect for life and life cycles. We look forward to new possibilities of reconstituting a culture which is non-hierarchical, which has not only the primitive respect for life and sense of interconnectedness but also those modern technologies which further peace and liberation. Peace is more than the absence of war, as freedom is more than the absence of coercion. They mean more than putting down the gun, taking off the shackles, or even just hearing and remembering. They are both ongoing processes which must be constantly attended to, criticised and expanded upon. Our movement is a process without end, much as life itself is a process without end.

The Conference on Women and Life on Earth and the Women's Pentagon Action where we mourned, raged, empowered ourselves and defied the chief architects of masculinist violence were only a beginning. They were only a beginning because more and more women are discovering that the therapy that *works* to heal self-hate and hopelessness lies in imaginative action and true sisterhood.

2

Unity Statement of the Women's Pentagon Action, USA

The Women's Pentagon Actions mentioned in Ynestra King's article were initiated by the Women and Life on Earth Conference on ecology and feminism which took place in Amherst, March 1980. They were organised by an ad-hoc group of feminist activists from many social movements and organisations in the north-eastern United States, and were the largest all-woman protests in the US in twelve years. In November 1980 and 1981, women surrounded the Pentagon for two days of nonviolent direct action against all military violence and against the sexual and economic violence in the everyday lives of all women. A Statement of Unity adopted by the original organisers of the action expresses the diverse concerns and politics of the eco-feminist movement, and has become a classic of its time as it continues to be distributed and used amongst women as an educational and political tool.

We are gathering at the Pentagon on November 16 because we fear for our lives. We fear for the life of this planet, our Earth, and the life of the children who are our human future.

We are mostly women who come from the north-eastern region of our United States. We are city women who know the wreckage and fear of city streets, we are country women who grieve the loss of the small farm and have lived on the poisoned earth. We are young and older, we are married, single, lesbian. We live in different kinds of households: in groups, families, alone, some are single parents.

We work at a variety of jobs. We are students, teachers, factory workers, office workers, lawyers, farmers, doctors, builders, waitresses, weavers, poets, engineers, homeworkers, electricians, artists, blacksmiths. We are all daughters and sisters.

We have come here to mourn and rage and defy the Pentagon because it is the workplace of the imperial power which threatens us all. Every day while we work, study, love, the colonels and generals who are planning our annihilation walk calmly in and out the doors of its five sides. They have accumulated over 30,000 nuclear bombs at the rate of three to six bombs every day.

They are determined to produce the billion-dollar MX missile. They are creating a technology called Stealth – the invisible, unperceivable arsenal. They have revised the cruel old killer, nerve gas. They have proclaimed Directive 59 which asks for 'small nuclear wars, prolonged but limited'. The Soviet Union works hard to keep up with United States initiatives. We can destroy each other's cities, towns, schools and children many times over. The United States has sent 'advisors', money and arms to El Salvador and Guatemala to enable those juntas to massacre their own people.

The very same men, the same legislative committees that offer trillions of dollars to the Pentagon have brutally cut day care, children's lunches, battered women's shelters. The same men have concocted the Family Protection Act which will mandate the strictly patriarchal family and thrust federal authority into our home life. They are preventing the passage of ERA's simple statement and supporting the Human Life Amendment which will deprive all women of choice and many women of life itself.

We are in the hands of men whose power and wealth have separated them from the reality of daily life and from the imagination. We are right to be afraid.

At the same time our cities are in ruins, bankrupt; they suffer the devastation of war. Hospitals are closed, our schools deprived of books and teachers. Our Black and Latino youth are without decent work. They will be forced, drafted to become the cannon fodder for the very power that oppresses them. Whatever help the poor receive is cut or withdrawn to feed the Pentagon which needs about $500,000,000 a day for its murderous health. It extracted $157 billion dollars last year from our own tax money, $1,800 from a family of four.

With this wealth our scientists are corrupted; over 40% work in government and corporate laboratories that refine the methods for destroying or deforming life. The lands of the Native American people have been turned to radioactive rubble in order to enlarge the nuclear warehouse. The uranium of South Africa, necessary to the nuclear enterprise, enriches the white minority and encourages the vicious system of racist oppression and war.

The President has just decided to produce the neutron bomb, which kills people but leaves property (buildings like this one) intact. There is fear among the people, and that fear, created by the

16

industrial militarists is used as an excuse to accelerate the arms race. 'We will protect you. . .' they say, but we have never been so endangered, so close to the end of human time.

We women are gathering because life on the precipice is intolerable. We want to know what anger in these men, what fear, which can only be satisfied by destruction, what coldness of heart and ambition drives their days. We want to know because we do not want that dominance which is exploitative and murderous in international relations, and so dangerous to women and children at home – we do not want that sickness transferred by the violent society through the fathers to the sons.

What is it that we women need for our ordinary lives, that we want for ourselves and also for our sisters in new nations and old colonies who suffer the white man's exploitation and too often the oppression of their own countrymen?

We want enough good food, decent housing, communities with clear air and water, good care for our children while we work. We want work that is useful to a sensible society. There is a modest technology to minimise drudgery and restore joy to labour. We are determined to use skills and knowledge from which we have been excluded – like plumbing or engineering or physics or composing. We intend to form women's groups or unions that will demand safe workplaces, free of sexual harassment, equal pay for work of comparable value. We respect the work women have done in caring for the young, their own and others, in maintaining a physical and spiritual shelter against the greedy and militaristic society. In our old age we expect our experience, our skills, to be honoured and used.

We want health care which respects and understands our bodies. Physically challenged sisters must have access to gatherings, actions, happy events, work. For this, ramps must be added to stairs and we must become readers, signers, supporting arms. So close, so many, why have we allowed ourselves not to know them?

We want an education for children which tells the true story of our women's lives, which describes the earth as our home to be cherished, to be fed as well as harvested.

We want to be free from violence in our streets and in our houses. One in every three of us will be raped in her lifetime. The pervasive social power of the masculine ideal and the greed of the pornographer have come together to steal our freedom, so that whole neighbourhoods and the life of the evening and night have been taken from us. For too many women the dark country road and the city alley have concealed the rapist. We want the night returned: the light of the

17

moon, special in the cycle of our female lives, the stars and the gaiety of the city streets.

We want the right to have or not to have children – we do not want gangs of politicians and medical men to say we must be sterilised for the country's good. We know that this technique is the racists' method for controlling populations. Nor do we want to be prevented from having an abortion when we need one. We think this freedom should be available to poor women as it always has been to the rich. We want to be free to love whomever we choose. We will live with women or with men or we will live alone. We will not allow the oppression of lesbians. One sex or one sexual preference must not dominate another.

We do not want to be drafted into the army. We do not want our young brothers drafted. We want *them* equal with *us*.

We want to see the pathology of racism ended in our time. It has been the imperial arrogance of white male power that has separated us from the suffering and wisdom of our sisters in Asia, Africa, South America and in our own country. Many North American women look down on the minority nearest them: the Black, the Hispanic, the Jew, the Native American, the Asian, the immigrant. Racism has offered them privilege and convenience; they often fail to see that they themselves have bent to the unnatural authority and violence of men in government, at work, at home. Privilege does not increase knowledge or spirit or understanding. There can be no peace while one race dominates another, one people, one nation, one sex despises another.

We must not forget the tens of thousands of American women who live much of their lives in cages, away from family, lovers, all the growing-up years of their children. Most of them were born at the intersection of oppressions: people of colour, female, poor. Women on the outside have been taught to fear those sisters. We refuse that separation. We need each other's knowledge and anger in our common struggle against the builders of jails and bombs.

We want the uranium left in the earth and the earth given back to the people who tilled it. We want a system of energy which is renewable, which does not take resources out of the earth without returning them. We want those systems to belong to the people and their communities, not to the giant corporations which invariably turn knowledge into weaponry. We want the sham of Atoms for Peace ended, all nuclear plants decommissioned and the construction of new plants stopped. That is another war against the people and the child to be born in fifty years.

18

We want end to the arms race. No more bombs. No more amazing inventions for death.

We understand all is connectedness. We know the life and work of animals and plants in seeding, reseeding and in fact simply inhabiting this planet. Their exploitation and the organised destruction of never to be seen again species threatens and sorrows us. The earth nourishes us as we with our bodies will eventually feed it. Through us, our mothers connected the human past to the human future.

With that sense, that ecological right, we oppose the financial connections between the Pentagon and the multinational corporations and banks that the Pentagon serves. Those connections are made of gold and oil. We are made of blood and bone, we are made of the sweet and finite resource, water. We will not allow these violent games to continue. If we are here in our stubborn thousands today, we will certainly return in the hundreds of thousands in the months and years to come.

We know there is a healthy sensible loving way to live and we intend to live that way in our neighbourhoods and our farms in these United States, and among our sisters and brothers in all the countries of the world.

3
Unholy Secrets
The impact of the nuclear age on public health

Rosalie Bertell

The nuclear issue is, for many of us, the entry point into a growing concern over other problems: militarism, environmental risks, health and the impact of technology on society. For the American bio-statistician Dr Rosalie Bertell it was evidence of the subtle but devastating impact of low-level radiation – the kind the nuclear industry routinely exposes us to – that first led her into the wider nuclear arena. As a speaker Dr Bertell is at once scholarly and down to earth, as the following piece, based on a speech she gave in September 1982 at Sophia University in Tokyo, reveals.

I should like to tell you about the unfolding of my own understanding of radiation health effects and how this took me from a concern about the medical X-ray to a concern about nuclear power plants and finally nuclear weapons.

I was originally trained in maths, physics and chemistry. This was during the years when all mathematicians were automatically taught physics and chemistry. In 1963, the United States National Institute of Health decided that they would sponsor mathematicians in order to begin to move their expertise into biology and bio-medical applications and so they offered me a doctoral grant in maths. I also worked for the equivalent of a Master's degree in biology and biochemistry.

After leaving university, I began to work in cancer research at one of the large national centres, Roswell Park in Buffalo, New York. I was asked to analyse a large study that had been done in three states, the Tri-State Leukemia Survey.[1] Information had been collected in New York State, Maryland and Minnesota. Sixteen million people were followed up over a three-year period and every leukaemia case which occurred over that period was included in the study; we had 2,000 cases and a random sample of 3,000 controls. The information gained from this survey was on 50 different variables for each person.

We had detailed information on what parents and grandparents died of; we had mobility history (every place at which the person had lived) and socio-economic status. We had the history of each person's medical ailments, their occupations, whether they lived in rural or urban areas. We had information also on medical diagnostic X-ray exposure, the ordinary chest X-rays, dental X-rays and so on.

The radiation-related data which I studied first was this medical X-ray information. I worked on the Tri-State Survey for ten years and for the first five years I did the general screening of the data to find out what were the factors that were influencing the leukaemia rate. Most of the things we discovered in the first five years of analysis would be of slight concern to the public health. Maybe two to five percent of the cases could be attributable to these factors. They were considered of minor importance though they were associated with some cases of leukaemia. However, when we reached the section on medical X-rays, the attributable proportions, depending on which section of the data you were using, ranged from 12 percent to 77 percent.[2] We realised this to be the major problem in the data.

During the second five years of analysis, we divided the team into groups specialising in the radiation-related health effects. I worked on the adult portion of the data, those over 15 years of age, and I worked on the non-lymphatic leukaemias. Non-lymphatic leukaemia is an old-age leukaemia. Acute lymphatic is the leukaemia which children get, and the chronic lymphatic is an older old-age leukaemia. I worked on what is called the non-lymphatic leukaemias in adults as related to ordinary medical X-ray exposure. I should say also that there had been three people before me who had worked on the radiation data and they had given up with it. It is very difficult data to try to unravel and I really stumbled into the key to unravelling it by accident.

In my early screening of the data, I had previously been looking at the leukaemia as an old-age disease and noting that the incidence rate increased very regularly with ageing at a rate of about 5.3 percent per year (like compound interest). We have very low probability of having non-lymphatic leukaemia at age 15. At 16 the probability is 5.3 percent higher; at 17 it is 5.3 percent higher. It does not become a large number or very dramatic until one gets to the fifties and sixties, because the rate one starts with is very low.[3]

When I first looked at the medical X-ray information I noticed the same type of phenomena. If I looked at only the males and only one age group, the leukaemia rate went up by roughly five percent with each trunk X-ray. The mathematical formula was similar. Once your rate went up, with another X-ray exposure, it increased by a percentage of the new rate. This gives a compound interest type of equation. After seeing that, I decided to ask a different research question. The usual research question is: If people are exposed to a given amount of radiation, how many excess leukaemias would you expect? That's the *usual* question. That's what I did not ask. Instead the question I put was: Since the leukaemia rate goes up with age, and it also goes up with radiation exposure, how much medical X-ray exposure is equivalent to one year's natural ageing for increasing leukaemia? Now when you begin to look at the data that way, it's surprising what you see !

First of all I found that, if the X-ray exposes the major blood-forming organs and the pelvic arch, then one rad of exposure to radiation (as measured in hospitals) is equivalent to one year of natural ageing. That one rad is about the dose you receive from a spinal examination. It's about the dose from a barium gastro-intestinal examination and from an intravenous pylogram. These are major diagnostic medical procedures, and the increase in the probability of getting leukaemia is about equivalent to the increase you would get from one year of natural ageing. If the radiation is in the chest area (the lungs, as with the ordinary chest X-ray), or the upper thigh area, one rad was equivalent to six-tenths of a year of ageing – not quite a year. In these examples one exposes less of the active bone marrow deposits. With dental X-rays, or arms or legs (i.e., the periphery), one rad is equivalent to a quarter of a year's ageing. Again, less of the bone marrow is exposed.[4]

After this research I began to look at low-level radiation in a very different way. I think I should probably have done this in the first place, but instead I kept to the usual research path for testing the effect of anything added to our environment. For example, if you put mercury in the water you will have an increased rate of Minimata disease – a very clear connection between the agent and the disease. Swine flu shots result in an increase in paralysis cases. It is therefore very easy to measure a dose and a response: so much of the hazard results in so many cases of illness. Radiation is different because it is our natural pollutant. Whether we like it or not we are exposed to natural background radiation from the ground, from the cosmic rays and from building material. Therefore if we make a slight increase in this background radiation we should not expect new and different sicknesses. We should expect more of those sicknesses we had in the first place.

Also, if we stop to think about what chronological age means, it is a very good measure of our exposure to natural background radiation. If you are 35 years old, you have been exposed to natural background radiation for 35 years and you can calculate the amount of exposure. If you are 65 years old, you have been exposed for more years and you can tell the difference. One experiences what has happened over the years. When you add to this an increased exposure by medical X-ray you really make the same breakdown process go faster. This is part of the ageing process – we say 'part' because we are not sure that it is connected with everything called 'ageing', but there certainly is a syndrome of old age that is directly connected with the actual background exposure: this is accelerated by medical X-ray exposure. Now, what I am saying is that the medical X-ray exposure is causing the old-age leukaemias to occur at a younger age. This looks startling to us. The leukaemias are occurring at an age where they should not be occurring according to our normal experience of ageing.

I tried a second approach to see whether there were other indicators of ageing that would be connected with this leukaemia effect. The ageing disease most common in the Tri-State Survey was the chronic ischemic heart disease. I carried out another study looking at the persons who had had heart disease five years or more before their leukaemia diagnosis, to see whether they were at high risk of leukaemia. My reasoning was that if a person was 25 years old and had heart disease, in a very real sense he or she was prematurely aged. If leukaemia was an old-age disease, he or she was probably at higher than normal risk. It turned out to be true. In general, people who have a history of heart disease are at higher risk of leukaemia.[5] The same is true for diabetes, asthma, severe allergies and arthritis.[6] There is a very specific set of diseases, also old-age diseases, which indicate higher than normal risk of leukaemia. I found that if you had these diseases you were roughly twelve times as susceptible to radiation-related leukaemia than persons who did not have the diseases.[7] The people who were already showing breakdown were at very high risk for further damage from the X-rays.

This has implications for workers who handle radioactive materials. One can say that if a worker starts to show one of these diseases, he or she should be extremely careful or totally stop handling radioactive materials. He or she is at high risk of leukaemia. It has implications for the hiring of people who will handle radioactive materials. It also has genetic implications, because the diseases which I mentioned (heart disease, diabetes, arthritis, severe allergies) run in families. They have a genetic component. It has also been demonstrated, and was seen in the Tri-State Study, that these diseases could be initiated in the next generation by radiation exposure of parents.[8] We are talking here about a hazard, namely radiation, which, when parents are exposed, can produce children with asthmas and allergies, or could produce children who have juvenile diabetes or heart disease, who will therefore be more susceptible to radiation damage than their parents were. It was actually that fact which first made me speak out on the nuclear issue. The long-range effect on the species will be even more serious than the long-range effect on the individual.

When I first began to work on radiation I was working very quietly in a research laboratory and I was not really in touch with either the nuclear power or the nuclear weapons problems. I thought nuclear power was the wave of the future. That we would have electricity too cheap to meter, and that the developing world would have unlimited sources of energy. I believed all of the things that we were being taught. I came right out of the era where we wanted something *good* to result from the nuclear age because we felt so badly about Hiroshima and Nagasaki. I think that this was a common attitude in the States.

My first experience with nuclear power plants was after a proposal to build one near my home in Buffalo, New York. The citizens who lived near the proposed power plant called the hospital where I was working and asked if someone could go to a public hearing and talk about radiation health effects. I went because the Department Chairperson asked me to, but I made it clear that I did not know anything about nuclear power plants.

So I went along to this public meeting, and it was quite an experience. As we went in the door we were handed a list of 12 questions which the local legislature had drawn up, and which we were expected to answer at that meeting. The people from the power company had had the list of questions for two weeks, but we only received them as we arrived. When I got to the front of the auditorium, I found that they only had enough seats on the stage for the men from the power plant. We were asked to sit in the audience. I asked for an overhead projector; they told me they did not have one. Meanwhile, I watched the men from the power plant put their movies on the reel in the remote projection room. The company had produced a printed programme for the evening listing the five speakers from the power plant, with all their credentials and everything they had written. Then there was a space in the programme marked 'citizens committee' to cover the rest of us.

I was the first speaker after the five speakers from the power plant had talked; I had watched their slick movie in which it looked as if everything in the nuclear power plant was operated by remote control. It was a very clean-looking white building and a very impressive film. The company described the health effects of radiation as non-existent. Everyone is exposed to natural background radiation, they said, and this was only a little bit more. There was no harm to human health. Their final radiation story stressed that it was just like a few X-rays. Of course, they are harmless! It was the first time I had heard their public relations pitch and what ordinary people were being told.

When my turn came, I went up to the microphone and asked if the people who had already spoken would mind going down into the audience to allow the other speakers to come up. That caused a little stir, but they did get up and let the other speakers sit on the stage. There had been five men from the power plant, and when the other group of speakers came onto the stage it was obvious that there were four women speaking for the citizens' group. I had not even been conscious of that before. I spoke into the microphone, 'I am sorry the issue broke down this way, into men and women; maybe it was concern for life.' I got tremendous applause from the audience, who had not applauded for the whole first part of the meeting, and after that the audience responded to practically everything that was said. It came out in the discussion that this power plant was to be built right next door to the Cornucopia Farms where they grow Gerbers baby food.[9] The impact of this information on the audience was startling! To cut a long story short, the next day the Niagara County Legislature voted the first moratorium in the States against a nuclear power plant.[10]

It was 1973. I was given the credit for this 'victory', and immediately my name was sent all over the United States and people started calling me up and saying 'Would you come to our place and talk about nuclear power?' Suddenly I was in a position where I felt I had to find out what was being said by this industry; what nuclear power was; what exposures the public was receiving; where the radiation exposure regulations came from; what science was supporting these regulations, and so on. As I searched back to find out where the nuclear industry's statements on health had come from, I always ended up with information generated by what used to be called the Atomic Bomb Casualty Commission Research Stations in Hiroshima and Nagasaki. They are now called the RERF, the Radiation Effects Research Foundation.[11] The more I tried to find out about the atomic bomb casualty studies, the more I discovered that they were based on data, basic information on the health of the people and doses they received from atomic bombs, which is classified secret for reasons of national security by the United States. It is still classified and has been so since 1945. It was my first experience of secret science. The only papers available to the public are the ones that were released because they did not pose a threat to the national security of the States.

When I looked back to see what the regulations were for exposure to radioactive material, I discovered that they were recommended by a committee set up in 1952, the International Commission on Radiological Protection (ICRP).[12] Of course, 1952 pre-dates any nuclear power plants other than the weapons reactors, which were operated in order to produce the spent fuel rods, the source of plutonium for the nuclear bombs. For example, at Hanford, Washington, eight nuclear power plants were operating from 1943 on, but they never gave anyone electricity. The military just operated the plants to get the plutonium from the fuel rods for making weapons. When the ICRP *was* finally established, it made recommendations for levels of radiation exposure to the general public and to workers in 1957 for external sources, and in 1959 for internal sources.[13] The commercial nuclear industry started after this and developed upon these guidelines.

The Commission, which made these recommendations, was called for by the US government. I need to cover a little of what occurred in 1950 – which was a global crisis year – for you to understand why it was felt that such recommendations were necessary. In 1950 Chiang Kai Shek had been ousted from China and China had declared itself Communist. The Korean war was being waged. The Chinese were assisting North Korea and the US was assisting South Korea. In the middle of this crisis the Soviet Union set off their first nuclear blast in Siberia, so the whole world knew that the Soviet Union now had the nuclear bomb. A war was in progress, and the US was afraid of losing military bases in the Pacific where it had been testing nuclear bombs. On 15 January 1951, Truman signed permission for the military to set off nuclear bombs in Nevada, at a test site about 16 miles northwest of Las Vegas. The military originally intended to detonate four bombs. However, since 1951, they have set off 600 – about 200 above ground, another 400 below ground – and they are still continuing to do so![14] One of the largest blasts occurred on 6 August 1982.[15] It was an affront to the world which was holding peace rallies in remembrance of Hiroshima. Nuclear bombs are being set off now at the rate of one every week or every two weeks; there are about ten days to two weeks between them.[16] They are rather large and there is a question about whether some are over the 150 kiloton limit.[17] They are certainly close to 150 kilotons.

Now 1951 was the beginning of testing on the North American continent. The American public was nervous – and they had every reason to be nervous – about the fall-out. The military was telling the public that they now knew how to control nuclear weapons. Fall-out would not hurt anybody. It was possible to set off bombs in Nevada with no harm to human health. Yet, the most recent developments downwind of the test site indicate that there are many excess deaths. There are about 800 claims in the courts from civilians, and over a thousand military claims.[18] There is also a general lawsuit by the Governor of Utah against the Federal government for the wrongful death of Utah residents. In just one blast the military wiped out 4,000 sheep.[19] We are dealing with gross stories of radiation damage.

In the middle of this 1950–51 international emergency, the military thought that it was permissible for them to allow random deaths downwind of the test site in order to prevent the dropping of an atomic bomb on US cities.[20] It is a bizarre kind of morality, but, given the mentality of the military, that was the decision they made. Some will tell you that rather directly. I have spoken to them. They thought it was justified to do this. They had to have some kind of universally-accepted radiation exposure regulations to appeal to, and they certainly would have no credibility if the US government set up the regulations for radiation exposure to the US general public for something like a testing ground for nuclear bombs, so the recommendations needed to be international. Moreover, because of the weapon testing, many concerned scientists not involved with the military were also calling for the formation of an international body to make the radiation exposure recommendations. This is how ICRP came into being and started to develop the papers that were the basis of the recommendations for exposure to the public and to workers from nuclear industries. ICRP has a very peculiar structure. It is not really a scientific society in the usual sense. Since everything that has to do with nuclear affairs was and is secret for reasons of national security, ICRP was set up in such a way that in order to become a member you had to be recommended by a present member and accepted by the present executive committee. Consequently it is a closed club. Friends are put in, one after the other, and there is no organisation in the world, even the World Health Organisation, that has the right to put someone on the ICRP.[21]

ICRP says quite openly in its documents that it is not directly a

27

public health commission. It is recommending radiation exposures as permissible or acceptable according to the economic and social benefits of the activity. This means they are not just talking about the health effects, but they are making the trade-offs for us. They are making value judgements as to what level of damage is acceptable to the public. This is all done pretty much behind closed doors, though some of the papers are available and the public can read some of the reasoning. The more I read of the papers that are published by ICRP the more upset I became at the decisions that have been made on our behalf.

Now ICRP has never spoken out on behalf of public health on any major radiological problem since the group was founded in 1952. It did not even have the courage to speak out about the above-ground nuclear weapon testing. Nor did it speak out for ventilation in the uranium mines, although the mining companies were saving something like six dollars a ton by not ventilating the mines.[22] In the States we have 1,100 excess lung cancers among the uranium miners – about one out of six has died as an excess lung cancer because there was no ventilation in the mines. This was a well-known problem, reported in occupational medicine for 100 years.[23] The companies knew it was not possible to mine uranium without being exposed to radon gas, but they saved some money at the cost of lives. This was during the big rush to produce nuclear weapons in the 1950s.

To return to the historical story, we are still using the recommendations ICRP made in 1957 and 1959 for worker and general public exposure to radiation now. The maximum exposure permitted to the general public from nuclear industries per year is 500 millirem.[24] That is equivalent to the bone-marrow dose from 100 chest X-rays.[25] Now that is the maximum. The industry does not operate at the maximum, but the regulation is obviously very protective of the company. It can give the public up to the equivalent of 100 chest X-rays a year within the law. Telling the public that the plant operates at only a small percent of the permissible level is outrageous, because even a small percent of the permissible level is too much! A worker in the nuclear industry can receive ten times more radiation per year – a bone-marrow-equivalent of 1,000 chest X-rays.[26] This means three to four chest X-rays a day for a year. It is very high from the point of view of protection of health. The risk is not only to the workers, but also to the worker's children, grandchildren and great-grandchildren. There has never been a formal study of the offspring of radiation workers.

In 1978 I began a study of immature infants (i.e., infants with a

28

birth weight less than 2,500 grams) in Wisconsin. Their death rate changes with the release of radioactivity from the stacks of the nuclear power plant upwind from their birth place.[27] This effect is, I think, a combination of respiratory irritation and a depressed white blood count due to bone marrow damage. The infants get both effects at the same time, and clinically it would probably look like a pneumonia death. I suspect the same thing is happening in the elderly, and it would probably be called a pneumonia death from old age. Similarly, early occurrence of old-age diseases is assumed to be 'normal'.

It is very easy to exploit people with exposure to radiation; a hazard which escapes our senses. If I get heart disease I cannot say I should not have got it for another five years. I do not have anything with which to compare my experience. We rarely keep track in society of the age at which the chronic diseases are diagnosed, so this could change rather dramatically in a population without it even being noticed or documented. We do not usually keep track of the number of children with allergies and asthma, and yet mild mutations are a very early indicator of environmental problems. So, from the point of view of public health, we are almost totally unprepared for the nuclear age, and we are almost totally ignorant and unmindful of the health effects that are occurring around us.

I would like to suggest an analysis, or a pattern, within which it might be possible to begin to deal with this problem, because what we have initiated here is a very serious health problem for the species. If something is not done about it, and done very quickly, it will soon become a deteriorating situation. It is not going to get better by itself. It is not going to go away. We are going to be producing children physically less able to cope, at the same time that we are giving them a more hazardous world with which to cope. We cannot keep doing that.

The model which I find most helpful is that of the labour union. I think the worker discovered rather early that industrial expansion was taking place and that the cost was the health of the worker. The hazards were in the work space. Frequently the worker did not know the kind of material with which he or she was working. Workers did not know what the hazards of the material were. They were not aware which of the health effects they experienced were connected with their work and which were natural until they began to compare notes. We are in very much the same position, since now technology and industry have so expanded that the hazards are in the *living* space. The whole community is at risk, not just the worker. We are talking about the same problem but it is now a much larger population being exposed.

It is also not as clear who is negotiating with whom. In the worker's situation you had the worker and management, and it was rather clear who was in charge and who was being exploited. When you try to look at the situation from the point of view of the community, frequently the polluter now is the government, and frequently it is the government's military programme that is causing it. The usual thing that citizens do is to look to the government to take care of them, but if government is the polluter then you have a direct conflict of interest. What has happened is what we see globally – people taking to the streets. I see the protest movement as the natural outcome of, or the natural extension of, the labour union movement. It is a way for people to say: 'We're not all right – we don't know what we are being exposed to. We care about our health, we care about our children, we care about the healthiness of the environment.' Citizen protest is not anarchy, it is the beginning of a new level of organisation in society which is going to be needed if we expect to survive. I think the church, for instance, has to stand with the citizen in this problem.

We have a basic right to information about what is being released into the air or the water or the land. We also need more protective action by public health officials. They are going to have to measure different health parameters. They are going to have to be much more aware of birth defects and chronic diseases. They are going to have to begin to provide the public with what I call base-line health studies before a hazardous industry is moved in, similar to the pre-hiring physical examinations which the worker has. I am frequently asked what happened to the health of the people at Three Mile Island, and I say, show me a piece of paper that documents their health before the accident and I will tell you what has happened. The people do not have a piece of paper that reports their relevant health statistics before the accident. They have only death certificates showing the first cause of death (a very gross way to measure the full life health history). For instance, one might have developed cancer and then have died in an automobile accident. We do not have any sensitive information on the health of the people of Three Mile Island before the accident.

We need new methods. We need to develop methods of conflict resolution, of negotiating between people and government. People need to be *part* of the decision-making, not just persons tolerated for show public hearings. There should be government accountability.

There should be binding arbitration. There should be mediation courts. There should be an extension of the concept of worker compensation, so that the children of the workers are covered. The wife who dies in a spontaneous abortion should be covered, and people exposed to the plant effluence -- those who do not work at the plant but who happen to live downwind of the stack or downstream of the water. We need to revise all these basic concepts and to extend them to cover the new reality.

That is my most optimistic scenario, that we do have the insight to do all these things. The most pessimistic scenario would be that we destroy ourselves totally in a nuclear war before we can get this kind of societal growth. In fact, I would like to touch on one part of the nuclear war issue which was very much on my mind as I moved from understanding medical X-rays, to nuclear power plants, to nuclear war. There are two events which moved me to conclude that the war issue is an emergency situation which has to be dealt with very quickly. One event was being invited to speak at the 1978 commemoration ceremonies in Hiroshima and Nagasaki and at a scientists' meeting in Osaka which preceded that commemoration. The experience of staying in the home of a survivor, of listening to stories of the people involved, and of seeing what happened there, was for me very deep and very moving.

The second event, one I found both moving and outrageous, was being invited by the US State Department to go to a special briefing in 1979 where they explained the SALT II treaty. They invited 500 women from across the United States. We do not know where they got our names from, but they invited us to Washington and we spent the day listening to information about their weapons – what the United States had and what the Soviet Union had. I presume you know some of the gross figures. Of the bombs dropped during the Second World War, the most-used bomb was the block-buster, which literally destroyed a city block. The Hiroshima bomb had 1,000 block-busters in one bomb. The hydrogen bombs which we have now are like 1,000 Hiroshima bombs. One bomb now is like a million block-busters. We have stock-piled globally 50,000 of these bombs.[28] It is absolutely unthinkable that these bombs would be used! They should not be built! No one should be threatened with them! They should not exist on the face of the earth! They have the capability of totally destroying not only the people of the earth but the life-support system: the air, the water, the land, the atmosphere, the oceans, everything. We have the ability to destroy totally the planet Earth.

At the end of that memorable day at the State Department, after we had heard about the MIRVs and MARVs and the ICBMs and the SLBMs, the Backfire Bombers and all manner of death-dealing devices, I asked a question: 'How many people die every year for the production of these weapons even if they are never used, if you count uranium mining and milling and transportation and enrichment, the nuclear power plants, reprocessing of the fuel rods, the separation of the plutonium, the building of the bombs, the testing of the bombs and so on? How many people die every year for this weapons programme?' There was great consternation on the stage. Everybody was looking at everybody else and finally the Secretary of State came to the microphone and he said: 'That's not our department.'

At that moment I knew that the military, which has never counted the cost financially, has never counted the cost in lives either. They are just spending the lives of the people to produce these weapons. We are on a death course, whether the weapons are used or not. We have already done severe damage to many parts of the earth. Probably the United States is the one that has received the worst damage. You cannot set off 600 bombs, build 100 commercial nuclear power plants and another 100 military nuclear facilities, as we have done in the US, without doing extensive damage both to people and to the biosphere.[29] It includes several effects.

The best documented is the brain damage to a whole generation. Downwind of the Nevada test site there is more brain damage than there is in other places in the US. It first showed up with the scholastic aptitude testing in 1967. Those children who were 16 years old in 1967, and started to take the exams, were born in 1951, when the above-ground weapons testing began. The aptitude scores have been going down every year and now there is a statistically significant difference. It is worse downwind of the test site – even the Navy has now admitted this.[30]

The second thing which you see is gross abnormality due to pollution from radioactive iodine. Radioactive iodine tends to concentrate in the thyroid gland and to destroy some of the thyroid tissue. If one lowers thyroid hormone in the body, the person gains weight. The American weight is now significantly higher than it was prior to the above-ground weapons testing and proliferation of all of these nuclear industries. There have been two major studies on calorie intake of food. It is now lower than it was, and is decreasing; yet the average weight is still increasing.[31] This is typical of what would be expected from radioactive iodine.

One can also see an effect in the fertility rate – one out of five males in the States is infertile.[32] It used to be one out of 20 or one out of 25.

32

One out of five pregnancies ends in spontaneous abortion.[33] Health effects are multiplied as chemical and biological military pollution is added to the nuclear pollution. These are serious health effects and they are only the beginning. We suspect it is the same in the Soviet Union and will soon become an acute problem for China, Polynesia, Micronesia and other areas. The survival of the species is at stake. The only course now offering a viable future is the total renunciation of war-making as human behaviour. Just as cannibalism, slavery and duelling, though once entrenched in human social patterns, are now totally unacceptable behaviour, so, too, war itself must be relegated to the history books. Alternative methods of resolving differences between nations can and must be implemented.

The long death

for Wendy Teresa Simon
(25 September 1954–7 August 1979)

Radiation is like oppression,
the average daily kind of subliminal toothache
you get almost used to, the stench
of chlorine in the water, of smog in the wind.

We comprehend the disasters of the moment,
the nursing home fire, the river in flood
pouring over the sandbag levee, the airplane
crash with fragments of burnt bodies
scattered among the hunks of twisted metal,
the grenade in the marketplace, the sinking ship.

But how to grasp a thing that does not
kill you today or tomorrow
but slowly from the inside in twenty years.
How to feel that a corporate or governmental
choice means we bear twisted genes and our
grandchildren will be stillborn if our
children are very lucky.

Slow death can not be photographed for the six
o'clock news. It's all statistical,
the gross national product or the prime
lending rate. Yet if our eyes saw
in the right spectrum, how it would shine,
lurid as magenta neon.

If we could smell radiation like seeping
gas, if we could sense it as heat, if we
could hear it as a low ominous roar
of the earth shifting, then we would not sit
and be poisoned while industry spokesmen
talk of acceptable millirems and .02
cancer per population thousand.

We acquiesce at murder so long as it is slow,
murder from asbestos dust, from tobacco,
from lead in the water, from sulphur in the air,
and fourteen years later statistics are printed
on the rise in leukaemia among children.
We never see their faces. They never stand,
those poisoned children together in a courtyard,
and are gunned down by men in three-piece suits.

The shipyard workers who built nuclear
submarines, the soldiers who were marched
into the Nevada desert to be tested by the H-
bomb, the people who work in power plants,
they die quietly years after in hospital
wards and not on the evening news.

The soft spring rain floats down and the air
is perfumed with pine and earth. Seedlings
drink it in, robins sip it in puddles,
you run in it and feel clean and strong,
the spring rain blowing from the irradiated
cloud over the power plant.

Radiation is oppression, the daily average
kind, the kind you're almost used to
and live with as the years abrade you,
high blood pressure, ulcers, cramps, migraine,
a hacking cough: you take it inside
and it becomes pain and you say, not
They are killing me, but *I am sick now*.

                                        Marge Piercy

4

Seveso is Everywhere

Women's Working Group on Seveso (Geneva)
Translated and extracted by
Frances Howard-Gordon

*In 1976, an explosion at a chemical plant in Seveso,
northern Italy, spewed clouds of highly poisonous dioxon gas over the
town and the neighbouring area. In 1983, waste from the accident was
discovered in a disuses abattoir in a French village, hidden there by a
contractor who had been paid to dispose of it and had failed to do so.
Local people, unaware of its presence, had milked their cows and
allowed their children to play near the barrels containing the poison.
Meanwhile executives of the Swiss-owned firm responsible for the
plant finally stood trial for their negligence during the original accident,
seven years earlier. The repercussions of Seveso, it seems, will be with
us for some time to come. What follow are extracts from a booklet put
together in the months after the accident by a group of feminists in
Geneva, making the connections between the incident and a whole
range of issues of concern to eco-feminists, from the military-industrial
complex to the question of control over our own bodies.*

In Vietnam, 75 percent of the population affected by the war were
women, children and old people. Chemical warfare has produced
large numbers of deformed children there. At Seveso too, the
children were the first who needed to go to hospital. The women
accompanied them, and had to wait in the dispensaries set up
especially for them. Women, with all their problems: contraception,
abortion, childbirth, children.

The firm behind the Seveso accident, Icmesa, was producing,
among other things, the defoliants destined for use in Vietnam: used
by those self-same Americans who today refuse to say what remedies
there might be for the terrible diseases resulting from dioxin. This
information is classified – a military secret.

After this, how can anyone dare say that the battle-zone and the
factory are the affairs of men? We do not need Seveso to tell us that it
is *our* business, and it is precisely because we still have so little power

36

that war and industry can go on developing in this way. From Vietnam to Seveso, from Malville to Geneva, the 'powers that be' are attacking our lives with a motivation that is utterly alien to us. They play us off one against another, dividing us amongst ourselves. The act of aggression committed at Seveso is not merely confined to one specific area. The effects of dioxin are all-pervasive and create mutants and horrendous deformities. At Seveso, the most deadly of principles has clearly struck at every level of our existence. Yet how can we find a response which measures up to this? How can we come together to act?

A Terrible Aggression Against Women's Bodies

The Women at Seveso

10 July 1976   A 'toxic cloud' escapes from the Icmesa factory.

14 July 1976   Flowers and plants within a radius of several kilometers dry up. The animals begin to die. The children start showing symptoms like 'nettle rash'. These are the first known effects of the poison cloud. The children are therefore the first to be physically affected, the first to cry because they feel pain. They are also the first to have to undergo medical examinations, doubly odious because no one knows how to take away the pain, because the role of guinea-pig becomes all too apparent at Seveso.

No need to tell the women what even one ill child, let alone several, means in terms of worry and overwork (visits to the doctor, special care, hospital examinations, etc.). Especially when one knows that the inhabitants of zones contaminated by the toxic cloud or exposed to the risk of dioxin poisoning will be *kept* under medical control for a period of *at least five years*.

24 July 1976   A 35-year-old Seveso woman, Maria Galli, dies suddenly at Cortina d'Ampezzo. She worked there as a housekeeper for an industrialist from Como. Every morning she would make the journey from Seveso to Como, and every evening she would return, crossing the most seriously affected zone round the Icmesa factory on foot. Thus, on the morning and evening of 10 July, just as in the days that followed, Maria Galli was breathing in toxic substances, even though her home was 'only' in Zone B. The doctor who performs the post-mortem at first refuses to say anything publicly. Then it is decided that the cause of death is an attack of bronchial asthma, an ailment from which she had apparently been suffering for some time.

Towards the end of July, people start talking about the risks of deformities to the babies still in their mothers' wombs. The doctors therefore declare that everyone must abstain from conceiving and avoid pregnancy for at least three months. The question of abortion arises. It is conceded that therapeutic abortions should be allowed to pregnant women from the most contaminated zone. It is Andreotti, President of the Council, who personally authorises the abortions, reserving the right of approval to a commission composed of two gynaecologists and one psychiatrist. The gaining of abortions is therefore made highly technical and bureaucratic, and the women – who, alone, are the ones who have to carry personal responsibility for interrupting their pregnancies – are left to face extra humiliation.

9 August 1976 The Archbishop of Milan speaks out against the 'eugenic' abortions at Seveso: 'If the women who are "bad Christians" do not want to look after deformed children, we will find "good Christian families" who will.'

At a special dispensary opened at the Desio hospital, we talk to two pregnant women. The first is Maria A, who is around 40 years old, lives at Desio, but was born and grew up in Reggio Calabria.

> In my life I have had two abortions and five children. My husband is often ill. Two of my children (13 and 11 years old) are handicapped. When the Icmesa cloud escaped, I realised I was pregnant. At the Seveso dispensary, tests showed that I had diabetes. I wanted an abortion. I went to the Mangiagalli Clinic in Milan and they told me to take care over my diabetes. Ten days later, seeing that nothing had happened, I left for the South. As soon as I came back, on 27 August, I went to the Desio dispensary. They did more tests which showed the diabetes to be worse, and now here I am – still being seen for diabetes. If I could have had an abortion in the second month, I wouldn't have hesitated for an instant. . .

We then talk to Marianna C, originally from Sicily, living in Zone B.

> I have a little five-year-old girl to whom I gave birth in the eighth month. I had another who was born premature and stillborn in the seventh month. Two premature births. On 15 September, I was in my fourth month of this, my third, pregnancy. In the second

month I almost had a miscarriage, and then it very nearly happened again while I was on holiday. I wanted an abortion, but last Thursday I came to the Desio dispensary and they told me that the baby was fine. On the other hand, they diagnosed 'kidney stones'. That's why I'm here having medical attention. They also told me that, as soon as I leave the hospital, I'll have to leave Zone B for a while. Now, you know, I don't think I'll be able to have an abortion. Too much time has passed, and I'm frightened. . .

At the very same Desio dispensary, a woman confronts the psychiatrist, saying: 'But what if I give birth to a deformed child?' The psychiatrist replied: 'Come now madam, don't you know that abnormal children are often happier than other children?'

29 August 1976   A Seveso woman gives birth to a dead child without a brain. Doctors declare that dioxin has nothing to do with it. Any woman who wants a legal abortion has to go through unbelievable tribulations. Everyone attacks her with their political beliefs and tries to con her on the theme of abortion. She goes through interminable trials, since weeks go by between the moment of decisiqn and the possibility of actually having an abortion. She experiences great pain. This is why some women have preferred to sort the matter out by themselves or have gone directly to an abortionist.

This is how Maria Chinni died. Several months pregnant and living in the contaminated Desio zone, she did not go to the dispensary with its reactionary gynaecologists. Maria was the sole breadwinner for herself, her sick husband and two children. She tried to induce an abortion by swallowing a substance which was supposed to poison the foetus. Dreading the legal consequences of her action, like all the women in her situation, she was only taken to hospital when already in a coma.

14 September 1976   The conference of Italian bishops officially condemns 'the dioxin abortions'.

29 September 1976   We learn that certain women from Desio, Seveso, Cesano Maderno have had abortions in Switzerland (Tessin and Geneva) in order to escape the anti-abortionist prohibitions of Italian doctors. In effect, out of 1,500 pregnant women in the contaminated zone, 730 were examined at the dispensary, 150 asked for abortions and only 25 managed to get them.

We, as feminists, have a long discussion about how to approach the local women, given that they live according to strict cultural conditions (e.g. very tied to the church, family, etc.). It seems to us that, despite our differences, it should be possible for us all, simply as women, to understand each other immediately on some matters. What follows is an extract from a discussion with one of the members of the Seveso feminist collective.

It's true, I did want to have a child. Only now, I'm waiting, because . . . I don't know . . . If there were reliable tests, blood-tests, for example, but there isn't a test which lets you know for sure, is there? Where does the dioxin go? Into the liver. And to examine the liver, you'd have to look at every bit of it, until there wasn't any left . . . if you wanted to be sure there wasn't any poison in it. It's the same thing for the earth. They analyse a bit of soil every 'x' metres or so, but there's no guarantee that in between the two spots, there isn't some contamination.

They do tests on rats, exposing them to dioxin, and their babies are born deformed. 'Well, it's only rats, maybe humans are different.' And yet drugs are tested for safety on animals all the time. Quite a contradiction isn't it? In Vietnam, it was apparently the women who showed no exterior signs of poisoning who gave birth to deformed babies. They don't tell us anything at the dispensary – it's impossible to find out the facts. When they are aborting foetuses younger than four months, why do they use the curetage method which can perforate the uterus? They say it's more certain that way, but really it ought to be we who make these decisions. One thing is certain. From now on, worker, employee, woman – we have to take matters into our own hands and not trust anyone else.

Then there are also the stories about people's immune systems breaking down when they have absorbed dioxin. That's frightening. And apparently it increases the risks from taking the contraceptive pill. It leads to an accumulation of toxic substances in the liver. Won't you have something to drink? A piece of bread? Not hungry at all?

Medicines in One Hand, Defoliants in the Other

The unbelievable chronology of events at Seveso (the delays, secrets, omissions, belated official statements, the clandestine NATO officials), raises the following vital question: what was Roche-

Givaudan really producing at Icmesa and who was Icmesa producing it for?

Someone high up in the Roche company (wishing to remain anonymous) contacted the weekly independent Italian newspaper *L'Espresso* on 30 July: 'Icmesa was not producing ordinary "tcf", but enriched "tcf" with the dioxin ("tcdd") kept in. Instead of the permitted 300 grammes of dioxin per week, Icmesa was producing 3 kilogrammes.' We know that the 'tcf' used in the production of hexachlorophine must contain the least possible amount of dioxin, since it is a secondary product which is undesirable, and must be eliminated. For that reason 'tcf' must be produced at the lowest possible temperature because it is heat which produces the derivative dioxin. One can only understand the production of 'tcf' at Icmesa in the following way: the 'tcf' produced by Icmesa was not destined to be uniquely for hexachlorophine at all, but also for the production of war weapons such as defoliants. In their attempts to conceal the true nature of their product, it would seem the conduct of Roche-Givaudan was dishonest, to say the least.

So who were the recipients of Roche-Givaudan's war weaponry? There is absolutely no doubt that it was NATO, according to the anonymous executive at Roche. Both the enriched 'tcf' and the mysterious 'Sp 121' have been used in Germany by German and American units for 'chemical defence'. The products reached there from the US and Great Britain – who had in turn received them directly or indirectly via Switzerland.

30 September 1976 We learn from the London *Daily Mail* of 21 September that the subsidiary of Givaudan in England, at Whyteleaf, pollutes the region so much that the fire brigade had to be called in to decontaminate the earth and rivers of the area. So far nobody is ill enough to be hospitalised. From the same source we learn that the defoliant '2–4–5–T' with its 'tcf' base is used by the British Army in Ireland against members of the Provisional IRA in the county of Armagh.[1]

With our thanks to the Chemical Industries

The History of Hexachlorophine – Thalidomide, Morhange, Seveso, Minamata, Baumol, Stalinon

When an 'accident' occurs, like the one at Seveso or the Morhange talcum powder incident, we are expected to believe that it is an isolated incident, a mistake. Obviously that is wrong. As things are, it is *impossible* for accidents *not* to happen *all* of the time.

The whole of industry, all the multinationals, functions in the following way: they try to find out, through market research and other studies, which products will be the most saleable. As a result, new products are created. A series of quick experiments and summary studies are done and then the new substance is launched. It is only when many people have consumed this product (we are only guinea-pigs for big business!), when reactions are evident in a large number of people or when people actually die as a result that things can no longer be kept secret and the summary studies are taken out of the drawer. Only then are similar, but less outrageous, 'accidents' remembered and only then is consideration finally given to the idea of restrictions and, if reactions are really serious, to a ban. It is the same for everything: additives in food, medicines, cosmetics, toiletries, insecticides, textiles. You have only to follow the black thread of all the 'accidents' to find the same names, the same multinationals, the same power and the same fundamental contempt for life.

Hexachlorophine is made, among other places, at Vernier. It is contained in the most common household and domestic products: in talcum powders as well as soaps; in the boric talcs; in various shampoos; in medications, including antiseptics; in many other soaps, shampoos, vaginal deodorants, etc. (especially those called 'antiseptic'); in tampons, toothpastes and mouth disinfectants; in detergents and in certain, so-called, 'sanitised' clothes. It is also used as an authorised additive in food and animal drink, as well as for the treatment of these animals, and is equally authorised in food prepared for human consumption.

To believe the publicity from Givaudan, and the others, you have to believe that beauty lays the world at your feet. A 'pretty' appearance is a guarantee of success with men and a successful social life. To be beautiful (and dumb) is the most important thing expected (and allowed) of us. Beauty, maternity, housework!

Western society has succeeded, backed by dollars, in imposing its model of beauty on the rest of the world. They want us all to be tall, long, white, supple, slim, perpetually young and charming. But how can we keep a fresh complexion when we are surrounded by pollution? How can we be smiling and accepting when our existence is ravaged by such a multitude of tensions? How can we stay eternally young when we work and motherhood ages us and . . . inexorably time passes?

We are forbidden to accept ourselves. We must transform our bodies, modelling them on an image, shaping them so that we are alienated by them. Denying them. And here the chemical industry comes to our rescue. It sells us youth in a jar, a fresh complexion in a bottle, slimness in a tube, happiness in a spray and cream against 'the aggressive outdoors'. A personality . . . with a million copies. And at what price?

In order to sell their product, through their advertising, they want to convince us that the cells of our skin are capable of digesting the chemical substances contained in these products. The truth is that if our skin absorbed these substances in their concentrated form, we would be poisoned to death! Research into the noxiousness of cosmetic products and the diseases they bring is long and complicated. The chemical industries hide behind their secret formulae. We have, nevertheless, been able to discover that, among the shampoos, perfumes and toilet waters, the skin lotions and deodorants, the list of dangerous products is long and tedious. We find that the more a perfume, soap or shampoo is 'refined', 'deluxe', or 'bio', the more noxious it is. Natural soap has never caused allergies! And yet these 'refined' products are sold to us as essential for our success and our beauty: what an irony.

One Solution Only: That We Control

The story of Seveso is black. The question of pollution is black. For the first time, we are thinking together about these things. We are planning how to act together. Gathering this information was difficult. It is difficult to read it too. But we could not say anything else. It needs to be said, even if it is nasty and could have a contrary effect to what we want: we have not written these pages to make our hands drop in discouragement, but to help our arms extend from woman to woman and to reach whoever can be reached.

The story of Seveso is true even if it is dreadful. It poses brutally the question of our (failing) power, of the usefulness and effectiveness of our struggles, of our discussions, of our existence as a women's movement. In fact, we are only grasping one part of the hurt done to us by the state and industrialists.

Our victories have been ambiguous and ephemeral. For example, we have fought for local anaesthetics to be provided when women abort in hospital. The sister who fought for this right got what she wanted. But the others? The same goes for the price of abortions: if we go in force to the gynaecologist, he does not dare charge too much, but if we go on our own, it is another matter and prices are going up! We wanted a women's centre, we squatted in one for three and a half months. But on the fourth, the cops arrived and destroyed it. It is true that what we gained from that occupation cannot be taken from us by anyone, but it is also true that we still have no women's centre. That is soon going to change! The Health Service will no longer reimburse us for our gynaecological examinations. We shall refuse to pay them also.

It is not a matter of underestimating what we have done or what we are doing, nor of in any way giving up. By living our lives and struggles as women, all of the things we have done, or are doing, are helping us to gain inches of ground.

But how can we increase our numbers, become stronger and more active? The alternatives we have been proposing now for several years have become far more serious in the light of what happened at Seveso and what it made us discover about medications and food. The booklets we have produced on 'abortion and contraception', on 'self-help', and the next on 'childcare', can become a real help and a way to escape from all those passionately interested in our health, such as doctors, chemists and big business. But there is still more to be written. 'Beauty care', according to our own ideas of 'care' and 'beauty'; 'hygiene and cancer'; 'pregnancy and birth', etc.

What is more difficult is to organise ourselves in such a way as to prevent this destruction. We need to force the closure of places which endanger the female and male employees or which pollute the environment. *We need first to destroy what is destroying us.*

For the moment *they* frighten us, and not the other way round. We intrigue them perhaps, we sometimes make them argue, but we do not frighten them. In other words, we have not enough power. That is why a women's centre is an indispensable instrument for us, in order to become stronger and more numerous. We should think about controlling our bodies in a more global way, as it is not only men and doctors who behave aggressively towards our bodies, but also the multinationals! What worse aggression against the body of women, against the children of women than that of La Roche-Givaudan at Seveso? From 10 July 1976, their entire lives have been taken over by the 'accident', and the effects are going to last a long time.

The story of Seveso shows clearly that it is either them or us who direct our affairs, and if it is not us, then the world becomes hell. It is a question of power over our own lives or their domination by others.

44

And it is every one of us, female and male, alone or all together who can do something to change the ratio of strength to our advantage.

5

The Politics of Women's Health

Nancy Worcester[1]

Control over and involvement in the kind of health care available to women, as much as concern over the environmental factors undermining that health, have been important items on the feminist agenda. From her experience in the women's health movement, Nancy Worcester draws some threads together.

Health is a political issue. Understanding and confronting the politics of health is central to the women's movement. Women call upon the health service more than men for a number of reasons. We live longer. We still tend to be the ones responsible for children's health care. We tend to be the ones (even when it is progressively labelled 'community care') responsible for older parents, the chronically sick and disabled. We are the ones who have periods, babies and the menopause. Normal healthy situations, like pregnancy and childbirth are too often medicalised and treated as illness. Real problems, such as period pains and miscarriage, are too often treated as normal. Women play an important role in the health service, but often that role is in low-status jobs which minimise the say that women have in decision-making. Women need to be both physically and mentally healthy in order to play a full, active role in society, but we live in a society where some women have a much better chance of being healthy than do other women. Only fundamental changes in society will mean that all women can realise their full health potential regardless of class background, race, or sexual orientation.

I want to look at some of the issues taken up by the women's health movement, and in particular to draw upon my experiences and discussions within the British women's movement. Where appropriate, however, I shall contrast our campaigns and struggles with those of our sisters elsewhere. Additionally, I shall look at China and Cuba as examples of where fundamental changes in society have affected the health of women and where specific women's health issues arise from the particular circumstances in these countries.

As women, we cannot control our own lives until we have control over our own bodies. Therefore, understanding and gaining control of our bodies has been central to the women's movement. Building on the principles of the wider women's movement, the women's health movement has been based on the practice of consciousness-raising; knowing, understanding, sharing experiences and oppression is seen as essential to changing them.[2]

The women's health movement is made up of a wide range of groups involved in different activities and campaigns. Health has often been a central issue even for feminists who have not consciously identified themselves as a part of this movement. Women are playing a crucial role in evaluating medical practice.

The health service in a country reflects the priorities and values of that society, so our critique of health services mirrors our analysis of what is wrong with society in general. Thus, different women and women's groups have directed their energies into health activities and campaigns in ways that are most in line with how they have defined the wider struggles.[3,4]

Liberal feminists view medical control over women's health as a consequence of the preponderance of men in medicine. Liberal feminists seek equal opportunities 'within the system', and work towards equal opportunities and employment for women in the health service (e.g. more women doctors). They are critical of the patronising attitudes of doctors.

Radical feminists consider the division between man and woman as the primary contradiction in society. They see current medical knowledge and practice as controlled by men and inherently patriarchal. Radical feminists have worked through self-help groups and women's clinics to establish women-defined and women-controlled health care.

Marxist feminists see women's oppression as inevitable under capitalism. Medicine, linked to the dominant ideology of science and capitalist interests, perpetuates the social class structure without serving the health needs of much of the population. Marxist-feminists emphasise that essential changes in health and health care are not possible without fundamental social and economic changes.

Basic Health Issues

We live in a society where some women have a better chance of being healthy than do other women. In the UK, the government itself has given us data showing social class differences in women's health.[5] For women who reach the age of 15, the risk of death before retirement age is 2.5 times as great in poor (class V) as in rich (class I) women. Of course, social class differences in health start much earlier in life. Low birth weight babies and stillbirths are nearly twice as common in poor families (social classes IV and V) as in rich families (classes I and II). Figures related to infant mortality (deaths in the first year of life) are usually considered an excellent index for assessing the health of a population. This figure will reflect the health of the mother and children's 'start in life' complemented with the back-up from the health care system. Infant mortality is at least 2.5 times higher among the poor. Girls are biologically stronger than boys, but class differences obliterate the sexual advantage so that, throughout infancy and childhood, a boy born to rich parents will have a better chance of surviving than does a girl born to poor parents.

On a global scale, social economic factors rivalling women's biological advantage are even more exaggerated. In many western countries, the average woman will live seven or eight years longer than the average man. In developing countries, e.g. India, a woman's lifespan is likely to be shorter than a man's. The average North American woman lives to be 77; the average African woman lives to be 50. These figures are useful in reminding us of the importance of social and economic factors in influencing health, but in looking at health statistics we must be careful to remember that they reflect more about the quantity of a woman's life than about the quality of that life. The women's health movement is concerned about both.

Groups of women in Britain have been looking at the relationship between specific factors and women's physical and mental health. The Social Causes of Women's Ill Health Conference recently brought together groups of women working on this approach to health issues. Topics covered included food/nutrition; lead; physical environment and housing; racism; stress; medically-induced ill health; unemployment; smoking; alcohol; sexuality; work hazards; and violence. Each issue poses many questions for women concerned about their relationship to health and strategies for change. In working towards a society where health is a priority, there can be contradictions involved in making demands specific to women's health issues. For example, when women are exposed to hazards at work, a short-term victory could be gained by emphasising the relationship of the hazard to the emotional issue of women's reproductive role. However, this demand again emphasises the role of woman as baby producer rather than worker. We know that protective legislation can ultimately be used against equality of working conditions and rewards for women. Fighting work hazards on the issue of risks to women's reproductive capacity also hides the relationship of work hazards to men's reproductive role, health hazards not related to reproduction, and the overall issue of healthy working conditions for all workers.

Other women's health issues arise directly from specific aspects of oppression. For example, a lesbian care project at the Amsterdam Women's Health Clinic observed, 'There aren't so many illnesses that are specific to lesbians as problems that are directly related to their oppression as lesbians.'[6] Women in Africa are working to get the practice of female genital mutilation banned, but see this campaign as a part of the wider struggle against women's oppression.[7] It is not easy to overcome health aspects of oppression. In order to do so, health services must be accessible to everyone regardless of their geographical location, class, sex, race or sexuality. A woman who cannot read or write will need to have details and 'choices' of medical treatment discussed with her more thoroughly than if she were able to read information herself.

Poverty is of course the world's greatest health hazard and killer. Even a superficial look at China and Cuba shows that changes in the social and economic structure of a country can drastically improve the health of women. The quality of life for a woman in pre-liberation China was determined by the ideals of Confucianism. Young girls had their feet broken and bound from the age of six to make them sexually attractive so that they could be sold into marriage. Chinese women would often have to go through numerous pregnancies, only to be forced to sell their children into servitude rather than watch them starve to death. Their life expectancy was short, with pregnancies frequently meaning death from problems in labour or puerperal fever. Pre-revolutionary Cuba was the playground for the USA. More than 70 percent of working women were stuck working as prostitutes and servants for the Americans. Many of them survived only on sugar and water for long periods of their short lives. In both countries, doctors and medical services were only for the rich, and women were held in such low esteem that it was hardly considered worth calling a doctor to see them if they were sick.

In China and Cuba 'good health care for the entire population' were battle cries of the revolutionary struggles. Both revolutions shared the recognition that basic socio-economic changes – improvements in public hygiene (clean water, sewage disposal), food distribution, insuring a basic adequate housing and education – were

49

prerequisites to improving the health of the population. Working towards provision of these basics was the major step in breaking the poverty → malnutrition → infection → death cycle, tragically familiar in both countries. Added to this, then, were the guarantees for good health-care provision based on preventative rather than curative medicine, and a commitment to changing the roles of women. Because of this combination of priorities, the health of women in both countries has improved drastically. Women's life expectancy in Cuba increased from 50 years in the 1950s to 72 in 1980. Infant mortality rates in China have dropped to below 30 in every 1,000, from a pre-revolutionary figure of 130 in every 1,000. In both China and Cuba women are able to play healthy active roles in the building of their socialist societies.

Preventative Health Care

The women's movement is concerned about health, not illness, so we have taken a *preventative* approach to health care. Critical of the curative, 'patch-up' approach of the medical world, we have questioned whether we have a National Health Service (NHS) or a 'National Sickness Service'.

Self-help and self-examination groups have been set up so that women can get to know their own bodies. These groups work from the premise that if a woman has confidence in her observations about her body, she will best be able to notice any changes in her body. These changes will indicate to her when she is ovulating, pregnant, or when her body requires a change of lifestyle. A woman in touch with her body will know when she should seek other medical treatment. Women's groups and classes have put an emphasis on the role of diet, exercise, sleep and lifestyle in maintaining good physical and mental health.

However, the women's health movement has recognised the limitations of this individualistic approach to health and, as discussed above, has recognised the wider social and economic causes of women's ill health. We have been critical that most health education materials virtually ignore the social and economic factors related to health. Their campaigns seldom go beyond the individualistic 'victim blaming', 'It's your own fault if you are not healthy' approach. With cuts in health service provision, we have to be careful of schemes which simply encourage self-help groups and 'look after yourself' projects as a way of shifting responsibility on to individuals.

Well Woman Clinics (WWCs) have been one of the most promising aspects of preventative women's health care within the NHS. They are clinics where women go when they are 'well' for a 'chat and a check up', extra time being allowed for general history taking and discussion. WWCs, set up in a number of different ways, have been available only on a sporadic basis depending upon local decisions, but they have proven to be popular with women wherever they have been set up. Many of us feel enthusiastic about campaigning to get more WWCs established. Unfortunately, with financial cuts in health services and increasing emphasis on high technology curative medicine, our fight is all too often to save the preventative services we have. As a doctor from a popular, oversubscribed WWC comments, 'We are very vulnerable. We may be closed soon because our statistics do not show that we find enough cancer.' How do we prove the value of a preventative health programme; who can put a price tag on a woman's peace of mind at having a negative cancer test?

In contrast to most western countries, prevention rather than curing is the basis of health programmes in both Cuba and China. China's use of traditional medicine, emphasising a 'whole body' approach to health care, blurs our distinction between health care and medicine. Herbs and acupuncture are used in many ways to keep the body in balance. Herbal remedies are used for period pains, to increase breast milk during lactation and to improve fertility. The role of exercise in health is also emphasised; Chinese streets and parks are full of people doing their regular exercises and whole factories may be scheduled an 'exercise session'. In both China and Cuba women are screened annually for both breast and cervical cancers. Cuban gynaecologists stress that cervical smears are available to *all* sexually active women no matter how young. They are routinely given to all women over 30. Contrast this to Britain where doctors are only paid to screen women over 35 years of age and in a few special categories. Cuba's 'Dispensarizacion' programme provides a model of how a preventative health programme can work. Small units in local polyclinics (evenly distributed throughout the country in relation to geography and population density) keep detailed health records of all members of the community. All individuals in vulnerable groups (children under five, people over 65, asthmatics, diabetics, hypertensives, etc.) have a fixed minimum number of visits with a doctor per year. Some of these visits take place in the home so that the doctor is aware of the home environment and its relationship to health issues.

My contribution here would not be an accurate reflection of preventative health issues in the women's health movement if it did not mention debates regarding the value of screening for women's

51

cancer. Women have questioned whether early screening for breast cancer is of real value.[8] Women are also emphasising that early *detection* of cervical cancer must not be confused with its *prevention*.[9]

Women and Reproduction

Many of women's special health needs are related to our reproductive role and our comparatively complex reproductive organs. Women are critical of the attitudes of patriarchal medicine towards these health conditions. Real problems – period pains, thrush, cystitis and vaginal infections – are too often ignored because they are not directly related to the reproductive functions of pregnancy and childbirth in which doctors have chosen to be interested. On the other hand, controlling our fertility, pregnancy and childbirth are the main reasons why perfectly healthy women come in contact with the medical profession; these normal healthy situations have however become overly medicalised.

Women's health campaigns have often centred on one of the numerous aspects of 'a woman's right to choose'. We have campaigned for safe, reliable contraceptives backed up by safe abortion. We emphasise that we require contraception, which is *both* effective and does not involve health risks. Too often contraceptives have simply been evaluated in terms of their contraceptive reliability; women have had to cope with undesirable side effects and health risks. Accurate information, written in a language and style easily understood, is essential for women to choose contraceptives most appropriate for their use.

We need a wide range of safe, reliable contraceptives. Contraceptive needs are very different from one woman to another, during various stages of a woman's life, in different kinds of relationships and from one culture to another. Some of the factors which we have found to influence contraceptive choice are:

(1) The importance of not getting pregnant A woman will be able to choose to use a less reliable form of contraceptive if it is not absolutely crucial that she not become pregnant or if she has the back-up of a safe abortion and feels able to make that decision.

(2) Types of relationships Some contraceptives may be more appropriate in some relationships than others, e.g. if the man can be trusted to take responsibility for contraception, all or part of the time, the choice is slightly wider. A 'use as you do it!' type of contraceptive may be more appropriate if intercourse is infrequent and the woman

52

is concerned about the 'continuous' health risks of the IUD, pill, or injectables.

(3) Climate Many contraceptives will deteriorate quickly in high temperatures. Reliable regular sources or refrigeration will minimise this problem.

(4) Attitude towards one's own body If a woman does not feel comfortable touching the inside of her body, she will probably require a method which does not involve this.

(5) Attitude of men If men do not 'approve' of the woman controlling her fertility, she will need to choose a form that men cannot sabotage. Apparently, some women in India 'choose' injectable contraceptives for this reason.

(6) Nutrition The pill is thought to increase some nutritional requirements, such as vitamin B_6, and the IUD can increase blood loss thus increasing the iron requirement. These methods will not be appropriate for a malnourished woman unless the diet can be improved.

(7) Availability Because of the USA economic blockade of Cuba for many years women in Cuba had to depend on a 'home-made' type of IUD made from fishing wire. (Cuba now makes the pill, but the IUD remains more popular.)

(8) Pattern of use In many western countries, young women use contraceptives for a number of years *before* having a child. In China, where pre-marital sex has been uncommon and late marriage encouraged, many women use contraception for the first time only *after* they have 'completed their family'. A contraceptive thought to interfere with future fertility will be far more appropriate in the latter situation.

(9) Age A woman's age may influence both health and social issues related to contraception. The rhythm method may be confusing and unreliable to use during menopausal years.

(10) Other issues A number of health and lifestyle factors will mean that some forms of contraception are less safe or appropriate than others. A woman who does not have appropriate toilet facilities may find it awkward to use the cap and contraceptive cream.

The 'woman's right to choose' campaigns have often worked around the demand for safe reliable abortions and the woman's right to be the *one* who decides whether or not she has an abortion. Early abortions are easier, safer and usually less traumatic for the woman. Our campaigns for the right to abortion and the availability of abortion facilities must also emphasise the need for reliable early pregnancy testing (a service which some NHS labs are actually cutting) and the accessibility of information on abortion so that minimum time passes between the decision to have an abortion and the actual procedure.

A 'woman's right to choose' must also mean that a woman can make the choice to have a child or as many children as she chooses. Economic and social factors may prevent a woman from being able to choose to have a child. For women to actually be able to make this choice, good childcare facilities must be available. Furthermore, she must have economic support for the child or be able to work for this, and she must still be able to play an active role in society. The choice to have a child involves the right to a healthy pregnancy and safe delivery. In order that women can attend ante-natal classes or clinics, these must be located in places easily reached by public transport, have childcare facilities and be open at hours convenient to women. Cuban women are given regular times off work during pregnancy to attend ante-natal clinics and the paediatrician and nurse will visit the woman in her home during pregnancy. The women's health movement in England has looked at ways to demedicalise the birth process and many women have been involved in campaigns for home deliveries. In contrast, Cuba is proud of her achievement in making hospital deliveries available now to 98 percent of her women. Women in the countryside can go to special maternity homes several days before their delivery so that they do not have to worry about the last minute journey. Women in Cuba are not asking for a return to home births, because housing conditions are still crowded and often inadequate, and it is only 20 years since women in difficulty died trying to get a doctor or midwife to help.

A 'woman's right to choose' campaigns have not always remembered that some women have not had the choice to have children. The women's movement is only starting to look at some 'forgotten areas of reproduction'. As women share their experiences of infertility, miscarriage and stillbirth we become aware of how common these experiences are. We need to know more about these situations and how to prevent, overcome, or cope with them. Women are setting up self-insemination groups so that women (e.g., lesbians and single women) who do not meet the medical establishment's qualifications for artificial insemination can still pursue this method of fertilisation.

We have been critical of racist population policies and population policies which encourage or discourage women's childbearing in relation *only* to the country's need. Depo Provera is an injectable contraceptive often given to women without their permission or without their understanding of the implications of being given this drug. The campaign against Depo Provera is built on examining the wider issues of racism in population programmes and the relationship between women's control of their own fertility and international population planning agencies.

Mental Health

Mental health is as important as physical health in enabling women to play their full role in society. Feminists are concerned with the prevalence of mental illness in women. We are also concerned about the basic causes of mental illness and the treatment of mental problems.

A number of recent studies have shown that depression is depressingly common in women and is more usual in working-class women than in middle-class women. More than twice as many women as men consult their doctors with emotional problems. Married women are more apt to suffer from a 'breakdown' than any other group.[10] Single women are less apt to suffer from a 'breakdown' than either married women or single men. Not surprisingly, married men are the group least likely to suffer a 'breakdown'.

Changing hormonal situations (after childbirth, pre-menstruation, during menopause) and their relationship to depression is an area feminists need to research. We must make certain that mood changes are understood in relation to the realities of women's lives. It is interesting to note that different cultural groups seem to respond in different ways to hormonal change situations. For example, Chinese women claim to have no post-natal depression and depression during menopause is not thought to be common, but Chinese women seem to suffer a lot from period pains. Feelings sometimes associated with menopause in western women may be more related to the changing identity/loss of identity of women in mid life in our society than to hormonal changes. Similarly, post-natal depression may be more related to the practicality of what motherhood means for a woman than her changing hormonal levels. Ann Oakley, whose research has found 'post-natal blues' and anxiety to be common in first-time mothers, has suggested that our understanding of this condition may be hampered by researchers looking for 'Why do some women adjust badly to motherhood?' We may learn more about both the realities of motherhood and post-natal depression by asking, 'Why do some women adjust well?'[11]

When women seek medical help with their emotional problems

they are far too often given mood-changing drugs which do nothing to alleviate the *causes* of their anxiety or depression. Few women have access to other forms of therapy and when therapy is available it may be directed towards encouraging a woman to adjust to unhealthy situations. As alternatives, feminists have initiated self-help groups. Self-help groups have been centered on such issues as domestic violence, rape, anorexia, compulsive eating, isolation as mothers and specific health issues. Women's Therapy Centres, providing feminist therapy to both individuals and groups, have been set up in England and the United States.

We would, of course, argue that women's mental ill health is related to our oppression as women and we are working to change this. However, as women working to bring about fundamental changes in society, we must also recognise that the changing roles of women, or more accurately our increased expectations but unchanged reality, will itself be a source of stress.

Women and the Health Services

Women are the backbone of the health service. Over 70 percent of the workers in the NHS are female. But, the role of women in the health service reflects the role of women in society. Men are in powerful, high-status positions and make the decisions. Women play a subservient role and are responsible for the 'caring' aspects of health care. This division of responsibility is partly responsible for the fact that patriarchal medicine cannot relate to women's health-care needs.

Women are the most affected by financial cuts in health services and by changing health priorities. A greater shift is being made towards curative medicine and special facilities for women are closing. Women are taking more responsibility for disabled and elderly members of the community as other services are cut. The growth of private medicine means that some women and children will have access to better medical care than others. And, of course, women's jobs are disappearing.

In a number of countries, particularly the United States and Australia, feminists have set up women's health clinics and provide feminist alternatives to conventional medical provision. Decisions are made collectively by all health workers. Services emphasise self-help, preventative and alternative health care. The philosophy of patients' rights means that patients have access to their own medical records, participate in decisions concerning their own health and are informed of test results, medication and treatment procedures. Education is seen as an integral part of health care.

The NHS, and changes in the NHS, provide a special challenge to the women's health movement in the UK. It has been crucial that we work in and for the NHS. For the most part, this has meant that we have tried not to set up alternatives outside the service, but have tried to bring feminist issues into our struggles to improve the NHS. Much of socialist-feminist activity has been focused on fighting cuts in the NHS, working to save women's jobs in the health service and trying to save special facilities for women. These campaigns have been full of contradictions for feminists as we fight to preserve a service which does not serve our needs. We often find ourselves in campaigns more related to the quantity of service than the quality of that service.

The Politics of Information

We have recognised that understanding our bodies is essential to having control over our bodies and our lives; we have also recognised that much of the power of the medical profession comes from their possession and use of knowledge and information which we do not have. Access to information is essential for us to make decisions about our bodies and our lives.[12]

While we are working to overcome our ignorance, it is crucial to understand that our ignorance is no accident and that we have to understand why our ignorance has come about. Some information is more available than other information, e.g. numerous leaflets are printed on hormone replacement drugs for menopause, but it is difficult to learn about the importance of diet and exercise during menopause. Information is often written in a style and language not easily understood; this perpetuates the feeling that the consumer is ignorant and important decisions should be left to the 'experts'. Most information is made available in order to *sell* a particular product or idea. Very little information is actually designed to enable us to make our own decisions about health care.

We see it as essential that women collect, evaluate and share information relevant to women's needs, making it accessible to other women. Information centres have been established by the Politics of Health Group (London), the Boston Women's Health Collective and other groups, precisely for this purpose. Many health activists and groups are involved in sharing information through women's health courses and feminist writing. The evolution of *Our Bodies, Ourselves,*[13] by the Boston Women's Health Collective, is representative of the women's health movement. The book grew out of a collection of papers put together for a course the group was doing. The course, the papers and ultimately the book, reflect a feminist analysis of health. Information is given in an easily understood way to help women choose health care appropriate to their needs and value is given to women's own experiences. The book has now been revised several times to reflect the movement's development. Special editions are appropriate to women in different countries, and the book is now published in Spanish, Italian, Dutch, Swedish, Japanese, German, Portuguese and Chinese. Feminists must also be involved in and influence basic research so that 'the right questions' are asked and medical knowledge is more accurate about women.

As feminists, we are concerned that basic social and economic factors are still the major factors determining one's chances of being healthy. Health services reflect the priorities and values of society. Therefore, we consider our fight for health care relevant to the needs of *all* women to be an integral part of our struggle for fundamental changes in society.

6
Feminism – Healing the Patriarchal Dis-ease

Jill Raymond and Janice Wilson

Homœopathy is an old and well established healing art and as such an important part of the holistic health movement. Here Jill Raymond and Janice Wilson make the connection between the deeper notion of health striven for by homœopathy and the health of our society as a whole. Feminism, they say, is a powerful homœopathic remedy. It goes beyond the symptoms to the deeper causes of our troubles: the imbalance between masculine and feminine energies, manifested in the ills of patriarchy.

In our current western societies, there is little or no understanding of the need for individual human beings to achieve balance on all levels – physical, emotional, mental and spiritual – if they are to be healthy. The same applies to the planet as a whole: patriarchal culture does not acknowledge the radical dis-ease in the world caused by the imbalance between male and female power, between man and nature.

The question is, how to redress this imbalance? We define feminism as the re-in-statement of the female principle in all her diverse forms, and therefore see it as the remedy to the planet's disease. And yet many people are confused about the way in which feminism works. Is it really effective? Doesn't it often make matters worse? It struck us that feminism is *not* a cure in the sense understood by modern, orthodox medicine (allopathic medicine). It is, in fact, far closer to homœopathy in form and effect.

Homœopathy, derived from the Greek *homoio* and *pathos* meaning 'similar suffering', is based on the principle that a substance which, in its crude form, would cause certain symptoms in a healthy body, can cure a sick body suffering from similar symptoms. A fundamental symptom of patriarchy is sexism; this means that male values are separated from female values and regarded as inherently superior. Any woman who wishes to be in a position of power under the patriarchal system must operate according to rules made by men, e.g. Mrs Thatcher. Women who wish to change this and see a balance between the sexes must first of all reclaim their own powers. It is in order to dis-cover female values and empower themselves that feminists meet separately from men. This can be seen as sexist and similar to the fundamental symptom of patriarchy. It is following the principle that 'like cures like' and is the remedy homœopathic to the disease.

The indicated remedy is prepared by succussion and dilution. Succussion is the shaking of the remedy in liquid form between each of its dilutions. The combination of succussion and dilution potentises the substance and releases its dynamic energy. Dynamic female energy, feminism, has been released through centuries of succussion. The greater the dilution and succussion the greater the potency. Though fewer and fewer particles of the original substance are left after every dilution, the energy and power of those particles increases. The potency of the remedy lies in the quality of the energy produced and not in its quantity.

As individuals, many feminists today are feeling a backlash to the latest rebirth and growth of the women's liberation movement . . . we are feared by many 'male-identified' women; sexual violence, actual and imitated, are increasing; orthodox or allopathic medicine (from the Greek 'other suffering') continues to invent new and more horrendous ways of immobilising our female bodies. Lesbians are accused of being unsuitable as mothers. Feminists are generally accused of man-hating and then promptly dismissed. On a political level, Britain alone has over three and a half million unemployed and many women are being forced back into the home, financially dependent on men or the state. The US Senate has failed to ratify the Equal Rights Amendment. Women in Iran are forced back behind the veil and off the streets as one of patriarchy's fiercest upholders revels in religious revival. If we see feminism as an applied remedy then we can recognise all the examples mentioned above as aggravations of the symptoms of patriarchy.

Aggravation of the symptoms is a homœopathic principle which applies only in chronic illness. In chronic illness the body cannot identify the root of its dis-ease; its view becomes obscured. The indicated remedy will stir up the vital force, sharpening and intensifying the perception of the symptoms, as a scene blurred through a lens becomes clear when it is focussed. 'The remedy creates for a time a heightened exacerbation of the symptoms which is the only manifestation of its action visible to our perception.'[1] Heartening news for feminists?

A far less well known homœopathic principle is that of miasms. It is difficult to grasp as it deals with the genetic history of the patient but it is particularly interesting. Miasms are taints of dis-ease inherited genetically throughout the history of man-kind. They can be likened to a room with flowers in it; when the flowers are removed their scent or taint will remain. Hanhemann, who formulated the laws of homœopathy in the eighteenth century, recognised three miasms: the psoric, the syphilitic and the sycotic.

The *psoric miasm* was universal in Hanhemann's time. It is the oldest and deepest taint and provides the foundation necessary for further dis-ease. It is characterised by underfunctioning and is physically sluggish, mentally fearful and lacking in trust. Its presence is indicated on the skin. The origin of 'psora' is taken to have occurred at the time of the 'fall from grace' as described in the Bible in Genesis. This corresponds, culturally, with the takeover of matriarchal cultures (i.e., Goddess-worshipping, woman-centered cultures especially apparent in the Mediterranian countries until around 2,000 BC) by the male-dominated, God-worshipping cultures that are now worldwide (astrologically, the Piscean age). This departure from the understanding and worshipping of the life-giving forces of the Great Goddess has left us open to destructive and life-sapping influences.

It is in the nature of living things to keep morbid influences as far from the vital organs as possible. The initial miasm, therefore, was present only on the skin (as sores, eruptions, boils, etc.), the most obvious example of which was leprosy. Skin problems are an unsightly mark of dis-ease. There is evidence that even in ancient Egypt attempts were made to cover up or suppress these outward signs by any means possible, driving the dis-ease from the skin's surface deeper into the body's tissues. Interestingly, one of the most common substances used for this was sulphur, which is now used homœopathically to cure skin eruptions.

The *syphilitic miasm* and the gonorrhoeal or sycotic miasm are both dis-eases of sexual origin. The syphilitic condition is characterised by cruelty, destructiveness, physical deformity and a lack of love. Outwardly it attacks the genital organs; inwardly it has a profound effect on the mental state. One of the homœopathic remedies for syphilis is mercury; this was used extensively by orthodox medicine to suppress the symptoms of syphilis until antibiotics replaced it.

Male-centered cultures became frightened and obsessed by woman's sexuality; her menstrual cycle, her ability to give birth, her changing powers according to the moon, were all beyond male control. Once female spirituality was perverted, female sexuality was

61

open to similar abuse. Our sexuality became the deformed and controllable property of men through monogamous and polygamous marriage. The cruelty of the syphilitic miasm can be seen in the persecution of witches that occurred in the middle ages. The male-dominated Christian church persecuted women ruthlessly . . . 'nine million menstrual murders'. 'Witches, whose natural crafts were midwifery, hypnotism, healing, dowsing, dream-study and sexual fulfilment'[2] were tortured and burned and their roles taken over by men.

The *sycotic miasm* is often called the gonorrhoeal miasm. It is characterised by overfunctioning: the sycotic person is never at peace – always wanting and producing more, insatiable and ambitious. The body expresses sycosis by growths, warts, moles and discharges. Layers of concrete, cars and industrial pollution are the expression, at a planetary level, of sycotic growths.

We can see the sycotic miasm in man's desire to control nature. Dissatisfied with the earth's riches, he must over-produce and create wealth for himself; expand his territory; get bigger; get quicker; get further; get more. The tree of life, or 'Thuja', is the most used homœopathic remedy for sycosis.

The Industrial Revolution is an example of the results of all three miasms. The (syphilitic) destruction of the natural environment and the interference in the balance of the planet's ecology is directly linked to (sycotic) over-production and greed. Physically, the industrial revolution provided a wonderful environment for dis-ease in city slums, with appalling working conditions and poor sanitation. A combination of the psoric and syphilitic miasms is seen in the dis-ease of the age, tuberculosis. The TB era saw destruction on a grand scale; two world wars, the Crimean and the Boer war all took place during this time.

Disease, having been continually driven deeper by suppression has now reached the stage where disorder occurs within the cell. Cancer is the condition where the cell continues to multiply itself far beyond its needs. Homœopathically, cancer is seen as a fusion of all three miasms and is a deeply chronic state. This stage has also seen man develop the ability to disorganise and split the atom, enabling him to completely destroy the entire planet. Scientists have finally dis-covered how to clone living things and create life in a test-tube; how to overcome death by mechanisation and the promise of resurrection by deep-freezing. The symbols of fertile womanhood, the womb, the ovaries and the breasts are being surgically removed as though they were no more than vestigial organs.

The nuclear age, its nuclear power, nuclear bombs and nuclear family have threatened the very nucleus of life. The nuclear family would appear to be the smallest viable unit in present society; yet women are splitting away from the male-defined boundaries which previously contained them, spinning off with incredible determination, releasing gyn-ergy (woman-energy). It isn't easy . . . hang on, the baby's crying! . . . but it is happening.

We have seen how historically the rise of patriarchy is balanced by the fall of matriarchy. Until recently patriarchy has ensured that only men have had the 'privilege' and power to be the explorers, soldiers and mad scientists. Within the procession of educated scientists, a certain exclusive fraternity evolved a replacement for the healers their fore-fathers had destroyed.

The doctors continue to refine their methods of suppression of the physical symptoms, at the same time surgically and chemically mutilating and invading women's bodies. Their ultimate aim is the takeover of the last layer of female be-ing: to create life in their test tubes and replace goddess-given birth. Similarly, they see death as an illness which they seek to control and master.

What are now termed 'holistic medicines', traditionally practised mainly by women, were replaced by allopathic medicine, traditionally practised mainly by men. But medicine is reflecting the re-claiming of the female principle. The 'new age' (astrologically, the Aquarian age) is exemplified by a re-vival of the female principle, and it is worth noting that the majority of young, apprentice homœo-paths, herbalists, etc., are women.

All these holistic methods of healing are inter-related, and not mutually exclusive, unlike allopathy, which is intellectual and rejects these more intuitive and spiritually-aware practices. Allopathic medicine takes power over and from the body and replaces it with drugs, whereas holistic medicine restores the body's own powers of healing. In the same way, it is up to women to restore the female principle, and this involves women dis-covering their own true powers, on all levels.

We see the holistic healing arts as female-principled and allopathy as male-principled. The female-principled medicines respect the cycle of life and death, whereas the ultimate power of the male-principled medicine is to control life and death.

Homœopathy recognises three levels of disease. Although we describe these layers separately they form an integrated totality, each dependent on every other and necessary for the healthy be-ing of the whole.

The first level affects the physical body. The second the emotional plane, e.g., moods, anger, depression, anxiety. The third level is the mental plane, which is traditionally the male preserve: the intellect. It is on this plane that changes in consciousness and understanding take place. Beyond these three levels are the spiritual plane and the will itself: the wish to survive, the life energy or the vital force. As Helen Caldicott has remarked, if we have lost our will to survive we are very sick indeed.

The potency of homœopathic remedies follows a harmonic scale that corresponds with these levels of disease. The least potent have an affinity with the physical body, those in the middle with the emotional plane and the most potent (i.e., those most dilute and succussed) with the mental and spiritual planes. The remedies highest on the potency scale can have repercussions throughout the system, percolating through the layers down to the physical plane.

As a remedy, feminism can be seen to correspond with this potency scale. The early demands of the women's movement at the turn of the century were for physical recognition (women's suffrage) and for better health and maternity care. At that time few women realised that this was not enough. Though 'dilute' in male provinces such as education, industry and politics, women gradually emerged through the emotional 1960s, angrily demanding equal rights, equal pay and liberation! The early 1970s saw the rebirth of women-identified literature, music and the growth of groups aimed at changing the consciousness and understanding of womankind.

The most recently deepened understanding of woman power is on a psychic and spiritual level – our quintessential state of energy. Women are linking their energies through feminism, which is leading many of us to play a strong and creative role in the peace movement in the face of the nuclear threat. Greenham Common Women's Peace Camp is a fine example of this connecting of energies.

How can we tell if our energy, the remedy, is having any effect? Well, homœopathically, the laws of cure state that symptoms disappear in the reverse order of their appearance: i.e., the latest symptoms are the first to be relieved. In the most recent male take-over of a woman's role – technological childbirth – midwives are reduced to technical assistants and mothers become spectators. The re-claiming of natural childbirth by an increasing number of women is beginning to re-instate birth as an experience of the power of the life force. This re-membering of birth is beginning to relieve the latest symptom of patriarchy.

There is one last principle guiding the prescribing of homœopathic

64

remedies, which is that the remedy must match every symptom if it is to reach the real cause of the imbalance. This may take several remedies, in turn and together, as they work through the different levels. Women are beginning to address themselves to all the ways they suffer in the hands of patriarchy. Women are understanding the true cause of the dis-ease we are all (women and men alike) sick with and sick of! In our different ways we are confronting our oppressions and their origin. Our real strength lies in our diversity, not in sheer physical numbers. It is the quality of what we are doing, not the quantity of it, that matters. As we try to use means that are compatible with our ends, feminists can become a potent remedy for society's ills. As any homœopath will tell you, only the patient application of remedies, which are appropriate to different symptoms and are of the correct potency, will bring about a deep and lasting healing.[3]

Ask a Stupid Question

(For the FBI agent who, inquiring about a sister, asked 'Who is in her network?')

Who is in my network,
what links us, to be exact?
Better ask to understand the force
that cuts through rock the water's course,
and binding like to like
makes also opposites attract.

Who guides the earthworm underground,
and makes the stubborn ants persist?
When wind and rain erode the land,
who calls the root work to resist?
And what clandestine hand inscribed
the coded message in the seed?
Who masterminds the spider's web,
and plans the strategy of the weed?

What inspiration could invent
the infrastructure of the vine,

the grass revolt against cement,
the rebellion of the dandelion?
What force undermines the walls
to make them crack,
or makes the branches of the tree
when cut grow back?
Who conceals the passages between death and birth?
Who leads the revolution of the earth?

Who is in my network,
what links us, to be exact?
Better ask to understand the force
that cuts through rock the water's course
and binding like to like
makes also opposites attract.

Investigate the daisies for invasion of the lawn,
or the ivy for trespass where it wants to grow.
Indict the sky for pouring out its rain,
contributing to the river's overflow.
Arrest the seagull for unlawful flight,
impose a boundary to confine the sea,
demand a mountain modify its height,
dare my woman-spirit to break free.

Susan Saxe
Susan Saxe is a political prisoner, poet and organiser.
This poem was inspired by a real-life incident.

7
Feminism and Ecology: Theoretical Connections

Stephanie Leland

The cross-fertilisation of feminism with ecology is a potential source for exciting social and cultural changes in the last decades of this century. Here, in an article originally written for the May 1981 issue of Resurgence *and subsequently developed for several other journals in the UK and overseas, Stephanie Leland traces some of the underlying themes giving rise to this phenomenon.*

Dualism, perceiving the world as a set of opposite principles, is an essential stage in the evolution of human consciousness. It is the recognition of the 'other' which signifies the birth of the ego out of the dark unconscious; as in nature, when the seed travels from the dark earth towards the light.

Within prepolarised unconsciousness there are no distinctions, there is no sexual differentiation. 'Sexual differentiation is not rooted in the constitution of life, but is a biological accident, a special device designed to meet certain conditions. This differentiation becomes marked in the higher organisms.'[1] Research into our earliest history has revealed the possibility that psychologically as well as biologically we began as unconscious hermaphrodites, reproducing parthenogenetically. In the simplest life-forms reproduction takes place asexually. As we move up the evolutionary ladder, in very primitive life-forms, such as ostracod crustaceans and nematode worms, the mode of reproduction is carried out by the female alone, parthenogenetically, or in pairs as hermaphrodites. In some species the male is entirely absent. 'Scientists know that the natural tendency of life on Earth is to be female. The female hormone oestrogen dates from early plant life, whereas the male androgen seems to be a recent invention and is produced by a minor alteration in the chemical structure of oestrogen.'[2] Human foetuses are all female until the eighth week after conception. If the foetus is to be male the hormone androgen occurs triggering the process which alters the female into a male. The 'Y' chromosome of the male is actually a stunted 'X' carrying very little genetic information of its own.[3]

Many of our earliest myths confirm this conception of our evolutionary beginnings. One of the oldest and most widely distributed Egyptian deities, going back to the predynastic era, is the goddess Net, or Neith. She is the personification of the original eternal female principle of life which was self-sustaining and self-existent. Yet she is also male, containing the seeds of an undeveloped masculine principle, and therefore is the prototype of parthenogenesis.[4]

As evidence suggests that a worldwide cataclysm, such as the shifting of poles or a sudden change in climate, is responsible for the extinction of the dinosaurs, it is also suggested that such a cataclysm caused the occurrence of sexual differentiation and reproduction. Whatever we may surmise, in psychohistorical terms, some mysterious evolutionary act of creation caused a revolution in our consciousness in which we began to view ourselves as separate from the cosmos. The striving toward individuation and independence had begun.

The birth of the ego, of conscious perception, is regarded in symbolic interpretation as the birth of patriarchal consciousness. It is the dawning of the intellect, of projecting concepts onto form. It is the division of unity into polarity: the evolution of the distinction between male and female, and between the polarities of the masculine and feminine principles in the human psyche.

As each culture imposes its own definitions and value judgements onto the polarities of masculine and feminine according to its own weaknesses and aspirations, it is necessary to clarify that the terms masculine and feminine should not be confused with sexual differences, are not to be interpreted as maleness or femaleness in the biological sense. Identifying masculine and feminine in terms of sexual differences has clouded the essential dynamic qualities and experience of the masculine and feminine principles. Though the essential nature of man is masculine and the essential nature of woman feminine, each of us is a reflection of the interplay and interrelatedness of the dynamic energies of both principles.

In terms of the polarity of the male and female principles, the urge to separate, to divide, to individuate, is a masculine impulse. Unfortunately, hand in hand with the positive evolutionary aspects of this impulse exist corresponding negative tendencies. The masculine drive to discriminate can result in extremism and conflict. Life is viewed as a battleground of irreconcilable opposites, such as masculine/feminine, subject/object, body/mind, good/evil, feeling/

intellect, black/white.

By conceptualising everything into conflicting mental images, a dichotomy of opposites is established which emphasises differences rather than relationships. Through focussing on differences we have become caught in a maze of intellectual definitions and symbols and have lost the actuality of the experience. Our primary, unitary feelings have become warped and prejudiced until feeling itself has become something to fear and avoid.

The emphasis on difference also creates insecurity and a corresponding need to belong in order to feel safe. Hence follows an identification with a chosen set of differences, which only serves to perpetuate separation and opposition. This behaviour is all too evident in our present-day society; obvious examples being teenage tribal gangs, minority ghettoes in our urban centres and blind adherence to religious sects. This reflects the erosion of our sense of individuality, whereby it no longer feels safe standing apart from the crowd, not identifying with a group or an ideology. What is lost is a sense of one's own centre and a belief in one's strength as an individual, as a single and very potent cell of the entire intricate web of life. The concept of safety as created under the influence of patriarchal consciousness is distorted and damaging.

The masculine urge to discriminate is followed by the tendency to dominate in order to feel secure in the choice of a particular set of differences. By placing greater value on one opposite over the other, a hierarchical system of values is created which filters into the social structure. Therefore, in contemporary western society, for example, to belong to the human species, to be white, to be male, to be rich, to be heterosexual, or to be adult is to be dominant. To be a non-human animal, or to be black, to be poor, to be female, to be homosexual, or to be a child is to be lower in the pecking order and to be subjected to oppression and a feeling of inadequacy.

Hierarchical social structure is fundamental to a society which is dominated by patriarchal consciousness. Within the dichotomy of Subject/Object, the prevailing masculine energy is Subject, and masculine thinking is considered superior, while that which is attributed to the feminine is considered inferior and becomes Object. Hence follows a social structure which favours the masculine and allows it full rein while suppressing the feminine. This has created a destructive imbalance within each individual which manifests itself on every level of our existence.

Perhaps the most distressing manifestation of this imbalance is created by the masculine drive for power. In its positive sense power

69

means 'the ability to do or act', 'vigour', 'energy'. But within a structure which depends upon dominance, on the concept of Subject/Object, power becomes used towards a negative end–for the purpose of subduing the Object in order to secure the position of the Subject.

This hierarchical power structure is the seed bed for the germination of the concept of oppressor/victim, friend/enemy. The creation of an 'enemy' is the fuel upon which the destructive fires of patriarchy depend. Without an enemy, there is no longer an excuse to subdue the other. Without an enemy, there is no longer a conceptual motivation for aggression and violence. Without an enemy, there is no war.

It is interesting and provoking to note how this concept of the enemy is used today by those in positions of power. The ramifications of the east/west Cold War are hypocritical and conceal deep-rooted corruption. Behind the extrovert aggression lies a web of economic and trade relationships which accrue vast profits for a small élite. While the west quietly benefits from state-controlled Gulag labour, the east benefits from the technological advances earned through the labour of western workers now being made redundant. Yet we are told that vast amounts of our resources must be utilised for building weapons against the very enemy we are in reality supporting.

In this light it becomes depressingly obvious that the politics of patriarchy is merely a game which distracts us from the real issues and only serves to perpetuate the hierarchical concentration of power in the hands of the few. Those few appear to have allegiance to no particular country or ideology but only to their own survival in positions of power. Yet the idea of nationalism is encouraged and exaggerated to the cost of many human lives and indeed to the detriment of the condition and quality of life of most of humanity.

Though aggression and violence expresses itself throughout Nature it is only in the human species that it is expended over abstract issues, such as religious or political ideologies. It is also only the human species that has learned to employ more and more cruel methods of violence on emotional and psychological levels as well as the physical. Throughout the rest of the animal kingdom violence, defined as 'an excessive use of force', is usually connected with reproduction and the defence of territory and serves the purpose of maintaining the delicate balance of nature.

By viewing ourselves as separate from nature, through seeing the earth as Object and ourselves as Subject, the earth has also become that which should be subdued, controlled, dominated.

Nuclear power is perhaps the deadliest manifestation of our dominance. Under the guise of the need for more energy to support, as well as supposedly to defend, humanity, we have created utility stations and an arsenal of weapons so dangerous that one malfunction of a computer can cause the destruction of all life on earth. If we learned better ways of living in harmony with the earth there would be no energy shortage. If we employed our knowledge and technology towards a greater understanding of ecology, we could learn to use the clean energy resources and power provided by Nature – earth, sun, wind, and sea.

We are now in a time of changing consciousness. The feminine principle has begun to express itself with the strength of conscious awareness; to balance the masculine urge to separate, discriminate and control, with the feminine impulse towards belonging, relationship and letting be. It is the strength of the feminine which can guide us towards a consciousness which, though aware of polarities, is concerned with their interplay and connectedness rather than their conflict and separation.

A positive and encouraging sign of this changing consciousness is the growth of the feminist movement which is seeking to challenge and change the artificial and hierarchical division between the sexes into that of a direct, autonomous and balanced relationship. Sadly, some sections of the movement are serving to support the dominant masculine consciousness by emulating some of its negative tendencies in their attempts to secure positions of power. However, many feminists are discovering that it is not enough to secure positions of power within the current masculinist structure because this is in effect only changing the content and not the form. They have begun to apply their perspectives and visions as feminists towards creating an entirely new blueprint for society.

Unfortunately, the media are quick to exploit any negative tendencies within the movement to their own advantage as the media is controlled by the white, male power elite and is simply a mouthpiece for maintaining the *status quo*. The feminist movement represents a threat to the *status quo*; therefore it is presented to the public by the media in a bad light. All too often feminists are seen as man-haters, home-destroyers, child-deserters, fascists, etc. . .

The result of this propagandising action by the media is the denigration and misuse of many significant words, such as ecology and feminism, creating misunderstanding and lack of communication. Both words have become loaded with meaning and elicit highly emotive reactions from every individual. This is interesting when one considers that the meanings of both words are inescapably connected.

Ecology is universally defined as the study of the balance and interrelationship of all life on earth. The motivating force behind feminism is the expression of the feminine principle. As the essential impulse of the feminine principle is the striving towards balance and interrelationship, it follows that feminism and ecology are inextricably connected.

The feminist movement is calling for a positive transformation and change in our consciousness. This change is not towards a state of static equalisation, but towards the full manifestation and vital interplay of the balance of life's energies.

As the domination of mankind continues to erode the balance and beauty of the earth, it is of the utmost urgency that we cease arguing over semantics and differences of opinions. We must turn our energies towards creating a consciousness of wholeness, in which we are concerned with relationship rather than difference, and in which we may learn how best to live together and to cultivate the earth out of love and a conscious understanding of the harmony of life.

8
Roots: Black Ghetto Ecology
Wilmette Brown

How relevant are ecological values embodied in, say, the holistic health movement, to the average Black woman living in depressed economic circumstances in the polluted inner city? In one sense they are *relevant, says Wilmette Brown, who in this article uses her experience as a cancer survivor as the starting point for a personal and political appraisal of her own and other Black women's situations. But in another sense, there is a serious danger in the doctrinaire approach of the white, male-dominated ecological movement, which ignores the reality of many Black people's lives. Indeed, in forgetting the role played by Black women, for example, to secure basic human rights in the US, the movement towards 'wholeness' is forgetting part of itself, part of its roots.*

Malignant Kinship

The politics of cancer is personal to me: I am a Black woman, a cancer survivor. But this is not 'the triumphant story of one woman's victory over cancer'. My cancer crisis was less the poetry of facing imminent death, than weathering the daily harassment of life in the 80s; less coming to grips with a medical diagnosis, than organising to overcome all the other cancers that Black women's flesh is heir to: sexism, racism, overwork and lack of money. The biological fact of cancer is a point of reference for the whole of my struggle to survive. For me the issue is how to transform cancer from a preoccupying vulnerability into a vindicating power – for myself and for everyone determined to reclaim the earth.

In the 1960s Martin Luther King described the 'malignant kinship' between racism and economic exploitation.[1]

73

No amount of gold could provide an adequate compensation for the exploitation and humiliation of the Negro in America down through the centuries. Not all the wealth of this affluent society could meet the bill. Yet a price can be placed on unpaid wages.[2]

Since the 60s, Black women's struggle, as part of an international movement of women, has finally established that whether we are in the metropolis or the Third World, sexism is inseparable from women's economic exploitation, from women's unwaged work; and that for Black women, sexism and racism are inseparable.

Women do 2/3 of the world's work, earn 1/20 of world income and own 1/100 of world assets.[3]

With Black women as a point of reference, statistics from the US show that cancer embodies the malignant kinship of sex, race and class.

Cancer is big business: medicine is the second largest industry in North America and the price of cancer treatment is more than $20 billion a year.[4] Everyone lives in dread of cancer. One in five people in the US dies from cancer, and one in four people may die if the trend continues over the next ten years.[5] But poor people suffer most: income is inversely related to mortality[6] and poor patients have less chance of surviving every type of cancer.[7] In all the most 'cancer-prone cities',[8] there are large Black ghetto communities.

Every mother is a working mother　Two-thirds of all poor people in the US are white, but the proportion of the population in poverty is greatest among Black people.[9] In the US, particularly among Black people, women and children are becoming the majority of the poor. According to a report by the National Advisory Council on Economic Opportunity, 'the poor who are in female-headed families . . . would comprise 100 percent of the poverty population by the year 2000.'[10] Worldwide, the woman-headed family is the fastest growing sector of the population;[11] and in developing countries, 50% of women are the main breadwinners.[12]

Because of the extra demands pregnancy imposes, nutritional and environmental diseases . . . take a severe toll on women, and can in addition adversely affect the growing foetus. The same is true of new health hazards accompanying modern industrialization: exposure to radiation and to toxic chemicals is particularly dangerous for pregnant women.

74

Women's heavy workload, particularly in traditional rural areas, but also in poor urban areas, increases their vulnerability to disease.[13]

Thus in Asia, Africa, the Caribbean, the Pacific and Latin America, 'development' means that degenerative diseases like cancer are developing in the new metropolis which is within the Third World; while in the US, cancer is ravaging Black people, women and children, the poorest of the poor, who are the Third World within the metropolis.

In the US, Black people's cancer death rate is 30% higher than white people's – Black men's is higher than white men's, and Black women's is higher than white women's.[14] Fewer than one-third of Black cancer patients survive for five years. At Harlem Hospital, one in five Black cancer patients survives.[15] Cancer is the major cause of death among middle-aged women, and among children it is second only to accidental death.[16] A fifteen-year study in Oregon showed that housewives have 'the highest job-related cancer death rate of any occupation'.[17]

In 1980, I had emergency surgery for cancer of the colon. I am alive thanks to the working class in Britain, who struggled for the National Health Service. I couldn't have afforded the treatment if I had been in the US, where cancer usually costs the patient over $25,000.[18] But whatever the country, whatever the amount of money for medical bills, as a cancer patient I am up against a world economic system that deprives everyone of health – discriminating between Black and white, women and men, with women of colour at the bottom.

The money required to provide adequate food, water, education, health and housing for everyone in the world has been estimated at $17 billion a year. It is a huge sum of money . . . about as much as the world spends on arms every two weeks.[19]

And less than the medical industry makes off cancer in one year in the US alone.

Having cancer is like being held hostage – the terrorism at gut level of living day to day in the military-industrial complex. Even the language of cancer is military. Recovering from my cancer crisis involved not only the emotional and physical work of learning how to be at home again in my own body – of which cancer dispossessed me – but the political work of negotiating the international economic order as it was practised at my bedside, in my hospital ward and outpatient clinic. Getting well means mobilising body and soul to defeat more than an illness or a disease; getting well means organising to defeat the power relations of sex, race and class that make cancer, illness and disease possible.

Cancer epitomises the crisis of health in our time. Cancer forces the issue of how responsible the individual can be for personal health when our every environment – from the urban Black ghetto in the metropolis to the tropical rain forest in the Third World – is continually being raped for profit by the military-industrial complex. Even as the military-industrial complex profits from our illness, it profits still more from our health: they depend on our work to keep running the world. The military-industrial complex depends on the working class being healthy enough to work – not healthy enough to be whole.

Being responsible for our health – repairing ourselves – enough to work for the military-industrial complex, without challenging the killing work we are forced to do, work which is destroying our environment and ourselves, can't finally achieve health. The challenge of health is the challenge of building new social relations among ourselves and our environment, from the ashes of the destructive personal, political and ecological power relations we suffer today. This challenge is posed most clearly in the situation of women, whose work it has been to mother people and environment – whose work producing and reproducing the workers of the world is the basic ingredient of all industry and all profit.

> The State, over and over, has put the responsibility for the well-being of other workers in our hands – for the young, the ill, the old, the man. As mothers, sisters, daughters, wives, we have put ourselves last and worked to join together what capital and its work tears asunder every day in factories, fields, offices, mines and schools. This has not been seen as work when there is no wage. It has been seen as dedicated work when there is a low wage. It is always work . . . and they have always blackmailed us into doing it. So far we have done it for love, not money. But the cost of loving is going up. [20]

> When the nurses shouted on their demonstrations, 'We can't put dedication in the bank,' they spoke for every woman. [21]

76

Housework: the home in the hospital

Whether we ourselves, children or men have cancer, it is women who are first and foremost responsible for taking care. Cancer demands a supreme effort – a 25-hour day – doing work that women are trained from childhood it is our 'nature' to do.

> Women are always made to feel completely responsible for whatever happens to those in our charge, and guilty for considering our own needs. This is a direct result of our wageless work in the home where we are always justifying our existence because we appear to be living off other people's (men's) labour. [22]

Cancer is very much a women's issue because health is still very much 'women's work' – beginning at home. Before it becomes critical, health is women's unwaged housework. After it is critical, health is still women's housework – in the hospital for low wages, whether as nurse, auxiliary or tea lady. Whether a woman is taking care of herself, or also taking care of others, whether she herself is a patient, or the friend or lover of a patient, women are held responsible for the housework of health.

When I was hospitalised for cancer, my friends did plenty of free housework worrying about me, keeping me company and giving me emotional support; helping to build relationships with the other patients; doing my laundry; bringing plants, palatable food and other necessities of life. They also did indispensable political work as my advocates: asking questions; getting attention and information from doctors and nurses; watching out for my interests when I had the least power to defend myself.

Convalescing meant doing a lot of physical and emotional housework for myself too – relearning basic bodily functions and developing patience. I had to face illness as my own childhood, disablement and ageing all at once.

I also did emotional housework for my friends: putting on a brave face to cushion the shock, and terror, and sadness of cancer; and political work too, struggling not to let physical weakness make me abdicate responsibility for my own decisions.

As a single lesbian woman cancer patient, I had to depend on women friends to mother me through my cancer crisis. As lesbians we struggle to survive not only the work and worry, the housework, of cancer. We struggle every day to survive the housework of being lesbian: the emotional and physical stress, this time in the hospital ward, of putting up with the half-hostile, half-curious, half-secretly pleased glances, this time of other patients and their visitors, who weren't sure whether they should disapprove of Black and white women who were being so blatant as to care for each other, in sickness and in health.

Bedside Manners

The NHS is not a service that the ruling class has granted to us, but a service which hospital workers provide for the ruling class in providing mentally and physically 'fit' workers. It is a service based on the exploitation of some workers, the hospital workers, and the manipulation of others, the patients. . . The fact that it is obviously in *our* interest to be seen by a doctor or go into a hospital, whether or not we have a wage and whether our wage is higher or lower, doesn't alter the fact that fundamentally the service is not for our benefit.[23]

Essential to the housework of being a patient is attending to your status in the hierarchy between patients, auxiliaries, nurses and doctors, in that order from the bottom up. The physical work of recovering – whether moving from bed to chair, coping with a catheter, swallowing hospital food or tolerating needles and drugs – is inseparable from working that hierarchy: you are most immediately dependent on them to survive.

The image of this hierarchy is the consultant, most often a man, on morning rounds with his entourage of anxious, sometimes obsequious, students (mostly men), and nurses (mostly women) straining to preserve and project dignity, but with proper deference to the certified (male) healers. The entourage inspects each patient one by one: washed and combed, each is at her bed in a fresh gown, hoping for an extra 30 seconds to ask a question, hoping not to be so intimidated as to forget what the question is; apologising for being ill.

Although my general practitioner and surgeon were kind and patient men, who were concerned to restore my confidence and make the best care available, there was the doctor in the outpatient clinic who told me the NHS was spending too much money on keeping old people alive who had cancer. I wonder what he thought about Black women.

In my experience, in spite of extensive NHS cuts, long hours and low wages, most nurses and auxiliary staff managed amazingly well to keep their good humour and not take out the pressure of overwork on patients. But women patients were sometimes expected to do some of the lighter physical housework involved in running the hospital – clearing away dishes, light cleaning, getting supplies, making tea for ourselves and men patients. We could expect to have a long wait if we pressed a buzzer or needed some special, or even routine, help. Without student nurses and auxiliaries – on trainee wages – the nursing staff clearly couldn't function. A nurse told me that the monthly attrition rate was sky-high.

Just as crucial to the unwaged job of patient, is establishing and maintaining good relations with other patients: they are your comrades-in-arms against the power structure in the hospital ward. As among other workers organising in sight of the bosses, we supported each other surreptitiously and shared jokes about our predicament, for example about the protocol of morning rounds. But it was hard work to build solidarity in the midst of unfamiliarity and physical weakness, dependency and pain. Being hospitalised together – sharing illness – didn't overcome the power relations we lived in the world outside.

Another cancer patient, a white English woman, told me, 'I don't mean you personally but' too many Black immigrants were using the NHS. While cancer brought us together, nationality, colour and money kept us apart. It didn't occur to her that all the American cotton my Black ancestors picked during slavery, on which the British textile and shipping industries and slave-trading ports prospered, and on which the standard of living of the ruling class in Britain was based, entitled me to be treated for cancer. But then their standard of living was not hers.

Welfare State

I grew up in Newark, New Jersey, one of the cancer centres of the US. Locally we call it 'cancer alley', because the petrochemical plants reek for miles around. New Jersey water is also highly carcinogenic. In addition, for years as a child I was given regular X-ray treatments for eczema.

When I returned to the US, after my cancer treatment, still unable to do waged work, I had to go on welfare. Newark is a little welfare state: one of the poorest cities in the US; about 85 percent Black and Puerto Rican; with a large welfare population of single mothers, children, and unemployed teenagers and men. Many of the workers at the welfare department were former recipients: they were Black or Brown; some were trying to help; others were rude with the insecurity of being one step away from welfare themselves. They had taken jobs to get more money; the state had hired them because they knew the welfare system from the other side of the counter. It was up to them to decide which side they were on.

The Welfare Department doesn't pay for your time: most of the time is spent waiting to be seen. It was better at a neighbourhood health centre where the welfare rights network from the 60s still had the situation organised from within. The health centre was also right 'on the block', rather than downtown, so the power of the surrounding community was a big protection. At downtown welfare offices there were police on every landing, with guns and billy clubs in case things got out of hand. Finally I was 'budgeted' with subsistence money and food-stamps. The struggle of Black welfare mothers in the 60s, who won food-stamps, had made it possible for me to have a little something to spend – if possible, at the healthfood shop. Newark is one big teaching hospital. Where once stood riot-torn tenements, brand new college buildings are just waiting for Black bodies to experiment on. Brand new medicine and dentistry facilities and students are eager to try out the new equipment on any welfare recipient who comes through the door. It's all free if you're on welfare.

Again the waiting. Again the tone of voice of people paid to be helping you, treating you like dirt. When I finally saw a doctor, he suggested that I have several tests, not only blood tests, but strenuous tests of every major organ, which involved multiple X-rays and coloured dyes being injected into my bloodstream. When I refused he was indignant: he said he would advise his wife to take them if she were in my situation.

How holistic?

So far in the holistic health movement there have been three visible approaches to confronting cancer: changing one's consciousness and lifestyle so as to take responsibility for cancer; self-healing therapies such as diet, exercise, yoga, meditation, visualisation or a combination of these and other techniques; and exposés of how the medical industry, and the military-industrial complex as a whole, are profiting from cancer.

The consciousness approach can amount to saying that cancer is our own fault.[24] For to ignore, or deny, that the military-industrial complex is continually projecting the view that Black people are disposable, and implementing genocidal policies against people of

80

colour all around the world, is to be part of the problem rather than part of the solution. Black people are entitled to expect more from the holistic health movement than confirmation of what the state always tells us, that our exploitation is of our own making. One of the ways we are taking responsibility for our consciousness and lifestyle, is by organising to end the conditions and the power relations which are set up by the military-industrial complex to destroy our health.

I am grateful to the holistic health movement for information about diet and other self-healing perspectives and practices from different parts of the world. This information has helped me and many other people. But apart from the fact that much information is still untried, or yet to be discovered, information and therapies by themselves are not enough.

Most people still lack access to the resources and techniques necessary for self-healing; and the poorer we are, the less access we have. Yoga and other classes at affordable prices are not widely available anywhere. The corner grocer or the supermarket in Black ghettoes, and most other communities, is no healthfood shop. Eating wholefoods means time for travelling, money for transportation, high prices, and the work of learning new eating habits and methods of food preparation – even buying new pots and pans. Foodstamps, welfare and low wages only go so far.

For women, especially women with children, the housework of holistic health is enormous. Women generally have too little time, too little money, and are too overworked for this kind of self-help. Yet lacking the time and money to research the information and implement the therapies, many women still feel guilty – as though cancer is women's fault, rather than the fault of poverty and overwork. And guilt is already one of the biggest obstacles to women's health. Self-healing for the few who can afford it, and guilt for most of us who can't, can hardly be considered holistic health.

The third approach has uncovered a wealth of information, which is a tremendous public service. But it leaves us with the question of what to do, how to organise. Without answers to these questions, except in terms of government hearings and lobbying, the more detailed the information about how the military-industrial complex plans for and profits from cancer, the greater the impression of their overwhelming invulnerability; as though they are able to anticipate, counter and/or co-opt our every move. If the balance of power is really so one-sided, which it is not, then we are doomed to keep dying of cancer – victims not survivors.

The information we most need is about how we are already organis-

81

ing ourselves against cancer, as a basis for moving further. Without this kind of information, fighting cancer is ghettoised to a single issue, the priority or privilege of a particular sector, deprived of the power and resources of the working class as a whole. Without reference to the daily lives of Black women, we cannot know how comprehensive the issue of cancer is, nor how comprehensive and powerful and capable the holistic health movement is of winning against it. Without reference to the daily lives of Black women, cancer wins – through our own sex, race and class divisions.

Black is green: the invisibility of the holistic health movement in the ghetto Even before Black women had taken organisational autonomy from men, in networks such as the welfare rights organisations of the 60s, the Black movement laid a foundation for all the issues which later became identified with the visible, predominantly white, predominantly middle-class holistic health movement. For the holistic health movement not to recognise and acknowledge this contribution by Black people in its perspectives and ways of organising today, is not to know its own roots, not to be holistic.

The most comprehensive meeting of East and West in our time has been the pooling of resources for liberation among the peoples of colour in Africa, Asia, Latin America, the Pacific, the Caribbean and the United States. One channel for this meeting was Martin Luther King's application of Gandhi's philosophy of nonviolent direct action and satyagraha, so successful against British colonialism in India, to fighting for the civil rights of Black people in the United States.

The pooling of ancient traditions with contemporary necessities has always been integral to the movement of people of colour within the United States. Immigrants always bring the visions and traditions of their peoples with them. Native Americans sheltered Black people from slavecatchers and integrated us into their nations. Black people in the southern United States, particularly Black women, still know how to identify and prepare herbs and plants to make remedies, a skill which survived the Middle Passage from Africa to the Americas, for which the Union Army used Black nurses like Harriet Tubman during the Civil War.

At the same time, throughout our history in the United States, there has been a debate – under many different names – within the Black movement, over the meaning of traditional culture. One key theme in this debate has been the question of what is a 'natural' or holistic way of life for Black people, as opposed to the culture imposed on us by white 'civilisation' through slavery and colonialism.

82

By the end of the 60s Black women had settled the question. By taking our autonomy from male-dominated organisations – whether by joining the welfare rights network, leaving Black power groups, initiating autonomous Black women's groups, and/or coming out as lesbian – Black women drew a line between tradititional cultural perspectives which repress women and those which help to make us free. We refused to accept as 'natural' any traditions that enslave us. Organising autonomously as women, we refused to identify Black Power with Black manhood, or to accept the notion that the 'natural' place for women in the movement was prone; we refused to equate liberation with sexual submission. We had decided that forced heterosexuality was no more 'natural' than racism or sexism. We had decided that the traditional cultures of Black people were going to have to be vindicated on other bases than the subordination of Black women to men. We had decided that women's unwaged work as personal and political servants was not 'natural'.

Taking our autonomy meant using our independent judgement to find in our traditional worldviews the holistic resources and tools for our struggle today. Thus a Native American welfare mother, an organiser of the Oh Gweh Oh (The Real People) Welfare Rights Organization in Milwaukee, Wisconsin, wrote:

> The dignity of the welfare recipient caught me as an Indian idea. The dignity of the individual says that no matter what a person's capabilities are, whether he is the leader or whether he is a person who is crippled or elderly or can't do anything, he still has a place in the tribe. Welfare Rights is an Indian organisation to me because I think a lot of things that Welfare Rights is going after are Indian ideas . . .[25]

Reparations – Pay Women, Not the Military

The welfare rights movement of the 60s was led by Black women and embraced poor people of all races, women and men. Welfare mothers made it impossible for the bureaucracy to carry on with business as usual by a mass campaign informing everyone of their welfare rights, and by refusing policing by social workers. They organised a mass invitation to share the wealth: the welfare rolls skyrocketed. They also took over schools to challenge the miseducation of their children. They also protested the Vietnam war. Young social workers like me, who were just out of college, had our consciousness raised by the struggle of welfare mothers, so that at least some of us knew we owed it to them, and to ourselves, to be their instrument against the Welfare Department from the inside. Today, more than ever, their struggle is my own.

The demands of Black welfare mothers brought about the first concessions from the American state of anything approaching free health care for poor people (Medicaid) and for elderly people (Medicare). The Establishment has been trying ever since the 60s, when these programmes began, to turn Medicaid and Medicare into a total defeat, but they have never been able to take away this bottom line of basic health rights for everyone.

Welfare mothers' struggle epitomises the determination of all women who are on the front line in the battle for health – first of all in our own homes: fighting poor food, drugs, rats and roaches, pesticides, dirt and disease; on the front line in hospital wards and clinic waiting rooms everywhere; on the front line against overcrowding, the emotional and physical violence of poverty, rape, and the degraded human relationships poverty breeds; on the front line outside US military bases, nuclear waste dumps and power plants – on the front line of health, campaigning for peace around the world.

Black welfare mothers have long been aware of how their struggle is an essential part of the holistic health movement:

There are many other fields – like the environment – that we haven't explored, that should be dealt with, but people are so busy making money off poor people that they don't have time to do the kind of thing they should be doing to benefit society.[26]

But is the rest of the holistic health movement aware of their need for Black welfare mothers as a point of reference?

The strategy of the Black movement in the US has always been, in one form or another, reparations. For a start, each Black person has yet to receive the 40 acres and a mule we were promised at Emancipation: none of us has forgotten. Black people, whether we talk out loud about it or not, continue to count on the mounting interest – and principal (principle) – of that debt. The victory of Black welfare mothers in the 60s was to make Black people's demand for reparations specific to the poorest in any Black community, women and children.

By taking organisational autonomy and demanding that their own needs be met first, Black welfare mothers refused the blackmail of free 'women's work': they demanded money as the power to refuse to work for free. They demanded money beyond the poverty of welfare.

84

They demanded that money go to women and children rather than to the 'poverty pimps': the social, health and legal 'service' bureaucracies, the 'community welfare projects'.[27]

Black welfare mothers demanded money for each and every woman in her own hands, as the first step towards everyone – children and men, Black and white, immigrant and native – having a decent standard of living.[28]

Beulah Sanders also travelled to Europe, because the welfare mothers were well aware that their struggle was part of an international movement in the 60s.

Black welfare mothers demanded money – the language the whole world understands – as the way to have the dignity of their work as mothers recognised with more than just the customary lip-service paid to motherhood. They demanded the same dignity as other workers, that at least their income be called a wage.[29] They demanded wages for housework as a way of taking back what is ours: as a right; as damages; as back pay for all the unpaid and unwaged work of plantation and domestic slavery; as reparations – a way of reclaiming the earth.

Cancer is the disease of our transition from the 60s to the 80s: the crisis of transforming ourselves into new people, fitter and clearer, fit and clear enough to win the new world. With the growth of the women's peace movement, symbolised internationally by Greenham, winning is again a living possibility, because white women are taking a lead from Black women in both the metropolis and the Third World, demanding that the military-industrial complex be disarmed and dismantled, and that the military budget be used to meet people's needs, beginning with women and children. Organising autonomously as women, the women's peace movement is refusing the sexist and racist assumptions and practices of the peace and holistic health movements once and for all. The women's peace movement – Black and white, Third World and metropolitan – are the 80s answer to the Black welfare mothers of the 60s, whose struggle is still giving leadership to peace campaigns and coalitions all across the United States. Power to the sisters, and therefore peace and health to all the workers of the world.

85

9

Seeds that Bear Fruit

A Japanese Woman Speaks

Manami Suzuki

Manami Suzuki is a twenty-four-year-old Japanese activist whose concerns range across a wide spectrum. Although in Japan there are still many divisions amongst those who make up a potential Green Movement in that country, Manami is an example of a woman who has intregrated within herself and so come to terms with the diverse ecological, political and spiritual elements necessary for a deep-rooted change in both her society and others afflicted by the dis-ease of the twentieth century. Here she tells her own story.

I was born and grew up in the countryside surrounded by animals and woods, so I have always felt very close to nature. My family lived near the coast and I spent a lot of time swimming and fishing. My school was an hour's walk (half an hour's run!) away from our house across some really beautiful countryside and I have vivid memories of making that journey on foot every day, watching the seasons changing the face of the land. Farmers on the way would greet me and sometimes give me fruit and other produce they had just harvested.

When I was 18, I went to college in Tokyo for two years. The only other time I had ever lived in the city was when my parents moved to Tokyo ten years before, and I as a child experienced such a culture shock that they had to move out again! Anyway, the contrast between the metropolis and the countryside is what really radicalised me about nature.

I then got a scholarship to study linguistics at Cambridge and so came to Britain for the first time. I did quite a bit of travelling around the wilder places in Scotland and Wales and this changed my view of nature once more. In Japan we have a very different attitude to nature from the British and other Europeans; look at our gardens, so formal, so carefully controlled! I became passionate about nature remaining wild and untamed. I also started working on an organic farm near Cambridge. By the time I returned to Japan I was really ready to become involved in the ecological movement.

My main interest was in the question of food and seeds. But I also became involved in the anti-nuclear movement because I began to do translation work for Friends of the Earth. The anti-nuclear movement is one of the main issues we are concerned with, since Japan is building so many nuclear plants and is planning to dump waste in the ocean. So I try to balance my anti-nuclear and heavily critical, political work with more positive things like the food issue.

Let me tell you some ways in which the food issue is central to the whole Green Movement. Soon after I had returned to Japan, the two biggest Japanese seed companies patented a range of seeds they had produced in their laboratories and received contracts from the government, which meant in fact that they had a virtual monopoly over the kinds of food grown in Japan. Now these seeds are not like natural, wild seeds which have survived climatic changes and other adverse conditions on the planet for millions of years. The new seeds are the result of genetic engineering by scientists, aiming at breeding only the strains that produce the biggest crop – even though these strains may in fact be too weak and specialised to survive if, for example, any severe climatic change should be placed upon them. They also have no relevance to the local land on which they will be grown – so by using them our society is getting rid of the whole notion of producing food suited to local conditions and which is organically diverse. Food is being turned, from something on which we know we can always subsist in our local communities, into a massive centralised industry.

The pattern is the same all over the world. Look at what the EEC is doing to standardise seeds in Europe. The petro-chemical multinationals, knowing the oil will run out, are looking for new ways in which to retain economic control. They are moving into agriculture, into seeds. They plan to retain their grip by selling us something that we once again find indispensable, because, of course, we will not have autonomous access to seeds once they are all standardised and patented and controlled by central authorities. In Japan, these industries, the government and the Japan Agriculture Corporation (which some call the Black Mafia) can control not only the food *we* eat, but also that of South East Asia, the Philippines, Korea and the Pacific, because we export very heavily to them.

There is an interesting series of connections in the Philippines which links the food, chemical and women's issues very clearly. A few years ago, a certain kind of pesticide was banned in Japan as being too dangerous for use. But Japanese chemical companies had already stockpiled large amounts of this fertiliser and did not want to lose out on their investment. So what do we see? These companies set up banana plantations in the Philippines, cutting down the rain forest to do it, just as do the industrialists in South America in order to graze cattle for hamburgers, until the land degenerates under the strain. And these Japanese companies are using the very pesticides that are considered 'too dangerous' in Japan, except here it does not matter because it is only Philippino people working on the plantation. Many of the men working there have become very sick and unable to work anymore. Because the families are so poor, the women are driven to the cities to find work which usually means that they get trapped into prostitution. Then along come more Japanese businessmen, become rich on just the kind of 'enterprise' that has exploited these people. They are taking a sex-tour holiday in Manilla, in which a girl is naturally provided along with the rest of the furniture in their hotel room. Finally, to stop these girls becoming inconveniently pregnant they are given the contraceptive pill, which in Japan is severely restricted because of fears about its side effects. Philippino women are obviously not considered in the same light as Japanese women! And nobody can protest because they live under martial law.

You can see why people become so angry when they find out these things. . . In Japan, our style of political protest is very heated, even confrontational. It is true that by talking to people, by making a big fuss, you can change the way they vote. But you cannot necessarily change their hearts or change the spirit of society that way. That is why I think food is so important, personally as well as politically: people's eating habits have an extraordinary influence on the way they behave! So as an individual woman trying to effect change, I realise that I have to work on myself and my own life-style, as well as campaigning on wider issues.

I first saw this when at about the age of 17, I had been very ill. The western-style doctors did not know what was wrong with me, whether it was my thyroid, my kidneys, or what. They operated on me, gave me drugs and I simply got worse and worse. Finally my parents took me to a traditional oriental-style doctor, who gave me herbal medicine and made me fast completely before putting me on a natural diet. Within a few months I had completely recovered. Now I take much more care about what I eat, though I try not to be as fanatical as some macrobiotic eaters who do not share food with anyone else in case it does not fit in with their diet! I fast for three weeks every year, which really has an incredible effect on my body and mind, especially since I have also started meditating. It is my most creative time of the year! I think I can be much more effective politically if I take care of my spirit and my body at the same time; this in turn has much more influence on the people I meet during my campaigning. For me, being at one with nature is the only way of being at one with other people, and that is the only way we will stop harming the earth.

Another country

When I visited with the porpoises
I felt awkward, my hairy
angular body sprouting its skinny
grasping limbs like long mistakes.
The child of gravity and want I sank
in the salt wave clattering with gadgets,
appendages. Millennia past
they turned and fled back to the womb.
There they feel no fatigue but slip
through the water caressed and buoyed up.
Never do they sleep but their huge brains
hold life always turning it like a pebble
under the tongue, and lacking practice, death
comes as an astonishment.

In the wide murmur of the sea they fear
little.
Together they ram the shark.
Food swims flashing in schools.
Hunger is only a teasing, endured
no longer than desired. Weather
is superficial decoration; they rise
to salute the thunder, romping their tails.

They ride through pleasure and plenty
secure in a vast courtesy
firm enough to sustain a drowning man.
Nothing is said bluntly.
All conversation is a singing,

all telling alludes to and embodies
minute displacements in epic,
counter-epic, comic opera, or the four hundred
forty-one other genres they recognize
as current. Every exchange comes
as aria, lyric, set piece, recitativo,
and even a cry for help is couched
in a form brief and terse,
strict as haiku.

Greed has no meaning when no one
is hungry. Thus they swim toward
us with broad grins and are slaughtered
by the factory ships
that harvest the tuna like wheat.

Marge Piercy

10
Thought for Food

Liz Butterworth

*In the west, most of us accept the food we eat without
question, although it is frequently both unhealthy for us and based on
the exploitation of people in other parts of the world. Yet it is possible,
as Liz Butterworth found, to trace a whole series of connections based
on a contemporary western woman's experience of food: from body
image, through the domestic role of women, the health effects of
refined and processed foods, to the role of big business in selling these
foods – not only to us, but to our sisters in the Third World, for whom
they may be even less appropriate.*

'Thanks to a survey carried out last year by NOP (National
Opinion Polls) we know what makes a woman happy, unhappy
and afraid.' (Birds Eye 1975)

I have always had an interest in food. I enjoy the sensual pleasures of
eating, particularly when I have not had to do the cooking, and the
social pleasure of sharing food with a group of family and friends.
Food is both an icebreaker and pacifier; it can be used to nourish your
body or to punish it; it can be given and received in love or used as a
weapon. It is a need common to all people.

It was not until my youngest child was two years old that I really
became aware of what the birth of four children had done to my body.
The changes were obvious, but I quite liked the altered physique and
maturity brought about by childbirth. Rather than losing my figure I
had gained a new one. The fact that I was over-weight was more of a
problem for others than for me, and I had consistently resisted
external pressure to diet, believing that only societies that produce a
surplus of food see slenderness as an ideal rather than a sign of
undernourishment. Yet while I seemingly enjoyed my years as Earth
Mother, my excess weight was beginning to make me feel unhealthy,
and, as no further children were planned, I thought the time had

come to readjust my figure and my health. Once my mind was focused on the idea of losing weight I began to notice rows of slimming aids in the shops, not to mention extensive advertising in the media. Women's magazines are bursting with ideas on how to feed the family, while offering women slimming aids and diet sheets on one page and fashion hints on the next. The concern is to keep your husband well fed and satisfied and yourself slim, fashionable and attractive for him.

Over a period of time I managed to remove, with a good deal of frayed temper, the weight I wanted to lose. At the end of six months I knew that I would have to completely review my eating habits in order to maintain my weight loss. It seemed essential to understand why I had put on so much weight in the first place, and slowly the reasons became apparent.

Quite simply, I felt trapped but had been unable to acknowledge or indeed save myself from the situation. All the aspirations and ambitions of my youth had become lost, forgotten, unconsciously put aside as the mantle of marriage enfolded me. I was, and still am, suspicious of those women who express satisfaction in their role of wife, mother, lover, cook, cleaner and gardener. I look at these women and ask them, 'Where are you?' And here was I, living just the same, but feeling an internal rage, a sense of injustice. My childcare activities appeared to have no social value. It is taken as natural and fulfilling for a woman to 'want' to have children, as it is natural and fulfilling for women to 'want' to care for and nurture a family. It is part of the female role that we are all brought up to recognise as our contribution towards maintaining the *status quo*. It is impossible to release yourself without engendering social disapproval. I had coped with this social imprisonment by ignoring its existence; but of course ignorance is not always bliss.

Perhaps some women are happy and content to nurture, but for others it may well be the only area wherein they receive any recognition; it fulfils and emotional need. The whole role of professional nurturer can become an unhappy and difficult area of conflict throughout the family life of women, often leading to unexpressed conflicts.

Having examined some of the causes of my weight problem I became concerned because, during a vulnerable emotional state, I had eaten a pile of foods which under normal circumstances I would not have touched. I felt angry and duped and this initiated a fascinating and anguished exploration of why we eat what we eat. Many women are now in part-time or full-time employment outside the home. By taking a job a woman has even less time for household tasks. For women with children, while they are now accepted as both workers and mothers, they are assumed to be less effective mothers because their work interferes with their mothering, and less effective workers because their responsibilities as mothers interfere with their work. Married women with full-time work in fact have two jobs: paid employment and housework. As women have less leisure time than their husbands the advent of convenience foods which require little preparation, has to some extent released us from the demands of the kitchen, but has resulted in our alienation from 'real' food. Food processing has erased from our memory such beloved little creatures as maggots and caterpillars. What we have now are prepacked foods with a longer shelf life, all carefully selected to avoid blemish or irregularity of shape and size, injected, moulded and polished, with added colourant and sweetener to suit eye and taste.

In any case, having been to a certain extent released from the kitchen, women are now being told by women's magazines, radio programmes and the rest of the media, that because of rising prices we should shop around for the best bargains. So now we have to lengthen our days searching out shops that sell the cheapest of everything, for if we mismanage our budgets we are not being Good Wives and Mothers. I wonder why we take it. As in all societies, women are responsible for the work of making ends meet. Whether this is seen in financial or emotional terms, it comes down to the basic task of nourishing others (in the broadest sense) providing the essential resources without which no one can survive.

In the modern world, the food industry is only too happy to cash in on the old adage, 'The way to a man's heart is through his stomach.' If a woman can produce a meal in the knowledge that it requires little preparation, and will be accepted by her family, whilst maintaining her own personal touch, then so much the better. The food industry is delighted to sell her such a product!

During the early part of the last century, food was in very short supply for most of the British population and what there was contained little nourishment. This poor diet was reflected in high rates of sickness and premature death amongst the working class. Women in particular suffered since most of the food went to men in deference to their role as 'breadwinners'. As wages rose and food became more widely available, so the diet of the population improved. Overseas expansion opened up new areas of the world and enabled the food industry to develop. However, although, on the surface, mass production appears to be a satisfactory method of feeding populations, it

93

depends for its success on exploitation of land and people; up to, and including, the present day that exploitation has been at the expense of the Third World.

We assume that the foods provided for us by the food industry are those which we most wish to consume – but are they? People have hazy ideas about nutrition and a 'balanced diet'; indeed because I structure my family's diet according to nutritional considerations I am viewed as an eccentric. I recently commented to an acquaintance about a virus all the children caught which left them ashen-faced and listless. She suggested that their susceptibility might have something to do with the food we eat in the family: 'After all brown rice can't be that nourishing, it's what starving people live on.'

The use of advertising by companies has greatly contributed to the rise in the consumption of convenience foods. A great deal of market research goes into the selling of food. A survey published in the Birds Eye *Annual Review*, 1975, suggested that 'tomorrow's woman will buy more convenience foods and prepared meals, expect to own labour-saving appliances and to shop less often in the future.' Have we been liberated? Far from it and our role certainly has not changed; rather it is being reinforced.

When examining some of the methods employed by the food industry in processing and production, I found many foods are positively harmful to our health. I am constantly amazed at the number of people who tell me that sugar is a vital part of a growing child's diet because it gives them energy. With the advent of cheap sugar production many foods are now preserved in heavy syrups and sugar is added to a vast variety of foods during the production process. We have only to look at the listed ingredients on labels to find a selection of white and brown sugar, caramel, syrup, glucose, molasses and treacle. John Yudkin in *Pure White and Deadly*[1] states that there is no physiological requirement for sugar. Yet it is sold as an essential food when, in fact, it is generally used as an additive. After sugar is consumed the blood-sugar level rises, giving a feeling of energy. It then drops rapidly – the greater the dose the bigger the drop – leaving a feeling of faintness and a craving for more sugar.

A mother recently asked the caterers at her child's school whether they really thought that jam doughnuts were a proper food to give young children as a dessert. The caterers replied that doughnuts were a complete, well-balanced food. They contained sugar, eggs and flour; all useful in a growing child's diet. Hannah Wright in her excellent series of articles entitled *Swallow it Whole*,[2] mentions that overconsumption of sugar can manifest itself as constipation, diverticular disease, piles, varicose veins, appendicitis, dental caries, gum disease, mature-onset diabetes, obesity (most women over 30 are at least ten percent overweight), coronary thrombosis, primary E-coli infection, urinary infections, gallstones, peptic ulcers, eczema, acne and causal contributions to bowel cancer.

Certainly the most prevalent disease of Western society is dental caries, an affliction related directly to the frequency of consumption of sugar. It used to be confined to the rich, but now few of us escape it. It is perhaps surprising that we allow a painful, disfiguring disease like dental caries to be more rampant in our society than the common cold. If this is not enough to set your teeth on edge, then consider the fact that the British Sugar Bureau produces a freely distributed nutrition teaching kit for schools, parents, technical colleges and student nurses, in which it actually states: 'Sugar is an important part of a balanced diet'.

If sugar is of no nutritional value to us, and is positively harmful, why do we accept it as an additive in our foods? Indeed, why do we accept any food processing? This ranges from the separation of the husk and germ from the wheat grain to produce white flour (when further processing is necessary to replace the vitamins removed with the husk); to the coloured dyes and artificial substances added to practically every food from bacon, cheese and fish to orange squash, table sauces and baby foods.

Unfortunately, evaluating the effect of additives on human health is not an easy matter. It should be remembered that additives have been used for centuries. Thousands of years ago the Chinese used ethylene and propylene, produced by combustion of kerosene, to ripen bananas and peas. Salt has also been used for centuries to aid preservation. Of course today's food industry does not want to poison its customers, and it will take great care to ensure that nobody actually drops dead holding one of its products. But the dietary causes of slow chronic illnesses are hard to detect and companies do only the minimum of research necessary. Even where there is clear evidence that an additive may be harmful, it is still permitted. If it were sold as a food, the breast milk of many American mothers would be banned because the level of additives from the mother's diet exceeds the permitted amounts. It has been revealed that, on average, a corpse in the United States contains such a highly concentrated level of preservatives that it can now be kept for a much longer period.

Lack of information on the part of the consumer has certainly aided the food industry in its bid to develop and produce new commodities. The practical experience of students is such that fewer now eat school meals because they find them unattractive and the choice restricted. Educational material is dominated by films, books and leaflets sponsored by food companies. The booklets most often given to expectant mothers in clinics and hospitals are financed by advertisements for baby foods or paid for by one of the sponsoring companies. Most of this information is paternalistic in nature, promoting a 'concerned' attitude which has little to do with real nutritional education and more to do with selling commodities to a cornered market. Women are particularly vulnerable. In fact what the food industry is interested in is profit. Health, it seems, is incidental.

But this is still only half the picture. We in the west belong to rich nations. Whenever and wherever they live, rich people eat first, and they eat a disproportionate amount of the food available. In Asian, African and Latin American countries well over 500 million people are living in what the World Bank describes as 'absolute poverty'.[3] Many well-meaning people will see the problems of starvation as the result of God-given acts, natural disasters, such as crop failures or flooding, over-population and in some cases laziness and lack of initiative on the part of the poor themselves. More likely reasons are revealed when examining the many exploitative techniques employed on the poor of the world. The western conscience involves various governments in formulating food-aid plans which do little more than control hunger-related actions such as revolution. Existing nutrition intervention concentrates on feeding the symptoms, not on dealing with the root causes which are usually found to be social and political. Concern for the hungry should mean concern for their social situation. Since the poor run the risk of being ill-housed, ill-cared for and illiterate, they will be less motivated to improve their own state.

Nutritionists agree that if a baby wants for sufficient calories and protein during the final intra-uterine weeks and the first months of life, she may be permanently damaged mentally.[4] Such children will, if they survive, grow into apathetic adults prevented by inherent hunger-related diseases from making any real contribution to their family and community.

A meaningful food-aid programme should be coupled with significant changes in the distribution of income or wealth in a country, a change in the consumption habits of the well-nourished portion of the population and a shift in economic development strategies and priorities.[5] If those who hold the power have no desire to accommodate these changes, then recipient governments of food aid will structure their policies to concentrate on the starving individual and his (medical) problem without giving consideration to the underlying causes. An impoverished, diseased people do not often rise up and challenge.

Western nations use food-aid policies for political arm-twisting. Using natural resources, instead of military forces, in power games is not new. In the 1950s oil was used as a political lever. Today the use of food is the most deadly weapon unsheathed by western society against the Third World. This message became clear in 1976 when the US State Department announced that it would consider the suspension of food-aid agreements with certain countries 'because of their attitude' in not supporting America in a United Nations vote on Zionism.[6] Since all of these countries were poor and dependent on American food aid, a breakdown in the programme could have resulted in political instability. Governments keen on retaining power necessarily had to compromise themselves.

Women in the Third World have traditionally been involved in subsistence farming, selling whatever excess they have in local markets. In some cultures the childcare and agricultural activities of women have been highly valued as work, providing the family and the country with a grass-roots economic base. Yet the perception and value of women's work is increasingly being eroded by the introduction of western agricultural methods leaving many women in a position of limbo. As their ability to nurture and provide for the family decreases, so does their status and negotiating power within their family and community leaving them vulnerable and open to abuse and exploitation.

Western agricultural policies followed in many of these nations is that of 'cash-cropping' – growing food for export rather than for home consumption. Since the 1950s and 1960s, the focus has been on economic growth, and foreign government investments aim at industrialising these nations. Any investments in the agricultural sector are usually devoted to cash-crop production with resources channelled to large landowners. Consequently, the poor suffer decreased availability of food and nutrition problems worsen. Many countries which concentrate on cash-cropping are now net importers of basic foods such as rice and wheat. In the Philippines 55 percent of farm land is used for export crops. In Senegal over 50 percent of the land is given over to growing peanuts and, during a recent famine in the area, export of peanuts actually increased.[7] Underdeveloped countries export about 3.5 million tons of high quality protein a year, roughly the protein needs of 300 million people, which the industrialised west uses to feed livestock (reared for their consumption) and even pets.

During the Sahelian drought of the early 1970s, women, especially pregnant and nursing women, were the hardest hit. Poverty and famine exacerbate many cultural traditions. As I have already pointed out, in all cultures women share the same responsibilities though specific tasks are different. Provision of food often involves everything from the cultivation of fields or the gathering of food, to the collection of firewood and water, to preserving, preparing, cooking and serving the food.

In their book *Woman's Worth*,[8] Lisa Leghorn and Katherine Parker refer to the fact that women often have greater nutritional needs than men because of long hours of physical labour, menstruation, pregnancy and lactation; but many cultures throughout the world do not recognise these needs and indeed follow dietary customs that are harmful to women. These customs originated in the belief that men should receive priority in nutrition as they are the wage earners. Women not only 'feed men and male children first in many situations, they may also prepare different meals for men, or abstain from certain foods that are reserved by religion or custom for men. Often these foods are higher in protein and vitamins than those which are permitted for women. . . In Northern India it is said that milk is good for boys but not for girls, contributing to a higher female mortality rate.' A 1974 study in India showed the extent to which women had internalised the male value system: 'Food distribution within the family arises from deliberate self-deprivation by women because they believe that the earning members (and the male members who are potential earning members) are more valuable than those who do domestic work and childrearing, which they consider devoid of economic value.'

This is the same fundamental dualism that we in the west experience, separating home from the outside world and making the former less 'important', so that only what has cash potential is valued. But with this level of acceptance of patriarchal values, women of the hungry nations face an added hazard. As western markets become saturated, the food industry, with its aggressive sales techniques, increasingly tries to foist their inappropriate processed foods onto the Third World.

The most notorious example of this scandal is the marketing of artificial milk for babies. The effect of bottle feeding a baby in the Third World can be lethal. To feed a baby on a powdered formula may greatly deplete a family's income which may result in the 'milk' being watered down. With the added risk of inadequate facilities for sterilisation and contaminated water supplies, babies develop a combination of malnutrition and gastro-enteritis. The advertising methods are directed specifically at women. A study conducted by the World Health Organisation (WHO) between 1975 and 1977 in nine countries, found the 'overall exposure of mothers to industrially-processed and commercially-marketed infant foods was extensive.' Dr J. Kreysler, WHO nutrition specialist in Botswana, said in 1977: 'The reason for the progressive decline in breast feeding is the massive propaganda of the milk companies which is particularly effective in the poor sectors of the population. The milk companies are creating a magic belief in the white man's milk powder.' Most companies take great pains to point out that they do not 'target' the poor of the Third World as potential customers, but it was only after a wide-spread public outcry during 1974–75 that any changes occurred. Despite the curbing of certain 'hard-sell' tactics, the sale of powdered milk to the Third World continues.[9,10]

Far from being a fact of life, starvation is a fact of man. It would be nice to think that the moral outrage of a few public-spirited individuals might alter this state of affairs, but it is in the end economic or military requirements which create change. In 1901 the British government could not find enough able-bodied men to fight in the Boer War. Poor nourishment in childhood had led to weak and enfeebled adults – the government therefore introduced free school meals to help ensure a fit labour and fighting force for the future. The notion of nation states feeding people solely so that they may become part of a war machine seems an indication of a gross lack of values.

Today many multinational industries are dispensing with their expensive western labour force and employing Third World labour. We in the west will not worry about the plight of the Third World until our own economic base is threatened. Equally, while the labour force of the Third World requires food as a basic ingredient for survival, they will remain cheap and expendable. Food may be seen as a basic human necessity but is clearly not thought of as a basic human right. What has been written here barely touches the many iniquities within the food industry's contribution to western food habits, starvation and exploitation in the Third World. There is a desperate need to redress the balance of power in order to combat exploitation of the weak by the strong for financial and political gain.

At the end – or is it the beginning? – of this whole chain is the woman of the industrialised nation who links the procedure by buying, preparing and serving the food in the home. Culturally women are accepted as the centre of the family unit, and every day they are reminded of this responsibility. Women are responsive to the emotional as well as the physical needs of their families, caring for the family members and upholding them in time of trial or conflict – in essence, supporting the family and keeping it stable. In providing these services for their children and their husbands, women are, in effect, producing time for them. If a woman cooks for the family it is seen as an act of love as well as one of duty. If someone were to do this work outside the home, for people who were not relatives, it would be seen by male standards as productive work and paid for.

As Leghorn and Parker observe in *Woman's Worth*: 'Women's burden comes not from their lack of access to men's work, but to the separation and division of power benefits and responsibility between men and women, which is rooted in women's role and work in the home.'

Historically food has produced enormous social upheavals and injustices. Alarming comparisons can now be made of techniques used by the food industry the world over in the production and sales methods used to influence their markets. Prevaricating western influences have certainly benefited the industrial nations, but clearly the nutritional standard of people throughout the world has not necessarily altered or improved, indeed in many cases it has become more precarious.

Education and the development of the feminist movement have rightly raised levels of expectation in women. The provision of food should be of concern to us all, not just to those who want to sell it and the women who have to deal with it. We must continually draw attention to the iniquities in the food chain, and take responsibility for getting back to the wider issue. If we remain enclosed in our limited world of the supermarket shelf and the kitchen, the system will not only expand, but we in our complicity will be helping to perpetuate it.

11
The Power to Feed Ourselves
Women and land rights

Barbara Rogers

Without the basic ability to feed ourselves, women will be forever at the mercy of commercial and cultural interests which put men first and take women's cooperation for granted. Here Barbara Rogers compares several examples of the dispossession of women, ranging from Africa and Asia to Latin America, demonstrating that a system of land tenure which does not acknowledge the rights of women can never be based on a sound ecological footing. Indeed, the experience of women from societies with remaining links to matrilineal traditions may prove instructive to feminists from industrialised countries who wish to explore a better relationship with the land.

Until women's work and resources are properly recognised, the healthy development of the Third World will never become a reality. This is especially true where land rights are concerned. Modern western laws see land ownership as an individual and not a community affair, with built-in incentives for the individual to work the land in order to maximise profit for him or herself. Common rights to land have dwindled to a tiny remnant of their former importance. Family property has been vested in the hands of the senior male. In Western countries, this tide is only now beginning to turn with the concept of jointly-owned property in a marriage partnership, and the development of various forms of cooperative ownership in which several people share responsibility for house or land.

In the world of 'development' projects and policies, however, individualism reigns supreme, untouched by even the concept of wives sharing property with their husbands. Land registration and reform is almost everywhere concerned with replacing systems of co-ownership with the concept of individual title to land, bestowed on the person seen as the 'head of household'. This is invariably a man unless the household in question is 'headed' by a widow, single mother or other manless woman. The hierarchical principle whereby even a family has to have a 'head' is deeply entrenched in development thinking, data collection and planning.

Because the official development philosophy, taking its cue perhaps from anthropology, assumes that the dominance of one person over others (dominance being invariably vested in men) is a basic principle of society, western-trained planners are seized with anxiety upon encountering any matrilineal, matrilocal or mixed society. It contradicts their basic assumptions about male supremacy.[1] Their anxieties are perhaps exacerbated by the fact that matrilineal systems are much less hierarchical than most patrilineal ones, with prestige based on personal accomplishment rather than membership in a particular family.[2]

A Kenyan sociologist, Achola Pala, has pointed out that in pre-colonial times, women could usually protect their own economic interests through their 'usufruct' rights in land and cattle, which were more effective than individual ownership would be. Usufruct, or the right to use, extended not only to the land itself but to other vital resources such as fish, game, salt licks, water, herbs, vegetables, fruits, fuel, clay and thatch. This ensured the economic rights of all kinds of people who could be squeezed out of a system of formal ownership: women, children, old people and the handicapped. In addition, since productive work was of more importance than formal ownership, the system guaranteed access to resources for all those who worked.[3] In fact, there was a much stronger incentive to work the land, and to care for its long-term fertility, than exists under a system of outright ownership which persists even if the land is over-exploited for short-term profit or left derelict. John C. de Wilde, writing about colonial changes in land tenure designed to create 'incentives' to make the land more productive, observed the opposite happening in Kenya's Central Province. Women were losing their customary land rights, and the right-holders now had no obligation to work their plots. He noted, even in this area of local enthusiasm for the idea of land reform: '. . .considerable areas which have been left idle or virtually idle. . .' The attempted solution was not to return the land to the farmers – mainly women – but to devise special fiscal penalties for men who held land titles but were not farming the land.[4]

One of the World Bank's favourite projects, the Lilongwe Land Development Programme (LLDP) in Malawi, illustrates the fact that the expropriation of women's rights to land is as common under development agency projects as it was under colonial administration. Under British rule, Village Reorganisation Schemes had been carried out in what was then Nyasaland, intended as an integrated programme for land consolidation and technical improvements in land use; by 1958/59 this programme had been applied to some 200,000 acres. During the next few years, however, the entire scheme had to be abandoned because of the fierce opposition from the local people. Among other mistakes, the colonial Department of Agriculture believed that the consent of the (usually male) chief was enough to indicate support from the whole area. John de Wilde, summing up the disaster, comments that there had been particular difficulty in obtaining the cooperation of the women who, in that matrilineal society, were central to any land reform and who were, he suggests, 'needlessly alienated' by the land redistribution.[5]

LLDP might be described as an updated version of this programme, now called integrated rural development. It also serves as a model for the World Bank's new policy, which stresses involvement of small farmers and a generally 'integrated' package. A Bank document states: 'The significance of LLDP for the IBRD [World Bank] is that the project typifies one of the Bank's two principal strategies for what are called "integrated smallholder development programmes" . . .'[6] LLDP management has determined, to its own satisfaction at least, that matriliny and the associated system of 'socialistic' distribution among an extended family is obsolete. Actual residence patterns indicate that it is very much alive. The administration is carrying out a programme of land registration to entrench ownership in a family 'leader'; this is within the framework of Malawi government legislation of 1967, based on western models, which provides the legal and institutional framework for the classification and registration of land in the hands of a relatively small number of men. The official objectives of the LLDP programme are to entrench individual 'security' in ownership of land regardless of the use made of it; and this in turn will be the avenue to credit and other inputs offered by LLDP. Now, however, there are reports of considerable local opposition to the programme, hardly surprising in view of the fact that people's land is in effect being expropriated.

It is in resettlement schemes, however, where a completely new system of land tenure applies, that women lose out most drastically. Jane Hanger's studies at an irrigated rice settlement at Mwea, in Kenya, show that:

'. . . the Settlement procedures treat the male head of household as if he were the principal labourer and decision maker for the irrigated fields farmed under a tenancy agreement with him,

103

whereas both traditionally and in present practice the women contribute the larger share of farm work within the cultivation system.'[7]

Having lost their right to land on which to grow the family's food, as well as being excluded from the system of cash payments for rice production, the women found the scheme an unpleasant place to live and work, in spite of all the government services available there and not elsewhere. The project as a whole was undermined by the women's refusal to devote the time needed to the rice crop, and their black-market trading in rice, the only source of income for them.[8] Another, even more drastic, response was for women to abandon the settlement scheme altogether; the researchers explained that 'many women have found Mwea an intolerable place to live'.[9]

A similar problem is described by James Brain in relation to a settlement scheme in Tanzania, were women accustomed to having rights to land were suddenly deprived of them and all the proceeds of land and labour were handed over to their husbands or fathers. At one scheme at Kingurungundwa women had revolted against what Brain describes as 'virtual serfdom' and demanded their land rights. The government's response was not encouraging; instead of listening to the women's complaints, it closed down the scheme shortly afterwards.[10]

Yet another example of this pattern is the resettlement programme of the Upper Volta government agency, the Autorité des Aménagements des Vallées des Volta (AVV). Faced with demands for exceptionally hard work on the cash crops owned by the men, and deprived of the means of growing their family's food or earning money by trading, women were unable to feed their children. According to a study by a Voltaic sociologist, Jacqueline Gissou: 'since women have no personal resources they are forced to condemn their children to constant hunger.'[11] It is not generally expected of the menfolk that they use cash income to feed their children. The result seems to be similar to that at Mwea: complaints from the women, a sucession of departures by some of them, followed by their husbands who could not manage the work alone.[12]

It is not only in Africa that women have lost their rights to land. That continent offers perhaps the most examples of this happening now, since in Asia and Latin America the process advanced much further under colonial rule, and legislation along western lines has dispossessed women on a massive scale. Indeed, in many areas women's history of land rights has largely been forgotten. India is a classic case of this: the land tenure systems of *zamindari* and *ryotwari* are those imposed by the British colonial administration, in alliance with the big landowners.[13]

In other Asian countries, land tenure is much more flexible than in India and might reflect patterns of land use which prevailed there before British rule. Women have well-recognised rights to land. In Ceylon after the Second World War, for example, a colonial settlement scheme selected only married men with children as participants; but when required to nominate a successor, 19 out of 43 of these men nominated a son, 13 a daughter and 7 a wife.[14] In effect, women were generally seen as having equal rights to the land which had been allocated by the British only to certain categories of men.

In South East Asia there has been a similar pattern. In matrilineal areas of colonial Malaya, for example, much of the land was traditionally passed down from mother to daughter. Under the British 'reform', the traditional code was allowed to apply only in regard to land seen as coming under 'clan' control at the time of the registration of land. The subsequent development of cash crops from rubber and fruit orchards was carried out on plots owned by individuals, with women largely excluded. Women have managed to retain their rice and house plots, but only as long as these remain without cash value, while vigorous family traditions back up the women's claims. In the event of women's plots acquiring significant cash value, as happens with commercialisation or 'development', no legal remedies are available to the women to enforce their rights over the land.[15]

In Latin America, women have virtually no claim to land on the basis of traditional rights, since land was from the beginning of colonial conquest and rule the focus of increasing demand by European settlers and commercial interests. It was acquired by *merced* (grant from the authorities), conquest, violent expulsion of native Americans from their land, and later also of mestizo and even white homesteaders from their private lands. Gunder Frank describes land claims as having been staked out by a variety of more or less fraudulent means, with the 'cash nexus', derived from profits in mining and commerce, ruling the land in Latin America right from the beginning of colonial rule there.[16]

Patricia Garrett has studied the situation in Chile between 1935 and the present. Under Chilean law, a woman's property passes to her husband at marriage, except in rare cases where expensive legal precautions are taken to prevent this. The law is closely modelled on nineteenth-century European concepts; the 1964 Civil Code indicated that 'the *potestad marital* is the set of rights that the laws

105

grant to the husband over the person and goods of the woman.[17] The Allende government in Chile, which laid considerable stress on land reform, failed to tackle this system; it remains in force, of course, under the present right-wing government. Failure to represent women's interests was probably an important mistake on the part of the Allende government, and left a vacuum which allowed right-wing propaganda to be particularly effective among certain groups of women.

Right- and left-wing attempts at changes in land tenure have all, up to now, hastened the process of dispossessing women who are working farmers, exacerbating the flight to the cities. In Latin America and some countries elsewhere many more women than men live in the vast slums these cities contain. Elsewhere, where colonial laws excluded women from the cities, the balance is beginning to change in the same direction. As Patricia Garrett observes in relation to Chile, it is 'practically impossible' for a woman to maintain herself and her children in the countryside if she has no adult male in the household.[18] Faced with destitution, the only way to survive is in too many cases prostitution or – often similar – domestic work in the cities. Land 'reform', often so well intentioned, is driving women, the poorest of the poor, from the land. Until it is radically changed to ensure their full participation, those who advocate it should be vigorously opposed.

12
The Land is Our Life

A Pacific Experience

Léonie Caldecott

Belau means 'our land'. The Republic of Belau (known to many as 'Palau' from its Japanese pronunciation) was born in 1981, though it is still administered by the US, which also has control over the other Micronesian islands in what is designated by the United Nations a 'Strategic Trust Territory'. In other words, an area of immense military value.

The Belauan Islands, situated at the westernmost point of the Caroline Islands in the Micronesian part of the Pacific, 500 miles east of the Philippines, have for the last four centuries been anyone's land but that of their own, indigenous people. The Spanish controlled them from 1598 until 1899 when Germany took over until 1919. Then came the Japanese, who occupied the islands under a League of Nations mandate; initially developing them commercially, then turning them into military bases during the build-up to the Second World War. Since the US won that war, they have taken over.

Under the terms of the Micronesian Trusteeship Agreement, drawn up in 1947, the US is meant to 'promote the development of the inhabitants of the trust territory toward self-government or independence as may be appropriate', and therefore 'promote the economic development of fisheries, agriculture and industries; protect the inhabitants against the loss of their lands and resources'; 'protect the health of the people'. Uncle Sam allowed himself a liberal interpretation of these obligations towards the Pacific peoples, conducting over 60 atmospheric nuclear tests in the Marshall Islands (at the opposite end of the Micronesian group from Belau) during the 1950s; then, after the Test Ban Treaty, they started using the lagoon of Kwajalein as a test target for their long-range missiles, evicting thousands of Marshallese from their homes on islands surrounding the lagoon in the process. 8,000 of these now live in cramped and dangerously insanitary conditions on the 65-acre island of Ebeye.

Meanwhile women who have been exposed to radiation from the nuclear testing are left infertile, have an abnormal rate of miscarriage or give birth to babies so horribly deformed that the women, in their shame, will not show them even to the men who fathered them. The babies usually die within an hour of being born. Similar things have, of course, occurred in Mururoa, where France is *still* conducting tests for the neutron bomb. The Marshallese make repeated attempts to return to their home islands, but negotiations with the US seem so far to have produced little improvement in their lot. They are paid a derisory sum for the use of the land from which they are forcibly exiled. The Kwajalein Atoll plays a crucial role in maintaining the nuclear capability of its captors; they will not give it up easily.

Belau, too, has suffered from the effect of other nations' aggressive concerns. During the Second World War, one of its islands, Peleliu, was completely denuded of its lush vegetation, its white beaches were turned into a bloodbath by the warring Japanese and American forces. The history books will tell you how many died on each side. They will not tell you of the thousands of Belauans who also died in a war which was not their own and which these essentially non-violent people would never have wished on themselves or anyone else. The population of the islands is now just under 15,000.

Bernadette Bedor was born a few years before the Pacific War began. She has hazy memories of the war, but fairly vivid ones of the devastation it left in its wake.

War is something very real to Belauans, not something we merely read about or see on television. We are also very aware of the health problems in the Marshalls – the highest rate of cancer and leukaemia in the world. I think this is what has made us the first nation in the world to have a specifically anti-nuclear constitution, which the US has not liked at all. They have forced us to vote on it several times over, but every time the people vote in favour – the initial mandate for it was 92 percent!

Bernadette will not tell you herself (it would not occur to her), but it is women like her who made that vote possible. Her brother, Roman Bedor, puts it very clearly.

Belau is basically a matrilineal society. We inherit through the women's line and women have a considerable amount of control over land rights. The reason we could have such a controversial and courageous constitution is entirely due to the strength of our

108

women, who campaigned for months on the issue, going from door to door and talking to the people. In our society, women are really powerful – the men can't do anything without their consent. That is why it is a peaceful society.

Bernadette is a biology teacher, and she became involved in the political struggle through her interest in education, especially as it relates to the indigenous culture of her own people.

Having spent some time in the US, I used to think that their way must be best. But then, as I began to teach kids back home, I realised that the US-influenced education system was not necessarily preparing them for life in their own country, let alone if it is to become an independent, self-sufficient nation. I saw that we were in danger of losing our own cultural values.

I have come to realise that education has to be more than just learning out of books. People need to know directly about what is affecting them, they need to learn how to exist in their own environment. I became interested in educating people about the specific problems that we as a people face in Belau, and that included the nuclear issue, since there are US plans to turn us into a forward base for the Trident submarine and the Japanese want to dump nuclear waste in the Pacific. I guess that's how I became politicised, though originally I thought of it merely as learning about the world I live in.

When we first started campaigning against US domination, resisting their plans to build an enormous super port for oil tankers here, we found the base of our support coming from older people in rural areas who are still in touch with our traditions. The reason they became active was precisely because they see those traditions being undermined by foreign influence. Our customary extended families and clans, for example, were beginning, in the developed areas like Koror, to break into small nuclear families. Instead of being able to exist off the fruit and vegetables we grow ourselves, and the fish we catch, as we have done for centuries, people are being made dependent on a money-based economy. Instead of doing things in order to serve one another, we do them for money. Schoolchildren are fed on American imported junk food, tinned meat and fish, instant noodles and canned drinks, and suddenly we have all sorts of health problems we had never heard of before – catching constant colds, getting dental caries.

Our traditional religion, *Motekgnei* (which means 'community'), teaches respect for nature. If you arrive at a river in the night, you first throw in a stone to warn the river of your presence, *then* you go in yourself. You pray before tilling the ground and talk to plants before picking them. The same respect extends to people. When we are campaigning we don't hold big rallies and harangue people from a platform. We go on foot from village to village, from island to island, talking one to one. That way people trust us, they know us and know we tell the truth. It can't be hurried. If the tide is not right, you wait until it is, then get the boat and go to the next island. We have no 'phones outside Koror, so if you want to speak to someone, you have to go yourself.

Now we are being asked to vote on a Compact of Free Association, which basically gives the US rights to military expansion on about two-thirds of our land. It is a way of getting round our constitution, which is not favourable to their interests. But how can we do this and still be able to feed ourselves? The water, which the Japanese want to pollute, and the land, on which the US wants to practise jungle warfare, is all we have. The land is our life. You can't sell your life.

The right of the Belauans to self-determination and the preservation of their own culture is, in my view, a worthy cause for women who yearn to create a world in which we play a full and powerful role. This is a culture from which we may have a lot to learn. We must surely do whatever we can to enable it to survive. Further information on this most urgent issue can be obtained from: Pacific Concerns Resource Centre, PO Box 27692, Honolulu, Hawaii 96827.

A Micronesian Woman

My baby, the fruit of my womb –
    for nine months I longed for it

  I sang to it
  I laid out clothes
  I dreamed sweet dreams

My baby, the fruit of my womb –
    it had no face for me to kiss

  Unheard my songs
  No eyes; no hands
  A bunch of grapes

My baby, the fruit of my womb –
    its heart beat furiously then stopped

  I held it tight
  I hated it; I loved it
  I hid it from view

My baby, the fruit of my womb –
    its father was the atom bomb

  He raped our land
  He killed our trees
  He saps my life

                Rosalie Bertell

13
Greening the Desert

Women of Kenya reclaim land

Maggie Jones/Wangari Maathai

*In 1977 the distinguished Kenyan biologist Professor
Wangari Maathai launched the National Council of Women of
Kenya's Green Belt Movement, a community tree-planting project
which aims to involve rural people personally in the fight against the
desertification and soil erosion which threaten their livelihood. At the
international public hearing on 'The Human Environment: Action or
Disaster' in London in June 1982, where she was a member of the panel
of judges, Professor Maathai was interviewed by Maggie Jones.*

Maggie: *You have said that it is rural women who suffer most from
environmental problems and the energy crisis. Could you explain this?*
Maathai: Poverty is the worst form of environmental pollution in
developing countries. This poverty is something that many men can
run away from – admittedly often into worse poverty in the cities –
while the woman and her children are left behind in the country. It is
she who has to worry about how to feed her family, what to cook with,
where she will get water from, why the topsoil is being lost, how she
will grow enough food and so on.
*It is often said that Africa is the most environmentally vulnerable
continent and that development in many cases results in the collapse of
local ecosystems.*
I don't know whether the African tropical ecosystem is *more* fragile
than others, but certainly Africa's poverty, ignorance and underdevelopment mean that once you destroy the natural ecosystems that
have been self-sustaining for centuries, it is very difficult for nature to
sustain or re-establish what is being at the same time consistently
destroyed – unless there is a new awareness from the people of the
meaning and value of conservation.
What do you feel about the question of population?
It has been emphasised many times at conferences that the major
problem facing the Third World countries is over-population or

112

potential population growth. Many Third World people prefer to look at it differently. What they see as their greatest problem is poverty, not really the rate of population growth.

Sometimes I find it very difficult to separate the two, or to say which comes first, like the case of the chicken and the egg. It seems to me that pressure on the land occurs because people in the Third World are poor and so cannot feed and clothe themselves properly and maintain a sound ecological balance. If the people were not so poor, they would be able to replenish their land, they would be able to exploit it soundly, and, overall, the continent would be able to sustain a much higher population, as we can see in other parts of the world.

The other thing I think it is important to understand is that, again because of poverty, security is found in children, and in numbers. Improved health care in some countries such as Kenya is also contributing to high rates of population increase.

What do you feel can be done to help reduce population growth – or to put it another way, to promote family planning?

First, I think we really have to persist so that we find better methods to control fertility. The techniques that we are currently using for family planning are not acceptable to everybody. We do not have enough information about the IUD, the pill or the injectables, and, like pesticides, we may very well be putting a lot of harmful chemicals into women just as we did into the environment. So one cannot completely blame the women who refuse to use these methods.

Secondly, there is another aspect, which is that the men in Africa are still very influential in the personal life of families, and I think that so far the family planning message has been aimed at the woman rather than at the man.

You have tried to involve rural women in trying to prevent the degradation of the environment in your 'Green Belt' scheme of reafforestation in Kenya's Rift Valley. How is this movement organised?

The philosophy behind it is to involve the people in solving the problems which arise from the pressures on fuelwood supplies. Kenya's forest cover is now less than 2.5 per cent of the land area. What the National Council of Women of Kenya does is campaign; it tells people why they should plant trees, and they have responded very well. They write to us and tell us that they want to plant trees. These trees are planted as a community woodland which we call a 'green belt', and each green belt must have at least 1,000 trees. The community must prepare the ground, dig holes, and provide manure and then must help to take care of the young trees.

The National Council of Women provides the trees and also a small

113

amount of money so that the people can hire a local handicapped person to look after the trees – our target is for five years, but at present we can only afford to pay for a year or two. We tried to have as small an input as possible and let the community do the work. We act as a catalyst and provide moral support.

The Government does not fund this project – most of the work is done on a voluntary basis, though we have had technical assistance from the Department of Forests. We asked people to sponsor trees at 100 shillings a tree.

Although initiated and promoted by women, the programme has to our delight involved all the community, including children and men, who usually do not become involved in women's projects.

How do you see this movement in the light of global environmental efforts?

I think it is very promising. One of the reasons why I think the tree-growing project has been so successful is that people can see the crisis – there are not enough trees and not enough firewood to gather – and also the trees we give them grow very fast, so that it is easy to see a result for their labours.

The main problem at the global level is that we are fighting an invisible enemy, often with invisible weapons. And I am afraid that it will be a long time before the invisible aspects of global environmental degradation will be reacted to.

The second thing is that we have a very short lifetime. Barbara Ward, Margaret Mead and others who alerted us are gone now. We need a new generation to carry out their work, but even they may not see the end result.

14

Greening the Cities

Creating a hospitable environment
for women and children

Penelope Leach

*Feminist debate on the subject of motherhood has been
fraught with controversy and Penelope Leach's work in this area has
been the focus of criticism by women concerned at the continuing
pressures on us to submerge our own identities in the interests of
bringing up children. Nonetheless, numerous women are, whether
they like it or not, engaged in childcare at this very moment.
Considering that they find themselves in a society that pays constant
lip-service to the value of what they do, it is scandalous that the urban
environment many mothers are forced by economic factors to live in is
so inhospitable to them. In this excerpt from* Who Cares? A New Deal
for Mothers and Their Small Children *(published by Penguin in
1979), Penelope Leach focuses our attention on urgently required
improvements in working conditions for any adult in charge of
children in our cities. Were such improvements to be brought about,
we might be on the way towards a genuine appreciation of childcare,
through which the whole of society would take responsibility for the
young, rather than lumbering women with what, all too often, proves
to be a frustrating, isolating, tour of duty.*

If you look around a suburban street in the daytime, a very large
proportion of the people you see will be mothers with children below
school age. Yet look at the street again and you will see that almost
nothing about it takes cognisance of them. It is as if no town planner,
councillor or architect ever had a young family. Or as if, and this may
be closer to the truth, no mother ever reached seniority in such a
profession. Over the past few years there has been increasing pressure on such people to make provision for the needs of physically-
handicapped people within the community. Yet few of them seem to
realise that life is almost as difficult for a mother with a pram or
pushchair as it is for an adult in a wheelchair. In my ideal society a
Children's Community Rights Act would be regarded as at least as

essential as a Sex Discrimination or a Race Relations Act. And if that sounds like a joke, I wish it did not.

But, as every social reformer knows, legislation is only effective to the extent that it is socially accepted. We could ban, by law, some of the most glaring injustices to mothers and small children; we could insist, by law, on the provision of some facilities for them. But what is really needed is a general recognition of their existence and of their worth. Their home conditions are their work conditions; they have no carefully-inspected factory, regulated as to light and heat, safety and comfort, to escape to. Their productivity is what they do together; and they have no employer anxious to get the best from them nor union to swop work for reward. If anybody cared, there are innumerable things which could be done to make their lives easier and to make them more fun. Many of them would cost nothing. The money spent on some of them could be recouped from the families themselves, while some of the most expensive measures would repay their cost through savings to the emergency services in accidents and family breakdown . . . Most of what I am going to suggest will sound – to everyone but a current parent – like trivia. Each issue is, by itself, trivial. But daily life with a small child is made up of endless successive minutes of trivia and each pin-prick adds to the next to make the soreness of being 'stuck at home' and 'bored out of my mind'.

The mother who does not want to be stuck in the house all day has to go out. To do so she has a few little problems nobody can remove like getting coats onto small reluctant bodies as well as her own, but having accomplished those she may have to go downstairs in a lift. It is designed to let adults in and out and it has no special gadget to hold the door open while she manoeuvres herself, a pram and a toddler safely inside.

If the lift is broken she, like other residents, will have to walk down. But unlike other residents she may be totally stuck. She cannot push the pram downstairs. Even if it folds and she can carry it, she cannot carry pram and occupant together nor leave a baby on the ground alone at either the top or the bottom . . . If she has a toddler as well as a baby she can neither carry both of them together nor leave either one alone at either end. Not a very good start.

Perhaps the lift was not meant for prams. Perhaps she is even provided with a pram store at the bottom? Fine, but babies use their prams as portable beds in, as well as out of, the house, so if that is the case she needs two. Does anybody who puts a young family to live in an upstairs flat give her a 'necessary second pram' grant?

Once down and out, she is in a street. Wherever she is going she will

116

eventually have to cross it. The traffic scene is beyond the scope of this chapter, but even within the present ghastly situation in which roads belong to cars rather than to people and those who drive them forget the times when they take the role of pedestrian, there are some measures which could ease her way. Kerbs are hell both for pram-pushers and for pram-riders. We urgently need more smoothed-out places where they can be avoided. At present kerbs stand proud of the road and flush with the pavement, the idea being that they keep cars from joining the walkers. But many road accidents to very small children take place because walkers join the cars. Why cannot kerbs stand proud of pavements, too? A four-inch rise would prevent that fatal dash into the traffic because the child who tried it would fall over instead. The new kerbs would make pram-life worse, but with more sloped crossings that would not matter. As a corollary to the new kerbs there should be a new, automatic and highly expensive traffic offence: that of driving any vehicle, under any circumstances, onto the pavement. At present putting your nearside wheels onto the pavement is an accepted method of getting your car – or delivering lorry – out of the traffic flow. Nobody seems to realise that wheels on the pavement make nonsense of everything parents try to teach young children about the pavement being safe and the road not being so. Of course if the mother we are accompanying happens to live in the country she may find herself on a road which has blind corners, large farm vehicles, drivers who assume that there is no oncoming traffic *and no pavement at all.* Just where is she supposed to walk safely with that pram?

Prams and pushchairs are designed to push rather than pull so when she needs to cross the road the mother must shove her baby into a river of motorised metal in order to demonstrate her intention to drivers. Let us hope there is a pedestrian crossing for her and that all the cars, even the ones in the far lane, really stop. In the middle of the road there will probably be a refuge but it will not be big enough to take the whole pram. It should be big enough for that and it should be partially railed too. Without rails how is she to keep her toddler safe while watching for the right moment to cross the second half of the road?

Panda crossings and their relations are a disaster and should be rethought. The time allowed for pedestrians is only just enough for the hale and hearty adult. If her toddler falls down the mother will be in trouble. When did you last hoot at a tiresome group which held you up after your light went green?

In a very busy area the mother may find an under- or an overpass.

But with a pram, she will not be able to use it. Without slopes instead of, or as well as, steps, these crossings cannot be used by many of the people who need them most.

Perhaps that mother would like to use public transport? Well, with a pram she will just have to want. Even a folding pram cannot be closed up with one hand while holding the baby with the other, even if the toddler will stay safely close by while you try. You cannot put a baby down on the pavement while you fold the pram, so it is hopeless. With a pushchair she can have a try. Not the tube, though. Folded pushchair in one hand, toddler in the other, on an escalator? No, thank you. A bus perhaps? Well, yes, if there is a conductor to help her on and somewhere to stow that pushchair once she gets aboard. Yes, again, if the downstairs seats were kept for her as well as for non-smokers and if the driver had been taught to glance over his shoulder to make sure she was seated before he let his clutch in . . . I wonder whether it ever occurs to the people who park their cars on bus stops to wonder how mothers with young children will enjoy getting out into the middle of the road?

Probably she does not need public transport but is only going to the shops. Fine, but will the shops let her take the pram in with her? Probably not. She cannot leave it outside with the baby in it or he may get snatched, jostled or teased so at present she will have to take him out and risk the empty pram getting stolen. Most shops could provide space for prams near the checkout counters, but they would have to get rid of their swing or revolving doors. A good thing too as both are murder when you are carrying a baby or have a small child at foot. You can get hurt or separated or both. Shopping is not much fun with a baby to carry and even less so if you have a toddler to steer as well. People only have two hands, you see.

'All shoplifters will be prosecuted' says the notice, but there, at the checkout counter, just where the toddler must wait in an incomprehensible queue, are the bars and bars of chocolate, piled into bins just his height. He did not shoplift that Mars Bar he is eating, paper and all, did he? She was always going to pay for it, truly she was. People with not much shopping do not see why they should queue for long so they have special express checkouts. But why should those children have to wait? Where are the special checkouts for them and their mothers? Rich ladies, who can tip, get their shopping carried out to their cars. But where is the packer who will help a harassed mother get her impossible load organised? How difficult would it really be to provide a few highchairs with safety harnesses so that she could park the baby while she found her money or went back for what she had forgotten?

Where next? The library perhaps. But there are steps up to the door (pram trouble again) and anyway the adult librarian will glare and say 'Ssh'. The Children's Library probably does not open until after the schools are let out and it may well have a minimum lending age of five. Many such librarians take their work extremely seriously and do a marvellous job in helping school-age children with books for projects and hobbies, as well as for pleasure reading. But dismally few provide the hours, the sincere smiles and the mats on the floor which would enable our mother to spend a happy hour there with her children. Anyway that toddler will certainly not be allowed to touch any books today because his hands are showing that Mars Bar. She would have to wash him first and where can she do that?

Every mother who gets out and about with small children needs public lavatories. Babies soil themselves and when they do, they stink, which is unpleasant for all. The only answer is to change their nappies and you cannot do that in the street. Toddlers who are 'dry' usually feel very strongly about staying that way but cannot do so for nearly as long as adults.

So we need more, many, *many* more public lavatories. But even when there is one, in the right place and at the right time, the parents' troubles are not over. A father with a small girl must choose between taking her past that uncompromising row of backs at the Men's urinal or sending her alone into the Women's. A mother with a small boy must either offend his dignity by lifting him up to *sit* on an adult lavatory or send him alone into the Men's. Perhaps we shall soon have unisex facilities as in most of Europe. Certainly every public lavatory should have a child-sized loo in a cubicle whose lock can be undone from outside with a coin when the child gets stuck. All our 'Ladies' already contain slot-machines for sanitary towels so why on earth not add machines to dispense disposable nappies and paper pants for the days when it gets left too late? We have mirrors and dressing-tables as well as washbasins, so why not a changing counter as well? Nobody has thought about it, that is why.

Neither has anyone thought about the fact that mothers might need a few places simply to rest, as, accompanied by tired and fretful children, they struggle through town. We provide shelters for people waiting for buses, so why not shelters or refuges, pavement bays if you like, where mothers could get out of the stream of people for a few minutes, sit down, wipe mouths, readjust loads, or just restore screaming muscles and tempers?

If the baby is breastfed such a public place is no good. With our negative attitude to babies and their needs the mother will be stared at, glared at and whistled out of countenance. She might even get 'spoken to' by a policeman. It is not actually illegal to breastfeed a baby in public but 'disturbing the peace' covers anything the law enforcer pleases even if a suckling baby is one of the most peaceful sights you are ever likely to see. Armed with a bottle, she can retire into a café if there is one. But the toddler cannot reach the table from the only available chairs and there is no room for both children on her lap. He wants orange squash and it comes in a sealed carton into which you push a straw. He has not yet learned to drink through a straw and taking off the lid so that he can use the container as a beaker sounds a great deal easier than it is, especially one-handed. The mother could have a cup of tea. Indeed if she is going to occupy the table she will have to have something. But the baby's hands are waving perilously close to the hot liquid and there is nowhere she can be put down while mother drinks it. Even without the special family coffee bars which I should like to see in every shopping centre, it seems extraordinary that ordinary local cafés do not cater for small children and their mothers. All they need are high chairs and/or baby seats; beakers with handles; half-portions on request; dampened tissues for mopping up and the kind of tolerance which agrees to provide a buttered role *without* the standard ham . . .

Probably it is time to make for home now, but as a walk with some fun in it. After all this is meant to be an outing. They walk along beside the railway and then over a foot-bridge. Of course that line has to be safely fenced-off but why must the fence be solid? Do people not know that children like to watch trains? On the bridge his mother lifts him perilously up to watch a train pass beneath them. Later he will climb, even more perilously, to watch. If peep-holes had been built into the concrete he could have watched in safety. In a society which realised that some of its members were small, every barrier which adults look over would have peep-holes for looking through.

Doing is even more important than looking when you are small. The toddler has mother's letters clutched in his hand and he recognises the friendly red postbox. But of course he cannot post those letters because he cannot reach. The postmaster tells me that special low slots would be 'inadvisable' because 'children would post rubbish'. Who is it that posts fireworks and french letters? Not people three-feet high but the five-feet people who should know better.

After the postbox they come to a remote-controlled crossing. It will be years before the toddler is safe out alone in his community, but his mother would like him to see the connection, again and again,

120

between pushing the putton and that little green walking man coming on. But he cannot reach to push it. He cannot reach *any* of the buttons which control this difficult, automated environment, not the ones at crossings or on buses nor the ones which summon lifts or ask people to let him in through front doors. So he cannot start to learn until he is much bigger. But think what could be done with this pleasure in posting and pushing things if anyone actually wanted toddlers to have fun. Rubbish bins could have posting slots and they would pick up sweet papers for the fun of posting them. Buttons to push could control a glory of tiny joys all along the street, like little mirrors whose covers slide back so that you can see yourself, or chimes that ring when you press. No, these are not meant to be *useful*; they are meant to be fun.

What else can they do on the way home? The corner shop is a favourite place and the shopkeeper is a familiar dispenser of goodies and therefore a good person to practise talking to. There ought to be an especially low section of counter for those conversations to take place across, but of course there will not be. Having a corner shop at all is luck these days. A few know all the local families by name, keep special pocket-money lines for children and care enough to keep the rules about who may buy cigarettes or fireworks. They serve as a vital link in the community chain with an importance far greater than their turnover would suggest. Yet one by one they are priced out of competition with the big chain stores and vanish, leaving their districts impoverished. If the local pub were forced to close by economic pressure from the road house a mile away, the uproar would fill the local paper. But the corner shops are only important to the old and to mothers and children. Nobody makes much fuss.

Perhaps there is a 'gardens'. If there is nothing, no patch of grass anywhere on which the family can pause, sit, play, look, then it is because nobody has thought or bothered. Most streets could provide a patch at least the size of an ordinary back-garden; even that is enough to make an oasis in the child's concrete world. Unfortunately most of our odd corners are devoted not to the grass children need, or to the cafés they would hold almost anywhere else in Europe, but to the motorcar.

If there is a gardens it may well be a pretty place to move *through* rather than a place *to be*. Neat tarmac paths will run through green and shrubbery which is somebody's pride and joy and firmly marked 'Keep off the grass'. The keeper will not yell at the lonely dogs who break his rules; after all they have to go somewhere, don't they? But let the mother spread a rug for that baby and produce a ball for the

121

toddler and he will move them on. It is for looking at, not for using. The children may see, but they may not do. If they try to feed the pigeons from their mother's newly-bought loaf, they will be told that they are messing up the paths. Pigeons can do damage in towns, so why are there no half-coconuts hanging in the trees to attract the smaller birds, first to their flesh and then to bathe in their rainwater? Why is there no dispenser, complete with reachable money slot and buttons, from which the toddler can purchase nuts or seeds to feed to them?

If he climbs on the seats he will be scolded for putting his feet where elderly ladies want to put other portions of their anatomy. But climb he will, so why not put something for him to climb? Those sharp metal railings could be cheap and friendly wooden post-and-rail and he could climb those to his heart's content. Year after year councils spend money on removing branches pruned from city trees. Pile them here and he could climb over, jump off and straddle them as they turn from horse to motorbike. Let them collect insects under their rotting bark; insects are part of his world and he needs an introduction. Let them gather moss for him to stroke.

Acorns and oak-apples fall each autumn and are quickly whisked away, with the dead leaves, as rubbish. But why? Leave the fruits and they will attract the squirrels and the bigger birds which could make this little urban gardens into a magic place for small children. Competing with them, children can make collections, grow the seedlings in jam jars, and find the leaves which have turned to skeletons. And those leaves: we are rearing a generation of children many of whom will never have spent an October afternoon jumping in a leaf-drift. To me that is almost as sad as believing that Cheddar cheese is mined from the Gorge as suggested on television.

Why is it all kept so neat, tidy, unused and sterile? Who is it for, if it is not for mothers and children? If you actually ask them, keepers either say that the gardens must be tidy for 'the old folk' or for the supervisor. But we pay that supervisor to use the land to fill our community's needs and mothers and children are needful members of the community. As for the retired people who may, or may not, sit there and contemplate the past, what makes us think that they want the gardens tidy and empty? Is this not the kind of place where young and old could meet and share?

So the mother and her young children make their way home. No disasters have struck. The mother did not drop her purse down a grating, up-end the pram with her shopping, lose the toddler . . . But it has been an effort rather than a pleasure and all three of them have got less out of the trip than they could have done. If we turn away from the realism of the kind of thing mothers do almost every afternoon, and look instead at the possible 'treats' in their lives, the opportunities which we miss on their behalf become even clearer.

Begin with parks. Britain is rich in them and London is world famous for its breathing holes. They are obvious places to take small children. A park offers wide open spaces and infinite potential for new experience, for excitement, for adventure – or does it?

'Our' park caters well for many other age groups. Their football pitches and running tracks dominate the scene and take up all the parkland that is close to the entrances. To escape organised sport, laden mothers must walk on. All the grass is mown and, to facilitate the machines, the land is kept as flat as possible. Lumps and bumps on which a small person could be King of the Castle are smoothed away and because the grass is kept so short, nothing *but* grass can grow. Left rough, that grass would be interspersed with wild flowers. A few packets of seeds scattered randomly in spring would produce a bounteous crop of wild things which could be legitimately picked. Late in summer there would be standing hay to crawl about in . . .

Dogs by the hundred spend their owners' working days loose in this park. I am sorry for them but much sorrier for British children whose list of phobias is headed by dogs and whose crawling, rolling and running is so often interrupted by a meeting with turds. Dogs must relieve themselves but on the whole they choose to do so where others have gone before. Ash pits would actually attract the neglected ones as well as providing a legitimate place for responsible owners to take their pets.

The park caters for children with a 'playground'. It is surfaced in concrete, roughened to be non-slip and apparently designed to ensure that every tumble draws blood from a knee. It contains the 'standard' playground equipment which leads to so many ghastly accidents each year all over the country. There is nothing in it which a child under five can manage alone nor is the place one where a pre-school child can possibly be safe unless an adult follows everywhere, foreseeing the flying feet on the swings. There are many surfacing materials available now which could be used for playgrounds; they range from hardwearing ryegrass to new kinds of synthetic rubber. There is a wide range of play equipment, too, which could be installed for the very young, ranging from play houses through sandpits to first climbing frames. But given that councils already equip such places and staff them, it would cost no more to break right away from the conventional 'Playground' model and instead provide tree-stump stepping-stones, a boat-sailing pool, a few rabbits or guinea pigs, a mound of earth with steps up one side and a slide down the other, perhaps even a couple of giant inflatable cushions to jump and roll about on. . .

Where else can a mother take small children at least for an occasional treat or expedition? Museum and art gallery staff are notoriously unwelcoming to the very young and, if challenged, express understandable fear of breakages. But their long, warm, carpeted galleries could provide hundreds of metres of toddling space for people who cannot possibly reach the display cases or the pictures and whose mother would actually like to look while they walk. Why should excited young voices make these righteous guardians of our national heritage bristle so?

A lot of towns, especially small ones, have special facilities which are expensive to maintain for occasional use and could also serve young children and their mothers. I can think, for example, of a number of covered markets which open only twice a week and are otherwise vast empty barns in which people could tricycle or simply run. I know several open markets, closed off from the streets and therefore not usable for car-parking, but complete with concrete sheep-pens and big auction sheds. They would be glorious places to play hide-and-seek, to climb and rush about. They could all be made into places to go, for fun.

If every mother with very young children had easy ways of making friends and obvious places to go in search of acquaintances, much of the outright loneliness which many experience would be lifted. If all these mothers came and went within a local environment which felt warm and accepting towards them and geared itself to their special needs, getting out and about, alone or with others, would be both less of an effort and more worth whatever effort it cost. If there were also places to go to make a special point to a day or a week, to make the most of sunshine or to let off the steam that gathers when it rains, then daily life could begin to feel positively cheerful. A full-time mother leads a life which is subject only to her own programming. She can decide what she and her children will do today; she has no boss to set her chores or deadlines. At present many mothers do not feel this as a unique freedom in their working lives because their choice is between going drearily out or staying drearily in. Remove the drear of the local environment and going out into it would become a positive choice. In parallel, staying home would become a positive choice, too.

15
Against Nuclearisation and Beyond

Statement of Sicilian Women

Areas targeted as bases for a new generation of nuclear weapons have also become the focus for a new determination on the part of women to stand out against the weapons and the forces giving rise to them – a much more difficult task in Mafia-dominated Sicily than in countries like Britain. The following statement was written by a group of Sicilian women shortly after the proposal to site Cruise missiles in Comiso, Sicily, was announced in the summer of 1981. It shows, as do the actions at Greenham Common in Britain, that women are delving deep to find the causes of the violence which has always threatened us and of which these missiles are but the latest manifestation.

We have asked ourselves if there is a specifically feminist way of looking at war and peace. Looking back over the last decade, as well as at the present and into the future, we feel the answer is 'yes'.

In our struggle for divorce; equality; social services; for a sexuality mindful of our sensibility as women, we have met with a new image of ourselves. This image is very different from the one demanded by males. We write here of some of the stages in our struggle for emancipation and liberation which, over the last ten years, has continued as a result of focusing on certain goals. The goals may seem a piecemeal approach, but nonetheless they are unified by a single thread. They pose – not for ourselves alone – the question of the *quality of life.*

What does quality of life mean? It certainly does not consist in the growth of consumption or in the mere multiplication of social services. Quality of life is respect for Nature. It therefore involves struggling against pollution, against the private ownership of natural resources. It is clean energy; the right to good health and preventative medicine; housing for all; dignified working conditions; social reintegration of the aged; respect for childhood; solidarity amongst the exploited; tolerance of physical and mental diversity; the abolition of sex discrimination under the law and in social behaviour, as well as many other things.

To attain all this, peace is necessary. Yet, let us be clear that although we oppose war, we also oppose a 'false' peace that ignores starvation and exploitation. We cannot accept a peace that benumbs conscience and builds empires upon women's labour. We know that because we are women, we are, in every society and social class, subjected to specific kinds of exploitation: sexual work, mother work, house work, unprotected and underpaid work. We also oppose that 'hypocritical' peace which creates the myth of the 'angel of the home'. Under this myth, women are made to stay at home to look after husbands and raise children for their country. It is this same mentality which boosts the myth of emancipation – when women are needed in factories and offices as cheap labour, or when, as now, unemployment and militarisation open the shining doors of military careers to women.

Our 'no' to war coincides with our struggle for liberation. Never before have we seen so clearly the connection between nuclear escalation and the culture of the muscleman; between the violence of war and the violence of rape. Such, in fact, is the historical memory that women have of war, wherever and whenever it takes place. But it is also our daily experience in 'peacetime', and in this respect women are perpetually at war. It is no coincidence that the gruesome game of war – in which the greater part of the masculine sex seems to delight – passes through the same stages as the traditional sexual relationship: aggression, conquest, possession, control. Of a woman or a land, it makes little difference.

We have reflected at length on this connection, and we remember our loneliness when we have to face the pain of an abortion. We also remember being accused of murder by the very same faction that today finds nuclear rearmament 'natural' and which is preparing the most absurd of deaths for us all. In this we perceive an idea of life which is no more than a 'planned death'. It is an idea that the Great Powers, and the states that passively support them, have in common, whether in the east or in the west; in 'real' socialism or in advanced capitalism.

When faced with the choices offered by 'planned death', women have the desire neither to be sweet or patient or resigned, nor to play Godmother to ships and guns, nor to be nurses nor, least of all, to be soldiers. Instead we are starting a movement which struggles for peace and self-determination, which rejects oppression and exploitation of one nation over another, of one class over another and of one sex over another.

Whereas the behaviour of states is apparently dominated by the logic of the 'balance of power' – for which they inflate fears of aggression in order to justify their nuclear rearmament – we on the other hand feel the strength of a presence, which has until now been utterly suppressed, growing all around us: the presence of women and children. It is with pride and hope that we use these words, which have so often been used in hypocritical and discriminatory ways. To us, this presence is the only ethical and political ground from which a courageous affirmation of life, capable of breaking the vicious circle of 'who is strongest', can spring anew.

We ask for unilateral disarmament now, because we firmly believe in the utopia of common sense, in courage without banners, in the fruitfulness of giving before receiving. We believe in paying close attention to the uniqueness and beauty of human life. *This* is *women's* culture.

We realise how difficult it is to say these things and to listen to them, cornered as we are between a false war-monger's peace and an abstract left-wing pacifism.

People have been slowly innoculated against imagining that there is any other answer to the rise in energy demand than the nuclear option. The energy demand itself has, in turn, been grossly exaggerated in order to prop up the profits, the habits and the myth of the opulent society. Many have believed this propaganda, fearing long freezing winters and mass unemployment. But now we can see that it was only the dress rehearsal for the imposition of missiles upon us as a matter of course, and for making our minds become accustomed to the idea of the neutron bomb – the 'clean' bomb that kills people but leaves the Coloseum standing for the delight of the American tourists.

We have to shake off the habit of accepting war; it is the first step towards avoiding certain death. *War is neither natural nor unavoidable.* Otherwise, what is the sense of giving birth, that experience which for many of us is our only creative outlet and source of identity? Faced with such unnatural options, why should we continue to believe in the 'natural' meaning of motherhood? Our answer to nuclear death, paradoxical as it may seem, could be a conscious refusal to give life. We therefore say:

No to the balance of terror

No to NATO and to the
Warsaw Pact
No to Cruise missiles in Comiso
(Sicily)

Yes to immediate unilateral
disarmament in Italy
Yes to talks for nuclear disarmament
Yes to multilateral disarmament for a denuclearised
Europe

Let military budgets be invested instead in a better quality of life
this is the message of women
– if it is not heeded –
we stop motherhood!

Catania, Sicily, October 1981

For the Hiroshima Maidens

I

Somewhere in these busy, honking streets,
She is commemorated in respectful aspic
– Fading photographs, snippets
Of cloth, concrete, newsprint, wax –
Appalling artefacts, grown hoarse with age.

A crackling newsreel recreates
This patient corpse in charred kimono
(How her hollow eyes have haunted me)
Neatly labelled, token victim,
With this reassuring epitaph:
'She will never smile again.'

And yet how you smile and smile
Hiroshima, virgin city, ripe still
For conquering,
Your heart locked
In the silent chastity of pain.

II

This, gentlemen, is the
Greater East Asian Prosperity Sphere,
Sprung anew like sickle-senna
On ground cleansed by history,
Watered with blood

And a few other things.
Imagine!
These impassive people,
Jovial in the myriad
Sushi bars at night,
Have walked through fire
To claim their great and glorious future.
What's done is done.

And you, sister,
Who lift your face to me today,
Keloid-kissed and brave beyond despair,
Speaking of your friend's leukaemia

And other cancers
– Have you survived by the grace,
As the clever men say,
Of natural selection?
But no, your urgent face
Affirms, there is
Nothing natural in this.

III

Shall I perform an autopsy
I who come here
With my sterilised hands?
Shall I strip you bare,
As this dome is stripped
Against its picture-postcard sunset?
Shall I enter your darkened house,
Creak across your sparse tatami mat,
Flushing you out
With my eager searchlight?

But no.
Your shame, sister, shames me:
Together we are monuments to it.
You with your patient witness
Here amongst the peace-park pigeon shit,
I with my untried body
And my tourist's lens.
As we stand, mountainous,
Irrevocably incarnate on this small earth,
Subtly (and not so subtly) altered
With every iodine release,
Every additive,

Every new encroachment
On the womb that bore us,
We too are exhibits, near extinct,
In the gaunt, ruined museum to
Science and Industry.
It is still standing, but then
So are we.

Léonie Caldecott

16
Gaea: The Earth as our Spiritual Heritage

Jean Freer

All too often, we create a dichotomy between politics and spirituality. Those of us who care about the one are deemed not to care about the other. Yet the more radical a political view we hold, and the more difficult the tasks we set ourselves, the more we need to base ourselves on fruitful sources of inspiration. A consciousness of the earth as our spiritual heritage can become, as Jean Freer explains, an integral part of our very real and practical efforts to save that earth.

Patriarchy has divorced us from the earth and turned our attention skyward. Modern technology has alienated us from our bodies and made us dependent on machines and chemicals. The Christian church, and other patriarchal religions, viciously suppressed pagan religions and gave us no rites or rituals with which to revere the earth. The gruesome threesome of patriarchy, male religions and technology have dishonoured the mother and countenanced the rape and pillage of the planet until she can barely support life. In the midst of this destruction the children of Gaea[1] are experiencing an immense spiritual hunger, a fearsome dread of isolation and meaninglessness. The tragedy of such inner emptiness is apparent to anyone who has ever experienced, however fleetingly, the celebration which is life.

In ancient times the people of Britain and Europe honoured the earth and gave thanks for her fruitfulness and protection. People were aware of their dependence on Mother Nature and tried to live in harmony with her. Much of this ecological way of life was instinctive and therefore unconscious. When science took over and began to champion 'man's mastery over nature', the need to nurture the earth was forgotten. Today she is force fed chemicals to increase her yield and hardly anyone has noticed the decline in her natural powers of fertility. These habits of agricultural destruction are being exported to the Third World in the name of progress. Science remains hostile to ecology.

The space programme is a perfect expression of the masculist[2] values of the late twentieth century. Based on militarist assumptions of conquering, it is used as a means of developing weapons' technology in the guise of 'taking a step for mankind' – while actually extending male dominance. The exploration of space forcibly turned our attention away from the earth and her needs. Even here man's disregard of the housekeeping requirements of nature – essential to collective living in a shared universe, to natural recycling and the creative unfolding of potential – was arrogantly displayed. Vehicles were left on the moon, littering her surface and adding insult to the injury of women. Plastic bags full of men's urine were sent to circle endlessly in the cosmos. How can they claim to be caring?

The fate of the earth is reflected in the health of all life on this planet. Unhealthy food creates unhealthy people living on unhealthy land. The atmosphere of this planet, the vibrations with which we are surrounded do not encourage a belief in life. This lack of faith breeds fear and fear breeds violence. The abuse of women cannot be separated from the abuse of the land. Both are intimately linked with the spiritual confusion of our time. Only by respecting the powers of life, without distorting them to support masculist assumptions, can peace return to the world. Only when we allow ourselves to give witness to truth will anxiety disappear. 'Truth' encompasses an acknowledgement of power, a recognition of the sources of power and a need to respect it and use it responsibly. Masculist power is artificial, based on brute force, threat and punishment, crude imitation and theft. Modern medicine and agriculture, chemicals and machines give witness to this reality. The power of the earth is awesome and is reflected in the power of women. An understanding of this power is available to all creatures who will approach it without pretentions and with humility.

Our ancestors had a consciousness of the cosmic power which could be channelled by people and our communities. Since at least Palaeolithic (Stone Age) times, myths of creation have revealed the interwoven links of all forms of life. Thousands of goddesses, abounding in the mythology and folklore of every country, attest to continuing awareness of the beneficent influence of women's energy. Some of the arts which utilise this force are still practised, more widely in the east and returning in the New Age to the west. Feng Shui is a geomantic art which uses earth energies to identify sites most suited for houses, temples and other buildings. Tai Chi is concerned with a direct use of natural power through the body, enabling the individual to hold her own space and to live in integrated harmony with the energies in her environment. Radiesthesia uses the energy tapped by dowsers and is now being applied to healing therapies. Spiritual healers have long known and worked with this power. The peace of harmonious living may still be ours if we cultivate truthfulness, courage, stillness and compassion.

How can we begin to return this joy to our lives? A wholefood vegetarian diet will immediately begin to increase our awareness of the cosmic web of life and to reintegrate spiritual awareness into our daily lives. Our bodies are the earth in miniature – a microcosm of the macrocosm – proof of the maxim 'as above so below'. The percentage of water in our bodies, about 80 percent, is the same as that in the whole earth and is influenced by the rhythms of the daily tides. If we can refine our perceptions we can begin to be consciously aware of the effects of these changes. If we can eliminate pollutants from our bodies we will be helping to eliminate them from the soil thus recreating a fertile environment in which to nurture life. The food offered by patriarchy is leached of its nutrients through extensive processing and reconstituted with poisons which are said to enrich it. Avoiding such food is an important step toward autonomous living. Eliminating chemicals and artificial stimulants from our lives, as far as possible, is essential to developing sensitivity to the influences of the unseen world. Personal practices, such as yoga and meditation, can help us return to our own centres. Recognising the self as source, with the wisdom to guide us through our lives, gives us political independence and helps generate an understanding of the dynamics of social responsibility, eliminating the need for centralised bureaucracies. Once we are emanating from our own centres we can begin to create meaningful relationships in our lives.

One of the most meaningful relationships we can make is with nature. We can make our interaction with the earth an expression of our sameness and a shared channel of healing for the world. A meaningful relationship with nature will bring us closer to the real world and help us to feel the life force in ourselves, intermeshed with all being. If we have a garden or allotment, or a friend who does, we can separate our rubbish and return organic matter to the earth. In practical ways we can show our respect for the earth and develop habits of commitment to life. Supporting life in our daily practices will help to save the world, and to create meaning in our existence.

There is, in the British Isles, direct evidence for the cult of wells, pools and lakes. Certain trees and groves of trees were also treated with veneration in pre-Roman times and earmarked places where the people gathered together to celebrate. Earth sites were also places of assembly and foci of power.[3] We must learn once more to be aware of the earth, to notice the seasons and to mark their changing. The old calendar, returning to wider use today, places the spring festival of Illythia, Goddess of Birth, on 1 February; summer is celebrated with May Day, the festival of Cardea (later Flora); autumn, the festival of Lamia, the Serpent Goddess, falls on 1 August; and the festival of Helle, the new year celebration, is on 1 November. All of these festivals begin at sundown the evening before and last until the next evening, so there is plenty of opportunity to sing and dance, make offerings and eat the foods in season. Your happiness and joy at these times is a gift to the goddess, a strengthening of the powers of life which reside in the earth, in her creatures, in all the elements and in the universe. Solstices and equinoxes are also times of communal gatherings and ritual.

The role of ritual is little understood today because the rise of the nation state has meant the suppression of the people. The repeated use of particular sites for honour and devotion increases the power of those places, as the repetition of songs increases their meaning. Dances, too, repeating patterns on the earth, especially if danced barefoot and with enthusiasm, enhance life-giving energy. Threading mazes was a way our ancestors made this connection, though most earth mazes have been destroyed by the demands of agriculture. Ritual properly observed will put the participants in touch with the timeless universal forces which weave the magical web of life. This awareness is indeed a huge threat to established temporal powers, and it is our best hope for survival.

The need to use our reclaimed power responsibly cannot be over-emphasised. Many women, so long denied any recognition, indulge in an orgy of influence when they first touch their inner strength. Such excesses feed the ego and aggrandise the personality at the expense of the more timeless and universal aspects of these forces. Caution is always wise, and attention to detail is essential for safety. Discipline is part of treading the narrow path, and your determination to be responsible must be strong enough to survive taunts of 'boring' and sneers of 'masochist'. The courage to live openly according to your spiritual beliefs in a secular misogynist world is a challenge to every woman.

In order to save ourselves we must regenerate our myths and reclaim our true origins. For women this specifically entails re-establishing a positive and creative relationship with the dragon. As Frances Howard-Gordon reminds us:

The spiral was a particular symbol of the Goddess faith. Spirals also symbolised the coiled serpent or dragon, both regarded as sacred in the old religion. The dragon or serpent represented the natural energies of the earth and the sky – energies which were cooperated with and revered. In the Shakti cults of South East Asia and China, dragons and serpents were associated with clouds and rain, and the Sumerian Goddess, Tiamat, was a sea-serpent and Great Waters Goddess. The Greek 'Mother of All Things' was the serpent Eurynome, who laid the world-egg. The dragon was also regarded as a manifestation of the psyche, in which the 'real' and the 'imaginary' are blurred and are, as in nature, only different aspects of Life.[4]

The dragon also symbolises wisdom, the strength of the dragon deriving from the power of her knowledge. A Persian proverb proclaims both women and dragons best out of this world.[5] 'This way of thinking is part and parcel of patriarchal notions that led to the slaying of the dragon and the conquering of the serpent power – the oppression of women by sexism.'[6] Mothers-in-law are characterised as old dragons; Eve was tempted by the snake, her sacred symbol of death and rebirth; Medusa's snake-hair was the source of her power, and dragon tales are told to frighten children and perpetuate the fears which serve the western patriarchy. But as a recent cartoon in *Outwrite*, the national women's newspaper, proclaimed, 'Some dragons are fighting back!' With a positive self-image and a creative relationship with our power, womyn[7] may begin to re-emerge as healers and oracles. When we can live in perpetual harmony with the cosmic rhythms of life we will have achieved an understanding of our true nature. In this awareness is strength, joy, wisdom and love.

17

He Wahine, He Whenua

Maori women and the environment

Ngahuia Te Awekotuku

*The search for ways of regenerating a culture that respects
the earth is a strong incentive for rediscoverng and learning about
indigenous traditions undermined and destroyed by white colonialism
and racism. In the growing eco-feminist movement in New Zealand,
this means listening to the experiences of Maori women such as
Ngahuia Te Awekotuku, who has made the connections between her
feminist awareness and her cultural roots as a black woman. This
article by her was originally published in the Autumn 1982 issue of the
magazine* New Zealand Environment, *which was devoted to women
and the environment.*

She deftly splits each blade of grey-green flax, drawing her sabre-
tough thumbnail down a straight impeccable line. Again and
again, until the intertwining leaves, dovetailed into the braided
weave beneath her sturdy foot, lie closely, tightly in a mass of thin,
even strands. And from this plaited base, she begins to weave.

From the historic swamps near Maketu, the flax is cut, the knife
slicing carefully through a rind-hard base. Trimming cautiously,
she ensures that the *rito* – the youngest, finest shoot that emerges
coyly between two larger parent leaves – remains untouched and
undamaged. The parent leaves are also respected, for they will
keep the youngest warm, and ensure the life of the plant. Anyone
who comes across the growing flax of a Maori weaver will immediately notice the quaint fanning of cut leaves, growing in a neatly
chopped delta shape up from the earth. Often, if the weaver lives
nearby, and certainly if the plant flourishes within her own garden,
the roots themselves will be fed. Bundles, bound and rotting, are
packed about the ground in browning, spindly piles. These are the
offcuts – the threads and thinning extremities, the freckled

unuseables, the blade spines and residue. Tied together, they are placed within the bosom of the plant – once again to ensure its life.

Observations such as those above form a basic part of the relationship of many Maori women – those of traditional society and those living a traditional lifestyle – with the environment.

Conservation of natural resources, particularly *harakeke*, the flax plant, was imperative. For from the flax plant came a variety of necessities. Garments: the shining *kakahu* and *korowai*, closely woven cloaks; the *piupiu*, multi-thrummed kilt; the *maro*, daintily decorative apron; the *rapaki*, worn wrapped around the hips. Also baskets, the *kete*, or kits of tremendous variety and function; and, of course, the *whariki* and *tuwhara*, mats for sleeping upon and rough surfaces for serving food. The medicinal properties of *harakeke* are also much acclaimed – a potage of roots, boiled to a pulp and served hot or cold, relieves chronic stomach upsets, cramps and dysmenorrhea.

Another plant whose gathering is controlled and steeped in certain practices is the elegant forest *epiphyte, kiekie*. Its strong, thin, supple blades are woven into fine mats, kits, hats, and form the contrast cross patterns on *tukutuku*, the lattice weaving of house interiors. A belief firmly held is that these beautiful fountaining leaves can only be picked when they are ready. Growing in clusters along sturdy runners, they sprout and dance among the *totara* and *matai*, creep and flourish across the hulking trunks of other, larger trees. Grasped resolutely with one hand, and turned against itself, the ready *kiekie* will snap off easily. Any resistance from the plant warns off the gatherer – she respects its growing, and seeks elsewhere, because *kiekie* that is unready can spoil, or split badly, and make one's work worthless. Taking from the plant as the plant offers itself makes the growth and ongoing lifecycle certain, and ensures further access to and use of these precious forest resources.

Certain prohibitions continue to be respected in varying degrees, although some women have begun to question them. During menstruation one should neither cut these plants nor work with them. Many have since defied the former *tapu*, but many more will not weave certain articles: *kete whakiro*, intricately patterned kits, or *whariki*, the fine floor and sleeping mats. The rationale, for a society in which menstrual protection was not absolutely reliable, made clear sense. Because the task itself demands a squatting position, often over the actual work, to accidentally stain it would be to damage it irreparably and cause the project indescribable shame. The risk was simply not worth it. Other prohibitions have nevertheless become much more mystified, and their origins, apart from the roots of obvious male fear, sadly obscured.

Much of the mystification comes from the colonising health system which has effectively disallowed one traditional – and essential – link of the Maori woman with the earth. The language sustains this; *te whenua*, the word for land and for afterbirth, are the same. One remains densely, dearly, part of the other. Yet, while hospitalisation and the secreting away of body matter in hygienic plastic bowls from a sterile birthing place continues to be the contemporary New Zealand (and therefore Maori) norm, this link dissolves, the relationship fades. No longer is *te whenua*, afterbirth, buried within and made one with *te whenua*, its element, earth. And we are left impoverished – cut off from the soil, cut off from the blood, alienated from ourselves and evermore convinced of our uncleanness. The mystery of menstruation remains though, and males cannot institutionalise *that* function; but with the mystery itself, a clutter of nonsensical, demeaning, prohibitive beliefs has survived. In previous times, the discharge of a woman's womb reinforced her connection to the earth, origin of all things. Each month, undeveloped beginnings of another human being came away from her . . . and thus it was considered inappropriate for her to cast them just anywhere. But as a new belief system, based firmly in male-oriented values and patriarchal concepts, imposed itself upon the Maori people, this essential wisdom was denied. Underlying her relationship with the land was the traditional Maori woman's perception of the environment as a source of emotional, spiritual and physical sustenance, identification and strength.

For the Maori, possession of land was merely custodianship, a caretaking for future generations, and an acknowledgement of the temporariness of individual human life. As the land remains, so do the people, who reflect its health, prosperity and creative vigour; the people, as a community of continuing generations, rarely isolated and identified individually, but seen rather as a collective grouping which embraces and is embraced by the nourishing earth of its ancient boundaries. If an area of land was heavily worked, then left idle for a period, the people maintained some regard for it, by the principle of *'ahi ka'* – keeping a fire glowing upon it, keeping the land warm. Should the fire go out, one's claim was relinquished and the piece lay waiting for another steward, another cultivator. By this custom, land was treated fairly and the hoarding and haggling typical of its twentieth-century inheritors were avoided.

Nevertheless, Maori society was a warrior society, and strife over land between those coveting, claiming, or caring for it was highly institutionalised. Warfare was glamorous – land, and women, were its spoils; pillage, rape and bloodlust were its practices. Both prizes are female: the Land being fecund, *Papatuanuku*, a Primal Mother Goddess whose consort was *Ranginui*, the Sky; and Woman, being herself.

As ravaging of the land – squabbling for its possession and striving to dominate, albeit in custodianship – was and is a masculine indulgence, so is the abuse of women and violence against them. This strong undercurrent in Maori society was a natural avenue for the infiltration of western attitudes toward land and women; with the descent of the Christian ethos, sophisticated technology and industrial 'civilisation', any semblance of precontact holistic balance promptly vanished. Female values were entirely eclipsed and chaos was unleashed.

Despite so much evidence to the contrary happening in Land Court hearings throughout the country, a vast number of Maori people, when questioned, will respond: *The land is my Mother. I cannot sell her – for if I do, I sell part of myself.*

But still the pillaging and rape continues. Layers of sand and sludge, piling up in poisoned effluent, laying waste a once immeasurably wealthy shellfish bed; pearly, cool, pebbled creeks widened and ravished; timeless, gentle trees torn down and dragged away; buoyant geyserfields whose warm fountains are concreted, piped and channelled off; these are pictures of contemporary Aotearoa.

One image is imprinted indelibly in my mind – an image of almost ten years gone when feminism was a fresh force raging in my spirit. Travelling up the Island, enjoying the voluptuously feminine shapes, the alluring contours and creases of the landscape, I suddenly encountered a scene of abysmal ugliness and grief. The leaking, stark clay scars of a formerly green and forested hillside, red soil exposed like bleeding viscera across a gaping, jagged gash of earth; singed and blackened tree stumps protruding helplessly from crusty slag piles; moisture rising dimly from the churned, uneven ground. And everywhere machines and noise and men. Obscenity – carnage – rape. Rape. I suddenly realised. That is what is happening to our world: to Aotearoa. By male greed, for male power and male gratification.

The Maori believes that the earth is the elemental womb to which we must all return. Folded within her, carefully placed, bones complete the cycle; for as she gives, so does she receive. And female in essence, she moves within the consciousness of many women.

For the future, despite the depletion and abuse of natural resources, we must find hope in the wisdom of the past. The past as it is preserved by the present – such as the work of the weaver of fibres, the woman who cultivates, gathers, recycles . . . the woman who knows and loves *Papatuanuku* and celebrates the bounty of the earth. This knowledge, if emulated and perpetuated, will serve as our strength and foundation for the times that lie ahead.

18
All of One Flesh

The rights of animals

Norma Benney

Hierarchical intellectual structures involve concepts of 'higher' and 'lower' in which the former inevitably exploits the latter. Feminist thinking challenges these hierarchies, and women are starting to realise that in the process of struggling for our own rights, we should not participate in the victimisation of those even worse off than ourselves in the patriarchal pecking order. We need to develop fresh ways of seeing the world, if we are to get out of the habit of ignoring the realities of how other, non-human, animals are living.

In Munich there was a feminist bookstore called *'Frauenbüchladen'*. In a room adjoining the shop there were seats where women could sit and read, and a pot of hot coffee. The room was pale and calm. White sheeting was used for the curtains and cushions, and I felt grateful to the woman who had placed green plants on the table. There was womenpeace in there.

But at the shop counter the peace was shattered. A German woman paid for her books, one of them entitled *Towards Women's Liberation*, and as she chatted to the woman behind the cash register, she dangled her car keys. From the key ring hung a fox's tail. It was a small tail. It must have come from a young fox. I looked at it without drawing any reaction from her. Then I asked her in diffident German, 'What is that?' pointing to the fluffy pale yellow appendage. The two women laughed. The customer pranced in the shop miming an animal. She patted her behind to indicate a tail. I asked her, 'You find that comical?'. She shrugged, still laughing, said *'Auf Wiedersehen'* and left. . .

The oppression of women is so much a part of the fabric of our lives that we need consciousness-raising sessions in order to perceive how from birth we are silenced, diminished and exploited. When we begin to know, we curse our gullibility and our trusting acceptance of the *status quo*. Then we begin to grow, use our voices and struggle for personal liberation and women's liberation in general.

But liberty is a holistic concept. It is neither fair nor just to claim freedom for ourselves, without at the same time claiming freedom for the creatures[1] which share the planet with us, who are cruelly oppressed from birth to death by patriarchal attitudes and systems, and who do not have women's power to organise themselves.

Since in the Women's Liberation Movement 'the personal is political', I would like to mention some happenings in my own life which brought me to an awareness of animals as oppressed beings. My consciousness raising in this respect was slow and solitary, and I relate only two of the many scattered incidents:

> As a child I spent summers on a farm. One morning, as I poured thick New Zealand cream on my porridge, I heard the adults saying that this was the day the men would kill the pig. The mother of the family was Danish with a direct gaze, and eyes of a blueness which made them seem young in a wrinkled face. She said, 'Oh no!' and wanted to know the hour of the killing so that she might block her ears against the scream. Her daughters made fun of her. 'Mother is always like this when we kill the pig.' (Not 'a' pig, but 'the' pig. The animal had so far lost identity as to become a composite pig with all the others killed before it.) That day for me was impregnated and heavy with the pig's slaughter, and I learnt the fear of waiting for a death cry.

> My mother told me of a lamb she reared as a pet. Her nephew was sent to slaughter a lamb for the Sunday roast, and it was not until the family was well into the meal that he mentioned they were eating my mother's pet, 'It was the only one that came when I called.'

In a private thought it occurred to me that if I were unable to bring myself even to enter an *abattoir*, let alone kill my own animals, I ought not to eat them. Based on this I tried to become a vegetarian. But the vague notions I had of rights for animals had no logical basis until I read Peter Singer's *Animal Liberation*[2] when my half-formed ideas were suddenly given substance. I was like a woman reading Kate Millett or Mary Daly, striking her forehead and crying, 'Of *course*! Why didn't I *see* that!' I became a vegetarian and later a vegan. John

Bryant questions this usual progression from vegetarianism to veganism as follows:

> In fact, although the normal route taken to personal 'non-reliance' on animal food products has been firstly to give up eating animal flesh and then later to drop dairy products and eggs, logically – in terms of suffering caused – one should firstly give up dairy products, as I am convinced that a cow endures much more suffering than the beef animal through continually being robbed of her young.[3]

Our enmeshment in chains of habit means that in this patriarchy in which we live, love, sleep, eat, cohabit and work, we must, as feminists, question our whole life – and this includes our attitudes to non-humans.

As a child, sister, at the same time as you were told to keep your legs together and that little girls didn't climb trees, you were probably told to eat up your meat, and heard vegetarians spoken of as cranks and sentimentalists. It is curious that this section of the public, for whom no animal is goaded to the slaughterer's knife, should suffer derision.

Awareness of injustices does not always take place as a sudden all-illuminating burst of light. It more resembles a burglar's torch which brightens one dark corner, leaving the rest of the room in obscurity. Some examples might be:

> Amnesty International, conscious of the rights of political prisoners, were once instrumental in having tests performed on pigs to obtain evidence regarding the torture of prisoners.

> Bertrand Russell, who has been called 'a complete man', whatever that may mean, when asked his opinion of vivisection replied, through his secretary, that ' . . .he [Bertrand Russell] is entirely preoccupied with cruel experiments on human beings, such as in Vietnam, and he regards this activity as more important than the activity against experiments on animals which you suggest' . . . a 'complete man' whose intellect was apparently incapable of considering two forms of oppression at the same time.

> The Vegetarian Society, especially conscious of the oppression involved in factory farming, and the Vegan Society, conscious of all animal oppression, both refused an advertisement in their

143

publications which would have acquainted female readers with the existence of a publication for isolated and lonely lesbians.[4] I should add that these societies are not exceptional in that most mainstream newspaper editors likewise refuse these advertisements.

Marchers with banners proclaiming friendship for the earth as such, and who picnic afterwards on ham sandwiches, show that they are concerned about the planet but that they are not concerned about the suffering of a sow who probably littered, clamped down and immobilised, in a device known in the pig trade as 'The Iron Maiden'.

Most causes are pleadings for humans, of one kind or another, and can often be equated with self-interest. The Animal Rights Movement is the only one which raises its eyes beyond human advantages and comforts.

Not so long ago women, blacks, the poor, the blind, the deaf – as well as all animals – were held to have no mind, no 'soul'. It is fitting that feminists, alien as animals are, in a male-dominated world, should not only raise their voices for non-humans but live a life which shows by example their contempt for patriarchal attitudes towards animals.

The early feminist movement numbered many animal rightists, who were, of course, vegetarians.

Shafts,[5] which was a magazine first published in 1892, covered, among many other issues, votes for women, sweated labour, marriage reform, while showing some evidence of awareness of animal oppression.

The 1892 *Shafts'* review of *Animal Rights* by Henry S. Salt, which has been recently republished a century later, together with new editions of John Stuart Mill's *The Subjection of Women* (originally published in 1869) bear testimony to the fact that just demands for rights for both women and animals, though slow of attainment, stand the test of time. The review, 19 November 1892, stated, 'The case of the animal is the case of the woman. The truest friends of the cause of equality of the sexes demand not indulgence towards women as such, but justice in all the relationships of life. . . This similitude of position between women and the lower animals . . . should ensure from the former the most unflinching and powerful support to all movements for the amelioration of the conditions of animal existence.'

Frances Power Cobbe (1822–1904), a feminist, was a strong anti-vivisectionist, although not a vegetarian. Not content with the 'gradualist' anti-vivisectionist policy of her day, she founded the British Union for the Abolition of Vivisection aiming for total abolition – an organisation most active today.

Anna Kingsford, Ms Cobbe's contemporary, studied in Paris to qualify in medicine *without* the use of animals. She had conceived the idea of studying medicine, not with the intention of practising it, but in order to make a scientific study of a diet that did not require the slaughtering of animals and to combat vivisection with a first-hand knowledge of the facts. At that time women could not obtain a medical degree in England, hence her enrolment in a university in Paris. Her professor deliberately omitted to call her name at the first roll call, and when she pointed this out to him he said, 'You. You are neither man nor woman and I refuse to write your name down.'[5]

It was a source of contention between the two women that Frances Power Cobbe was not a vegetarian. Anna Kingsford finally disassociated herself from the suffrage movement, saying 'these women are deluded because they cannot see that universal peace is impossible to a carnivorous race.'[6]

When Mary Wollstonecraft wrote *Vindication of the Rights of Women*, Thomas Taylor, a contemporary writer, tried to reduce her arguments to sheer absurdity by publishing anonymously in 1792 a volume entitled *A Vindication of the Rights of Brutes*.[7] Were Taylor alive today he would find that clear and cogent arguments are now accepted for (in his terms) the rights of 'brutes'.

The Animal Liberation Movement, as it is known in various translations in different parts of the world, is based in English-speaking countries upon the philosophy of Henry Salt[8] and of Peter Singer's book *Animal Liberation*. Singer writes: 'Bentham [a social philosopher] points to the capacity for suffering as the vital characteristic that gives a being the right to equal consideration [of interests].'[9] Animals have amply shown a capacity for both mental and physical suffering in millions of psychological tests and pain experiments in vivisection laboratories.

Animal rightists are both more radical and more militant than animal welfarists. Briefly, animal welfarists seek to ameliorate the lot of (sometimes only a group of) animals. Animal rightists strive to eliminate the primary cause of the oppression, and are themselves vegetarian or vegan. The Animal Liberation Front and the Northern Animal Liberation League, whose members break into battery farms, vivisection laboratories, breeding establishments of animals for vivisection, fur shops and mink farms, etc., are the escape valves for all other animal rightists' frustrations. 'Yesterday's illegality is tomorrow's accepted morality . . . When [change] is too slow, the frontrunners in the movement for change will be driven by frustration and the mounting pressure behind them to throw themselves at the barrier of inertia in an effort to move it.'[10]

You will realise that the Animal Liberation Movement is concerned with all aspects of animal oppression, yet it is factory farming and the animal as food that I am mostly concerned about here. Our *eating* of animals is responsible for all the other forms of oppression, since our treatment of them as recipe ingredients, instead of sentient beings, eliminates from our consciousness any notion that their interests should be considered. The animal's 'inferiority' is established by our treatment of it as an inferior. Hitler's extermination of 11 million Jews, gypsies, ethnic groups, homosexuals and political prisoners took place after his first persuading his followers that these unfortunates were sub-human and of no account. This notion was then reinforced by the subsequent treatment of them as sub-humans and of no account.

It is, of course, the *female* animal which is the most exploited. The Royal Society for the Prevention of Cruelty to Animals believes that of all the female inmates of factory farms – more even than cows and battery hens – it is pigs which are probably the most cruelly treated. Sows are kept in crates for most of their gestation period which has a duration of almost four months. With no room to turn, they only lie down, get up and eat. Peculiar habits develop such as bar-chewing and foot-stamping because, intelligent and curious as they are by nature, they suffer boredom and frustration in the unnatural environment of a restraining crate. Piglets were once taken from the sow at eight weeks, this period was reduced to five, and then one month, and now experiments are being carried out on weaning piglets in 24 hours. Some farmers slaughter a pregnant sow just before full term and the litter is removed with the placental membranes. This is to obtain a high health status piglet. Just as women suffer induced birth to suit hospital hours, sows are injected to produce litters to suit the stockperson's working day – or pub hours. The reason for all this unseemly rush is, of course, the profit motive. The sooner the litter is weaned, the sooner the sow can be mated and produce another litter; when the whole cycle will begin again for the sow, only *ten days* after she has been deprived of the piglets. Factory farm animals are bred by mechanical rape, castrated, docked, imprisoned, forcibly fattened, forcibly made anaemic, horribly murdered, and the end product is a cutlet on an overfed human's plate.

One has read in male science fiction of balloon-like women who are kept as breeders and who, with bloated bodies worn by childbearing, lie on cushions producing one baby after another from male-selected studs. But there is no need to seek fictional situations for comparison.

After spending $200,000,000 to get rid of the Indian 'problem', along with killing the natives, Thomas Jefferson, Benjamin Franklin and others urged the white Europeans to displace the Indians by outbreeding them. They encouraged the new settlers to breed rapidly in order to take over the land and create a homogenous white society from coast to coast. This was relatively easy to do since Indian women would not have sex except when they chose to (women generally feel the most sexual at their least fertile times) and also because Indian women had knowledge of herbal contraceptives and abortifacients. The white European population increased 500 percent in only 50 years! . . . Among the casualties of this perverted view of sex (besides the natives) were thousands of European women who died before 30 or 35 literally worn out from childbearing.[11]

The patriarchy tends to choose certain animals which can be labelled 'cute' and one sees them in the media *ad nauseam*. One such is the panda. Heavily protected since there are only about 15 of them in semi-captivity, it is acceptable to gush over their black and white fur and cuddly appearance because one can do so with a clear conscience knowing that they will not end up flattened by a hunter's gun or in a slaughterhouse, and this also helps us bask in the notion that England is an animal-loving nation. However, were there more pandas and were the fur trade suddenly to promote panda coats, you may be sure that the panda would instantly disappear from the media. This selective vision is closely mirrored in the patriarchy's treatment of us. Women who are conditioned to conform to the male 'ideal' are extolled and heavily featured in the media for their male-defined attributes, while our general oppression is ignored. At the Tyrrhenian resort of Tropea in Italy, the Mayor proposed that women 'who are, let's say, no longer full-bosomed' should no longer be allowed nude on the beach.

The Fur Traders' Annual Dinner held at the Savoy Hotel in London is always picketed by animal rightists. Police protection is accorded the fur traders. Rolls Royce follows Rolls Royce to glide up to the hotel's back entrance, and as a further symbol of wealth=success, each fur trader emerges with a woman cloaked in furs from neck to knee . . . silver fox, mink, white seal. . . One of these women walked along the picket line in her mink coat looking at the tennis-shoed feet of the demonstrators. In the rare instance of an activist wearing leather shoes, she commented on the fact. The point had already been taken by animal rightists who, as I wrote earlier in this article, are mostly vegans in any case. 'To those who may argue that cows are killed for their meat "so it's all right to use their skin for leather" I would say that cows are slaughtered *both* for meat *and* leather. In any case, the fact that an animal is killed for a double motive doesn't make the act of slaughter any more acceptable – on the contrary it should make it doubly condemnable. Did the gassing of Jews in Nazi concentration camps justify the use of their skin for lampshades or hair for brooms and brushes?'[12]

Bearing in mind the market value of tiger skins, it is all important when killing a tiger that its skin not be marred. One system used is to pull the animal by the tail until his tail is completely out of the cage. While two men pull hard to immobilise the animal, a white hot iron is inserted in the animal's anus. In this way it is killed without marking the fur.

A feminist group on a protest demonstration carried a placard 'A rapist is an animal. Put him behind bars where he belongs.' In nature, of course, animals do not rape. Unless the female is in oestrus and receptive, no intercourse takes place. The rapist is only one form of the rape of women's lives, as we know, but he is not an 'animal' in the common meaning of the word. Nor is an animal's place behind bars.

Rape is an oppression that women and animals share, and rape has always been a male joke. Until feminists protested, a local well-known store sold men's underpants inscribed 'Your favourite rapist'. A recent television series inferred the rape of a chicken as a comic event. The 'rape rack' is an established piece of vivisection equipment for impregnating primates and, according to the Kinsey Report, eight percent of men use animals for sex. 'Linda Lovelace mentions in *Ordeal* that Hugh Hefner's collection of human/animal films includes films with chickens, probably those in which the birds are literally disembowelled by the human actor's penis.'[13]

In pornography, women are treated as meat, and a recent centre-fold of a music magazine showed a naked woman, spread-eagled and chained on an operating table in a butcher's shop surrounded by hanging animal carcasses and butchers' knives and cleavers while a man in a red, rubber, butcher's apron prepared to divide her with an electric saw.[14]

One can understand that, as feminists, we resist the use of the word 'victim' since it has a connotation of passivity, and makes women feel frightened and powerless; hence 'rape *survivors*' and 'incest *survivors*'. Alas, animals in vivisection laboratories, on factory farms or royal estates geared to hunting, or bred for the fur trade, are always *victims*. There are no survivors.

In vivisection laboratories, to prove what most women know and certainly every mother knows, namely, that young ones need the love of their mother, primates were separated from their mother at birth in the infamous 'maternal deprivation' studies. They were placed in chambers where they saw neither humans nor non-humans (their food being sent to them through a small hole) and taken out after six years, crazed by isolation.

Queen Victoria's reputed ignorance of the existence of lesbianism so that it is largely excluded from the laws of the land, is something I suppose lesbians may be thankful for. However, Queen Victoria was certainly not ignorant of the injustices of vivisection, and wrote to Gladstone, the then Prime Minister: 'The Queen has seen with pleasure that Mr Gladstone takes an interest in that dreadful subject of vivisection, in which she has done all she could, and she earnestly hopes that Mr Gladstone will take an opportunity of speaking strongly against a practice which is a disgrace to humanity. . .'[15]

Brigid Brophy wrote: '. . . to hold vivisection never justified is a hard belief. But so is its opposite. I believe it is never justified because I can see nothing (except our being able to get away with it) which lets us pick on animals that would not equally let us pick on certain groups or classes of humans (who would be more useful) or, for the matter of that, on a few humans of any sort whom we might sacrifice for the good of the many. . .'[16]

One would think there was a Great Adult Conspiracy to keep children's books from revealing what really happens on farms. And in fact, there is. Children who may see the worst of violence in comics or on television are carefully protected from a knowledge of what farming means in real terms. In a book *A Calf is Born* by Jane Miller[17] children are shown photographs of the birth of a calf in a field, which is all very well – it is good for them to see the birth of anything – except that most calves never see a field. The deceitfulness involved in depicting farm animals in a cosy way, is that they only exist for very non-cosy reasons, namely, for life-long exploitation as milk or breeding machines, or for chemically-fattened slaughter. Although the relationship between cow and calf is a very close one, no mention is made in the book of the anguish experienced by the cow upon separation from her calf. It might also have been educational for the

149

young, future Wiener-Schnitzel eaters to follow the fate of the bull calf as it is dragged, tottering, from its restraining crate where it has been confined and deprived of iron to produce white veal and despatched to the slaughter-house.

The nomenclature of the end product of farm animals is interesting: 'pork' instead of pig, 'veal' instead of calf, etc. The definition of a cow is so related to her output that she is only called a cow when she has had two calves. Before that she is a 'heifer'. Men refer to women as 'chicks', 'pets' and 'bunnies', and their vaginas are 'beavers' or 'pussies'. Derogatory terms used are also 'bitch' and 'cow'. If hypocrisy is the homage that vice pays to virtue, according to La Rochefoucauld, then guilty silence must surely be the acknowledgement that conscience pays to *abattoirs*. The collective guilt of adults on the subject of eating dead animals must be strong indeed judging by the total exclusion of the real facts of factory farms from books written for children. In a children's book about wolves, where a wolf kills a deer for food for the pack, the no doubt carnivorous author sanctimoniously commented '. . . this made me quite sad . . . but I thought that it was hungry and had to.'

A friend of mine who is an animal rightist has a rejoinder for people who say, on the rare occasions that a stray cat in her garden manages to catch a bird, 'There you see, it has eaten it.' My friend asks, 'And what did you have for dinner?' To people who claim to her, 'I only eat a *little* meat,' she retorts, 'I'm sure the animal is obliged.'

Kristie Neslen writes: 'In our society women are forced into the perpetual babyhood of economic dependency. Men, meanwhile, are forced into the (in some ways more serious) perpetual babyhood of physical and emotional dependency.'[18] Milk drinkers are in a state of perpetual babyhood, drinking milk never intended for them, but for a baby cow. In constant search of a virile image, man hunts, shoots and fishes. To see a gross, over-fed angler leering beside a long, silver-scaled fish is always to ask oneself, 'Which is the nobler animal?'

The Royal Family, adored as they are by a section of the community, could ease somewhat the lot of animals and appease to a certain extent some of their critics if they so chose. But could one imagine a royal vegetarian? That royal children are 'blooded' on their first hunt with the blood from a mangled animal, and that Prince Charles and his spouse engage in blood sport is a fair indication of the attitude of the Royal Family to sentient non-humans. England, acclaimed as an animal-loving country, may blush in the knowledge that the future monarch first met his wife at a 'shoot'.

There are no occasions, fêtes, ceremonies, celebrations, or

reunions which do not involve the slaughter of non-humans. The Christian festivals of Christmas, Easter and Thanksgiving are preceded by overtime rates in the slaughter-houses. I never trust any pronouncements by preachers, secularists or philosophers who speak their views through a mouthful of dead animal. Oppressed, smothered, disadvantaged, silenced as we are – women, the 51 percent 'minority', – let us not forget that there is an even wider band of oppression, the non-human animals, beneath us on the bottom of the pyramid.

A future matriarchy would mean a world changed, but there is a change we can effect now. We can change the patriarchal dietary pattern – not forgetting that in most 'households' it is still the woman who shops, cooks for and feeds the family. For once women are provided with a positive base for political action; that of being able to refuse to cook dead animals.

The overthrowing of the patriarchy is the feminist's *raison d'être*. We write, organise, activate, oppose patriarchal life-patterns and edicts, and work towards an overthrow of the system. But if while aiming for this change we do not become aware of the sufferings of non-humans, then I feel we will not have understood the concept of liberty. If we struggle to free ourselves, without realising that we are also crushing the most oppressed and exploited creatures on the planet, we can only fail.

19
The Mothers do not Disappear

Marta Zabaleta
Translated by Jackie Roddick

Cortazar called them doves. The Argentine military call them the Madwomen of the Plaza Mayo. Internationally, they are known simply as the mothers and grandmothers who stage a weekly protest in front of the presidential palace.

In Argentine society, of course, motherhood supposedly confers all sorts of protection and rights on those who accept the limitations imposed by their femininity. And it is true that to belong to this very special association, one does have to be a mother or grandmother: mother of one of the 16,000 adults or grandmother of one of the 600 children who, as they say themselves, 'were made to disappear by the very same forces who kidnapped them, for political reasons'.

But it would be wrong to see these women as taking refuge in traditional roles. If there is a traditional female conduct in political matters – submissive, passive, dependent, far from the channels through which power is exercised – the task they have set themselves cuts directly across it. In the context of Argentina's social crisis, their demands are uncompromisingly radical and dangerous: 'Let the "disappeared" return to us alive!'

They began to organise themselves about five years ago, a handful of women meeting every week to support one another in the frightening task of trying to locate their children's gaols. As the numbers of the disappeared grew, the task became more complicated. New mothers had to be integrated into the group, bureaucratic complications multiplied – and they, themselves, began to suffer from problems of repression.

That original group was formed by women over 45 years of age, the same generation which had benefitted from a whole series of new rights for women in its youth: the right to vote, for instance, and the right to stand as a candidate for public office. But on the whole, like

152

most Argentine women, these were basically housewives. 'Individually we found it daunting, we weren't prepared. We left the cooking, the washing and the ironing to take this up.'

They found they needed a collective focus. Without any prior theoretical discussion, they were about to take a step whose advisability has been hotly debated by feminist movements throughout Latin America. They formed themselves into an autonomous organisation based only on gender, making no distinctions between social classes, to achieve their tactical objectives and encourage the active participation of women in the process of social change.

Today, there are more than 3,000 members. They have a centre (The House of the Mothers) and three years ago began to publish their own bulletin. Now they are not simply pacing the squares of Argentina but gathering world-wide support for their cause. They offer help to political prisoners, while reminding the Argentine people of the existence of secret concentration camps.

It was perhaps the example of these women which inspired the creation of the Mothers of El Salvador. Within Argentina they have created a symbolism which does more than give them a public identity. Their white kerchiefs, each embroidered with initials of the disappeared relative they are seeking, bear witness to a hope of justice which the people of Argentina have still not abandoned. If they never receive an answer it will not be for a lack of trying. The fact that their founder, Azucena Villaflores Devincenzi, has 'disappeared' is itself mute testimony to that.

In some senses it has already been a fruitful struggle. They have come to understand a reality which, before they combined to challenge it so courageously, they may have had little idea existed. They condemn the doctrine of National Security adopted by the Argentine armed forces, because 'the horrendous practice of making opponents disappear is one of its logical consequences.' They know very well that the Argentine military are not the only armed forces to adopt this doctrine, and Argentina is not the only country suffering as a result.

They believe that 'only the union of peoples across Latin America' will make it possible to eliminate the new tactics of repression being practised throughout the continent and in other countries around the world. For these women (in common with allies of theirs, such as, Simone de Beauvoir and Michele Mitterand) understand that the techniques of imprisonment and disappearance being practised in South America are only the reverse side of new models of domination being tried out in the cause of a new 'international order'.

Today, the mothers criticise the Catholic Church because, as an institution, it has cheated them. 'In Argentina, it has not responded in an evangelical spirit, as it has in other parts of Latin America.' They point to the solidarity of the first Argentinian trade union to take up the case of its disappeared members – the power workers, last December at Luz y Fuerza. The two groups then joined in protest and the mothers have faith that this type of activity will be the augury of a 'new practical relationship with the trade unions'.

These women are not afraid of anything. Not the violence of counter-protesters on the one hand: during the period when Argentina was at war with Britain their slogan was, 'The Malvinas are Argentinian, so are the Disappeared!' Nor the dangers of a possible sell-out by Argentina's political parties on the other: 'because we don't belong to any political party'. Superficial changes in political circumstances will not deflect them.

If there is some kind of future for the Argentinian people, it will be in large part thanks to the persistence of this group of women. One can only hope that in the aftermath of the crisis they will not allow themselves, once again, to be relegated to a secondary sphere . . . as has so far been the pattern of women's struggles in Latin America.

20

Invisible Casualties

Women servicing militarism

Lesley Merryfinch

Militarism has always taken a severe toll on women's lives, both directly and indirectly. Women are not only expected to clean up during and after wars, to nurse the wounded and replenish decimated populations; they are also expected to service the manufacture of the weapons used to carry out those wars. Even now, in the midst of a supposed period of 'peace' (as far as the West is concerned) women are fulfilling these functions. Most of us do not notice them: Lesley Merryfinch says we must.

My mother worked as a nurse in the air force during the Second World War. She joined up without any nursing experience and in 1944 was stationed on the south coast of England to receive the butchered, mangled and dying bodies of young men who were taking part in the D-Day landings. There seemed no end to the shiploads of human beings pouring across the Channel, hour after hour, leaving her no possibility of a break to come to some sort of terms with the ghastliness of one death before the next body was wheeled in. Even after four years of nursing the wounded in wartime conditions, she had never had so much demanded of her.

I grew up on my mother's wartime stories, but she never really described what went on around D-Day. There were anecdotes about losing Matron's dog, cycling trips in the English country lanes without signposts, and occasional names of airmen who were stationed in the same place and then 'lost touch'. It all sounded rather jolly, like an extended Girl Guide camp. As I grew older, pregnancies and over-enthusiastic American soldiers began to creep into the stories, but still the details of the D-Day time remained vague, and, I sensed, unspeakably awful. She was one of those specially selected to nurse in that situation as she was one of the more competent; so competent that she could not be promoted to officer rank. That would have meant posting her elsewhere and she was too valuable to lose. Yet after the war she had no officially-recognised qualifications, received no piece of paper to testify to her skill. She was never able to work as a nurse again. The military world had extracted its utmost from her.

Thirty-five years later, she was able to tell me that throughout her early married life she had been diagnosed as chronically shell-shocked. Only in 1982 was she able to cry about it. We were in the middle of the Falklands War and it was a re-run. Untold memories made her weep, but I was simply stunned. It all made too much sense.

I have always thought that my mother was a war victim in a special sense, and that war enters our lives in more ways than is generally recognised. Having been brought up as girls, our concern for peace is, for many of us, indivisible from our care for the physical well-being and survival of others. In the books we choose to read, in discussion with others and in the leaflets and pamphlets some of us produce, we concentrate on the awful physical effects of war. We know about the suffering of the people of Hiroshima and Nagasaki, about the danger to human beings, especially babies, of low level radiation and we want our children, nephews, nieces and grandchildren to grow up. There are many reasons why it is women who are so specifically concerned about these aspects of war and nuclear technology, but I shall not go into them here. Let us just accept for the moment that it is so. Yet I have always felt that there are other features of war and the war machine which demand a specific response from women. If we take motherhood and nurturing life as the concern at the root of our peace action, then concern for the way women pay the higher price for war should also be one of our 'roots'. This 'higher price' is that of being an invisible casualty of war and also, as I shall discuss, of those periods of absence of hostilities called peace.

By 'invisible casualties' I mean suffering in ways that are either not officially recognised as having anything to do with war, which are hushed up, or which are not even recognised as suffering. The millions of people who die anonymous deaths in concentration camps and the millions who perish in air raids are also invisible in one sense, but I do not include these because their sufferings are recognised to be within the scope of the terrible facts about war that are already part of the whole debate about war and peace, armament and disarmament. What I want to point towards are less widely discussed facts about war, when military powers dominate civilian life and those who are second class citizens in that civilian world are dominated even more.

Here are a few examples. Munitions work is always dangerous and during the First World War it involved using materials that were not only explosive (in all over 200 women died in munitions factories' explosions and other incidents) but also highly toxic. Munitions work was also seen as women's patriotic alternative to joining the armed forces. By 1918, 948,000 women were employed in munitions compared with 212,000 in July 1914. But you can not make complaints about patriotic duty, indeed you have to be glad of a chance to do it. So, toxic and explosive substances in the factory process just have to be accepted.

'Canaries' was the name given to women whose work filling shells with TNT poisoned them and turned their skin yellow. It was lethal. Aircraft wings had to be sealed with a substance known as 'dope'. Its fumes caused dizzy spells, nausea and eventually death. Women who lost production time by popping out for fresh air had their wages docked. Complaints were made but little was done to enforce better practices.

> The tool room hours were 7.30 a.m. to 1.00 p.m. and 2.00 p.m. to 8.00, Saturdays to 6.00 p.m. There were no intervals for lunch and tea, though tea could be sent for from the canteen and drunk standing. These hours are of course longer than those laid down for women in the Factory and Workshops Act, but I was unaware of this at the time, and in any case I knew that women as a class were being sampled in me, not only for their work, but for their behaviour, time-keeping, endurance and general adaptability, and had I known [what hours the Act laid down] I should have done nothing to have them shortened. (Account by Dorothy T. Poole, 1919.)[1]

These women then had to suffer illness and death in circumstances which virtually forbade complaint, and where deaths were not regarded as war deaths. This means no pensions for dependants. The price of the nation's war effort was simply extracted from them.

Invisible casualties are still with us. Take another example from the more recent past. The Americans stationed some 6,500 women nurses in Vietnam, nurses who, like my mother one generation back, worked in casualty-clearing stations. They too were continuously surrounded by distressingly wounded, agonised and dying young bodies. 'We had to be strong. If we allowed ourselves to experience that kid lying there without an arm or leg, we would be no use to him at all. We just shut out the pain,' writes one nurse.

These women came back quite unnoticed. Despite reams of material written on the readjustment of male Vietnam vets, no one has studied the women who served in that war. Many of them are still completely unaware of their veteran's benefits, yet nearly 7,500 women vets are coping with delayed-stress syndrome (violent flash-backs, nightmares and drinking bouts) and other problems, such as the effects of the defoliant Agent Orange. They brought home their traumas, fears and illnesses as individuals; they were unaccustomed – and not encouraged – to see themselves as a group which had been abused.

Peace has its invisible women war casualties too, such as those whose work is essential to the war machine. Two recent examples will serve to illustrate this. Three women who worked at the laundry of the Aldermaston Weapons Research Establishment were found to have plutonium contamination of the lungs. The laundry cleaned protective clothing from the active area but, and this is directly related to the prevalent notion that 'women's' work is always inferior, they were not considered radiation workers and so were not required by law to be monitored regularly for radioactivity. The severe risks to their health – and in a way they, themselves – were invisible.

Perhaps even more frightening is the electronics industry. Here, much as in the munitions factories of the First World War, women constitute the bulk of the labour force (justified by our alleged suitability for fine dexterous work) in manufacturing processes that are both dangerous in themselves *and* which have a lethal end product. The clumsiness of shells has been replaced by missiles which are increasingly sophisticated. This sophistication makes them more dangerous because they are more accurate and such sophistication is entirely due to the so-called advances in military electronics. As weaponry and war-fighting techniques progress, the role of electronics is likewise growing, not only in making for greater accuracy, but for training simulators, communications and surveil-lance. It is no longer figurative to talk of the electronic battlefield; it is already with us.

Dangerous chemicals are used in the production of some micro-chips and the work demands a high standard of eyesight which, after a few years of such work, not surprisingly fails. With it goes the job. Electronics manufacture is heavily concentrated in the developing world, in particular the poorer countries of South East Asia – Indonesia, Thailand, Malaysia and the Philippines. It relies on low labour costs and a high unemployment rate. For thousands and thousands of women it means appalling conditions, interminable hours, a frenetic rate of working and dismissal at the slightest sign of unrest. In South Korea, for example, 12 and 13-year-old girls work up to 18 hours a day, seven days a week, for as little as £12.00 a month. A high turnover of women workers is nothing unusual, it remains unnoteworthy. And the fact that to a great extent it is preparation for *war* that has claimed these women's sight and livelihood goes unnoticed. They are after all very far away. Far enough to be invisible.

As I have suggested, much of the reason for the invisibility of these women war casualties lies in the fact that we are encouraged to regard ourselves and our experiences as individual, and not to see patterns of exploitation behind them. Another reason is that work done by women is regarded as inferior, not to be compared with the 'real' heroism of the trench, the cockpit or the burning deck. If we have been let down by health and safety legislation, by trade unions in which male domination still persists, and by a prevailing ideology that no price is too high for patriotism, then we have also been let down by the peace movement generally. Starting as it does from political or religious convictions, it has not yet contributed an analysis of peace and war that gives sufficient importance to women in roles other than those dictated by popular culture, even though it recognises how much that culture is tied up with the war machine. It has colluded in making women war and peace casualties invisible. But now we, as women, are finding the roots of our peace action within our own and other women's experiences, rather than in purely reasoned or religious standpoints. The high price of suffering paid by the invisible casualties can be part of our experience too. It *has* to be, because it is being paid right now by ordinary women the world over, just as it always has been paid by women like my mother.

21
Alternative Technology: A Feminist Technology?

Chris Thomas

The development of alternative technology (AT) is one of the most hopeful signs of a changing relationship between human beings and their environment. Yet any technology reflects the values of those who develop it, and this may mean that women's concerns and needs are not always taken into account in the planning of AT projects. Because this is such a broad area, we wanted to tackle it from the perspective of several different women. First, Chris Thomas gives the background to the growing feminist critique of AT.

Women have a history of little involvement with science and technology. As we've grown up, we've learnt that technology is not for us; and yet women have always been technologists and may have even been the earliest technologists. Women were responsible for developing many of the early survival technologies of food gathering and preservation, shelter building, clothing production and healing, as well as many of the early implements to carry out these tasks:

It is frequently suggested or implied that the first tools were, in fact, the weapons of the hunters. . . However, since we really do not know what the early stone tools such as handaxes were used for, it is equally probable that they were not weapons at all, but rather aids in gathering. We know that gathering was important long before much animal protein was added to the diet, and continued to be important. If, however, instead of thinking in terms of tools and weapons, we think in terms of cultural inventions, a new aspect is presented. I suggest that two of the earliest and most important cultural inventions were containers to hold the products of gathering and some sort of sling or net to carry babies.[1]

Technology today however is commonly perceived as a masculine activity, this belief is expressed by Ruth Wallsgrove[2] when she states that: 'The philosophy of our age is scientific rationalism, and it is clearly masculine. It is objective, logical, independent, brave . . . rationality and its ultimate refinement, science, are undeniably masculine. Science is not a womanly subject.'

The masculine image of science and technology is also commented on in literature produced by the GIST (Girls into Science and Technology) project,[3] which refers to the personality characteristics of a typical scientist tending to be those society encourages in men and discourages in women. They express concern about the significant effect this can have on adolescent girls anxious about their identity.

This introduces two areas of argument, both discussed and debated in depth elsewhere. These being: are men innately more masculine than women? And, is science and technology innately masculine or has it developed that way because of its domination by men? Whatever opinion you hold on this question of why, I feel it is important to acknowledge that science and technology is seen as a masculine, and a predominantly male, activity. Because of this many women have developed a fear of, and alienation from, technology. Women have suffered the resulting manipulation in an increasingly technological world. Women's lives are dependent on technologies they do not control; and control of technology represents, and equals, power in our society.

Two distinct responses have emerged from the women's movement to the development and use of technology. Some demand greater access to technology for women and argue that women must become involved in and take control of technology rather than be controlled by it. They are concerned with the need for greater education and training to help overcome the alienation felt by many women, and to correct the historical imbalance of access to and control of technology. This concern with access to and understanding technology is prevalent in discussions of 'new technology' (i.e., computing and microelectronics) which is seen by many feminists as particularly important for women. Jan Zimmerman[4] summaries this dilemma:

> . . .women could use computers to: ease housekeeping responsibilities; reduce time spent running errands; lower transportation and energy costs; encourage the adoption of flexible working hours; support shared-parenting responsibilities, and gain access to information resources crucial to political change. Or computers could use women, just as other technologies have. They could

push women into even more alienating, low-paying jobs or out of the workplace altogether; they could double women's bind to the home, and make it impossible for women to acquire control over the information being used by others to make decisions about women's lives.

At the other end of this spectrum of opinion women have expressed concern that technology is not 'neutral'; that it has developed to reflect the values of those who control it. They reject the values of scientific rationalism and the philosophy of control associated with technology, and they reject what they see as 'masculine' technology. This has led some women to adopt an 'anti-technology' attitude; where others argue for the development of a feminist technology reflecting the values and ideals of women.

The critique of contemporary technology inherent in this latter response, whether from anti-technologists or those concerned with creating a feminist technology, shares much in common with that developed by the environmental and alternative technology movements. Both reject technology which has resulted in nuclear power, polluting emissions and ecological disasters; and which attempts to exploit and control people and nature. Both are critical of 'experts' and the lack of access to control of technology to those served, and affected, by it. Feminists have often emphasised the obvious parallels between the exploitation in our society of nature and that of women; Susan Griffin in *Woman and Nature*[5] chronicles the history of how the association between women and nature has been used to dominate and manipulate both. Western science is based on the concept of understanding nature in order to control it, and has been since the time of Francis Bacon in the seventeenth century. It is this concept that both environmentalists and feminists must challenge. Rosemary Radford Reuther[6] stresses this common aim:

Women must see that there can be no liberation for them and no solution to the ecological crisis within a society whose fundamental model of relationships tends to be one of domination. They must unite the demands of the women's movement with those of the ecological movement to envision a radical reshaping of the basic socioeconomic relations and the underlying values of this society. The concept of the domination of nature has been based from the first on social domination between master and servant groups starting with the basic relation between men and women.

162

The alternative, or appropriate, technology movement grew from a belief that social and political changes alone, without technological changes, were not sufficient; and a concern to develop new forms of technology rather than devise new forms of social control of existing technology. Rooted in the belief that technology reflects the values and interests of those who control it, AT enthusiasts are concerned very much with promoting a technology which is more accessible to decentralised or local control. Other issues central to AT are that technology does not exploit natural resources or people, and that it enhances local self-reliance. The social and political framework in which alternative technology could develop, is also considered by many proponents of AT to be as important a factor as the technology. Technological change without social and political change is not enough either, as David Dickson[7] emphasises: 'While an alternative technology . . . may well be a necessary prerequisite for creating a non-alienating, non-exploitative way of life, the development of such a technology is not, I maintain, sufficient to ensure that this state of affairs will be brought about.'

AT has been described as 'soft' technology, and is often associated with what our society considers to be feminine characteristics, such as caring and being in harmony with nature, in contrast to the 'hard' masculine characteristics of conventional technology.[8] Because of this many women have seen in the AT movement the roots of a feminist technology, not only in respect of its non-exploitative aims but also in respect of its concern with local control and organisation. Ruth Elliott expressed this ideal some years ago in an article on 'Women and AT':[9]

> . . . production should be based on small local units. The advantage of this is that the differentiation of roles between men, women and children could be considerably reduced. All can be involved in the productive technology of the community; both men and women can combine productive work with domestic and child-rearing functions, since home and work would not be spatially divided, and children too could be involved in the process of production as part of their education and socialisation.

Has this promise been realised? Has AT developed as an appropriate technology for women, is it a feminist technology? The answer to these questions must unfortunately be 'no'. The AT movement is, and has always been, dominated by men, and hence (inevitably?) reflects their priorities. There has been little acknowledgement that a

163

gender bias exists in technology, or realisation that technology does *not* affect men and women equally. It is not therefore surprising that the specific relevance of AT to women's lives has often been overlooked.

Feminists involved in the AT movement have come up against a number of conflicts of interest. Judy Smith[10] describes here what is perhaps the most common one:

> The role models for women provided by the AT movement are not very inviting. The back-to-the-land, long-skirted earth mother baking bread and feeding children in the kitchen doesn't attract much admiration from women interested in expanding their life options. This evokes images of stepping backward into rigid sex roles and sexual division of labour – a retreat from new options for women and a denial of the growing consciousness that housework should be shared by all who live in the house. Though women often enjoy participating in the traditional female technologies of food production, they want their participation to be by choice, as one option among many.

The emphasis often placed by AT on the desirability of more labour-intensive, rather than energy-intensive, technology at a domestic level could, unless accompanied by social change, reduce women's options to move out of our traditional roles. Typically women have expressed concern about replacing synthetics by natural fibres, as this might increase time spent on washing and ironing, and that replacing cars by bicycles would mean decreased mobility, a serious restriction for working mothers, as this statement illustrates:

> I recall watching college students bury a gas guzzling car on Earth Day 1970 thinking that they had never raced in such a car to an emergency ward on the other side of town at 3 a.m. with one feverish baby in the front seat and its healthy sibling sleeping in the back seat. Nor did they have the harried daily routines of driving miles in one direction to the only available childcare centre, miles in another direction to get to work, back to the centre before it closed, and off in yet another direction to pick up some food for dinner. Nor had they probably ever tried using bicycles to shop or do laundry with two kids in tow.[11]

Clearly then the impact of the technological change involved in, to take one example, reducing energy consumption at a domestic level

164

could be significantly different for women and men. AT has not so far included in its criteria for determining what is appropriate the effect of that technology on women; it has still to ask the question of whether it re-enforces existing power/role relations and restricts women's options, or creates the possibility of expanded options.

AT does not necessarily mean restricted roles for women, and in many instances may in contrast lead to increased freedom and autonomy; but it is up to us to begin to define what is appropriate for women, and become involved in developing that technology. 'As women analyse the relative impact on their lives of high and low energy-intensive systems, they will need to set their own priorities for technological development. To ensure that these priorities receive full consideration in spite of pressures to reduce energy consumption, women will have to become involved in all phases of appropriate technology from policy planning to invention and application.'[12]

Therefore, although, as expressed earlier, a feminist technology should encompass the aims and ideals of AT, it seems that AT falls short of being a feminist technology. A feminist technology must develop from an explicit assessment of the impact of technology on sex roles, asking questions such as: Does it expand options or reduce them? Promote equal employment opportunity? Affect gender-role expectations for either sex? Result in an equal distribution of economic and social benefits between women and men?

It would be more correct to call this assessment a feminist critique of technology, as it is difficult to envisage what a feminist technology might be, or to develop one, in the absence of a feminist society. Just as often it is difficult, or even impossible, to determine whether it is the application or the inherent nature of the technology that is masculine. Criticising, assessing or evaluating technological developments is an activity that we all increasingly find ourselves involved in, whether in campaigns at work about the adoption of 'new technology', about nuclear power, or over medical issues, etc. Being able to bring a feminist critique to these issues could help in laying the foundations for a feminist technology and, by chipping away at the edges, in making technology less masculine and more completely human. 'When masculinity is seen as an incomplete and thus distorted form of humanity, the issue of making science and technology less masculine is also the issue of making it more completely human.'[13]

22
Safety and Survival

Margaret Wright

What is safety? Can it be secured by surrounding ourselves with high technology and the presence of 'experts'? Margaret Wright's experiences – working with women learning to assert their own feelings and instincts in the face of a medical profession unsympathetic to those needs, and with the tragedy that struck her own family – have led her deep into these questions.

For the past eight years I have been helping women who wish to give birth at home. Such women are routinely told that they are selfish and irresponsible, that they are not thinking about the well-being of their unborn baby, because it is *safer* to give birth in hospital. At the start, I accepted this statement, although I knew very well that I felt safer at home. This seemed a trivial sentiment, however, to set against the full might of the local medical school and its ranked hierarchy of obstetricians.

However, in time, research was carried out which cast doubts on the 'safer in hospital' assertions. It has become clear that a policy of one hundred percent hospital births has been enforced without undertaking any substantial research to prove it to be safer, even on the terms of those running the service. I had been involved for several years before it occurred to me that the 'safety' which women were being sold was nowhere defined. I have therefore looked into the nature of safety in our society and have discovered a tap root leading further and further down below its foundations which are shored up on sand.

I take my examples from obstetrics since this has been my own personal starting point, but I hope it will become clear that safety, as a concept, is applicable in every aspect of our lives. Let us first consider, therefore, what obstetricians mean by safety. They say: 'If you put your trust in us, in our environment, we will strive to ensure that

166

neither your wife nor your baby, born or unborn, dies.' This statement is made to the father of the child, even though it may be spoken to the woman. It is a promise made man to man. They are in effect saying: safety means 'non-death'. By this promise the safety of the baby will not be left to 'nature' – that is, woman, unassisted by modern technology. If anything 'goes wrong' they will be able to say they did all they could. They will be protected from the fear that life, at its deepest level, may be outside their control. They need not feel responsible for whatever goes 'wrong', nor indeed need society feel responsible. We are all absolved. We may thus avoid this opportunity to come to terms.

The safety obstetricians offer, and upon which their power depends, exists in zones which are under their control. These zones are known as hospitals. A baby born on the way to one of these zones is considered 'safe' since the mother was attempting to reach it. If a baby is born quickly, unattended, at home, this baby is considered 'unsafe', and an ambulance will be sent to remove mother and baby straightaway to safety within the zone.

The politics of the Flying Squad illustrate very clearly this way of thinking. Flying Squads were set up in the 1930s in Britain. Their purpose was to take medical care, available in hospitals, out to pregnant women should an emergency arise. The beginnings of radio communication and the greater speed of the combustion engine enabled this service to be offered. Early pioneers of the Flying Squad considered it perilous to move a labouring woman under dangerous circumstances, and so the skilled personnel and the equipment went out from the centre into their homes.

During the war years, when the men were away, women attended women – whether as doctors or as midwives. The improved mortality statistics of that period have been claimed by the patriarchy as due to improved understanding of scientific principles, the brown loaf and National Dried Milk. The fact that women attended women has been altogether overlooked.

When the doctors returned, they brought with them the technology and the new breed of experts who were able to transfer the use of the technology from inanimate to animate objects. Thus ultrasound came to be directed at the bellies of pregnant women after it had been used to track submarines. They also returned from serving in the forces with a strong attachment to the hierarchy of control. Efficiency meant control from the centre, from the HQ. The very sophisticated, immobile technology of modern obstetrics reflects the feelings those at the centre have about their crucial role in childbirth. They reflect

167

the belief that birth cannot be said to have occurred without their sanction.

The Flying Squad continued to go forth but, rather than going out from the centre, it was used to bring women in. Until eventually obstetricians refused to make it available at all: once more retaining absolute control over their 'safe' territory. During this time women lost the safety of the territory of the home and the right to make decisions about how they gave birth. Women are beginning to spend more of their time 'resting' in hospital beds during pregnancy. The development of more sophisticated diagnostic techniques, notably ultrasound, continues to ensure that problems will be discovered for their expertise to right – and to fill their hospital beds.

An examination of the technology which has been developed reveals much about how obstetricians perceive themselves, and also much about the nature of their power and the safety they would have us accept. Consider the difference between the 'old-fashioned' midwife, listening to the foetal heart either by the primitive method of placing her ear directly against the woman's belly, or by the use of the trumpet to magnify the sound, and the modern 'safe' method which uses a battery of electronic equipment to monitor the foetal heart. Tracings, recording the information, are produced on paper which is fed out some distance away from the woman in labour. But this information may only be obtained by rupturing the membranes surrounding the unborn child and screwing a foetal scalp electrode into its scalp. The wires then protrude from the woman's vagina. This procedure, this technology, renders childbirth 'safe'. There is no way that it can be used without it affecting the relationships of all the people involved – including that of the baby and its parents.

The attempt of The Short Report to reduce the resistance of some women to technology to that of a 'communication problem' belittles the opposition's case. There is no way this system can be humanised since its whole ethos is quite deliberate dehumanisation. Touch will be eliminated, conversation will be limited to the interpretation of machines, and instructions must be obeyed coming as they do from someone higher up in the hierarchy. The ability to make a decision and to accept responsibility are removed. Normality is being defined by the machine. A woman's ability to be in touch with her body and her feelings must be destroyed if modern obstetrics is to succeed. Reality is mediated by the machine, by the interpretation of a trained technician, who has certain very limited skills. The threat that if one accepts responsibility, one can be blamed if anything goes wrong, takes on a sharper focus. Under the present system we are being

168

forced to depend upon machines. Machines cannot accept responsibility. They can only go wrong.

Epidural anaesthesia is a logical expression of obstetric safety. The ability to respond directly to the contractions of labour is removed by the injection given into the spine. The strength of 'real' contractions is measured on a graph. Medical attendants can then tell the woman in labour 'how she is doing'. The baby will be spared the dangers of the vagina either by the safety of a caesarian section or the protection of a forceps delivery. Techniques perfected by men, with women in mind.

Ultrasound, sold to us as a completely safe technology, ensures that the professionals attending a pregnant woman will have a greater knowledge of her unborn baby than she has. The accurate estimation of gestational age, the normal development of the unborn, can be monitored. No one is looking at the effect this is having on the perception of the pregnant woman, on how she feels about herself and her child. No one, that is, except the multinational companies who are making the equipment, or the obstetricians whose research projects multiply as its use extends. We are therefore being sold a 'safe' technique whose safety is in doubt, allowing pregnant women to be manipulated by the interpretation of what is on the screen, and affecting the perception of pregnant women in ways we do not understand. It is already not uncommon for normal babies to be aborted because of false readings. Operator errors. This is being carried out in the name of 'safety'. It must be a powerful master.

It is clear to me that obstetricians seek to protect us from the loss of a baby. But they have gone beyond. They have managed to set up the expectation in society that, because we are civilised and advanced we are *individually* entitled to healthy, full-term, 'perfect' infants. They need do no more. Responsible adults now see it as their job to accept whatever tests, whatever intervention is necessary to bring this about. So we are able to improve on nature, to be free of her mistakes.

We live protected lives. Protected from the dangers of natural hazard – from death, famine, drought, the ravages of disease – cushioned from pain by a sophisticated technology of drugs, protected from grief and emotional trauma by this same assiduous drug industry. Why suffer when we can be so well protected? If reality is painful, then let us obliterate it. We will then be safe.

There remain two points in time, two gates. We enter our own time through one and leave through the other. For centuries it has been the work of women to assist at the opening of these gates. Our safe society continues to search for ways in which to prevent women from carrying this out. We live in an age when the midwife can no longer wait, when the act of giving birth reduces women to passive spectators, and when death must be defined by a professional or else it cannot be said to have occurred. We give birth objectively, watching a western on TV, and die to the sound of ice-cream chimes. These profound mysteries are being rendered safe – they are under control. Yet the two gates remain. Sometimes, by chance, we rediscover their meaning, and we are renewed, as I was in the spring of 1978

It was March 1978 when my youngest daughter Alison fell ill. I was annoyed. It was inconvenient. I was isolated with her, by her infection, and had to stay indoors. At first I sat there with her on my lap as she was content to lie still. I was able to read all the things a lively toddler had prevented me from reading. A doctor came and went. I had a strange unease.

One day, I went to collect something I had had printed. My mother stayed in to look after the child. I went to the door of the printshop and found a notice flapping in the breeze. It read: 'Due to bereavement this shop is closed until further notice.' I found myself laughing, behaving in an offhand way. I cycled home.

My daughter was not getting better. The doctor reassured me: yes, she was ill, but she would get well. Yes, he had seen the illness before. I had nothing to set against what he said – only the grey-pale child I held. I was sitting still by now, holding her all the time. I had things to read, but I was finding it more difficult to concentrate. I put on the radio. If I moved her she cried with a weak cry. She was very sick. I was having to remain very still so that she was not distressed. When my husband came home from work he would hold her. I had been sitting so still that I would run up and down stairs as fast as I could to regain freedom of movement.

Sometimes, when the doctor called, I would say: 'Could you turn off the radio?', because I had put it on when I first sat down with her when I brought her downstairs and could not move to do it myself. I was hoping all the time that someone would realise that I was trapped. But no one did. The terror I was pushing away reached its peak. When my mother came every day to cook for the other two children who were at school, I would say to her: 'Leave the door open will you, so that I can call you if I need you. Please come back in a few minutes.' By now, after three weeks, I was afraid of what was happening to the child. I was afraid of being left on my own with her. I had this terrible secret. I was hysteric. She was going away from me. I was taking her somewhere, but I did not know where it was.

I took her brother and sister out to a big store one weekend when her father was holding her. I always thought of her as a ladybird. I bought a large, stuffed ladybird and handed it to them and said: 'Here you are. This is for Alison, to help her get better; but in case she doesn't, you can have it yourselves.' I felt very close to these two. They were on the inside. That same day I bought a tin of olive oil – it was from Greece. The next week as I sat by the fire with her, I opened the oil, fetched herbs from the garden, rosemary and thyme, put them with it into a glass bowl, and warmed it by the fire. I massaged her with it, very gently. I remember she stretched out a very, very thin arm and smiled. I knew exactly what I was doing and I was on my own.

One evening I sat with her watching the late film. My husband went up to bed. The film was 'The Sandpiper'. I remember it clearly. I became interested in the film, my mind was on something else. But, suddenly, I had a blinding understanding that this was a film. That it was not happening 'now', that some of the actors may even be dead. I began to cry and cry. I could not stop. I knew I was alive in the present moment; I felt more sharply alive than I had ever been before, and I was sitting, watching television, holding a dying child. I wanted to run away. I attempted to do so. . . Whenever my husband came home I left the house.

The next Saturday I went into the centre of town. I was distracted. There was nothing more I could do for her. I bought a scented pillow and a bright new dress. As I handed over the money for the dress my thoughts were clear: 'She can wear this dress if she gets better – or she will wear it as her shroud.'

When my husband took the other two children out to a party the next afternoon, I was able to be open to the reality of the situation again. I cried for a long time. I rang a friend who was a nurse: 'Come over, come over.' She came. I had given up trying to get the doctors to hear. She rang a doctor for me. He said: 'Do you think I should come?' She said yes. She was a nurse. She could say yes and they would come. He said one word, 'Hospital'. I cried again.

I had known for such a long time. And I was right. They diagnosed meningitis straightaway and began treating her. But when they realised they had failed, suggested she be allowed to starve to death under sedation, the feeding tube and the antibiotics having been withdrawn. I had been right all the time. I had done everything for her, but I had not known that the treatment existed. I only had an understanding of life and death. I kept repeating, 'I carried her into this illness and I will carry her out to wherever she has to go.'

171

I knew that I had to grieve or else I would be destroyed. I rejected any drugs offered to blur the reality of the agony which was all I had. So I have been able to go on responding to it. The slow working through of grief in my own time has sharpened my sense of being alive. To sit and hold one of my children reminds me constantly of my finite existence. I am open to the possibilities and the pain of my present moment. One of my children has taken me to the Third World – where women sit and nurse their starving children till they die. The experience has had a profound effect on my life. I have only one level in which I can relate to people. Nobody is more, or less, important than myself. This has come about directly as a result of my daughter.

I have begun to run workshops entitled 'Verbal Disarmament'. The technique was learnt, in crisis, to deal with the doctors who wanted my daughter to die. I found myself speaking from the thoughts I had always had. When they put her on a high dosage of valium, I was able to send for the consultant and say, 'Doctor, I am in no fit state, emotionally, to argue about this drug. Would you please tell me what part of her brain you are affecting with it and what the normal dosage for an adult would be?' He was honest with me. He did not know the answer to either question.

When she left the hospital to come home, the same consultant came to our cubicle. He said, 'I will not make a routine appointment for you to bring Alison to see me. When you feel it is right, let me know through your GP. There's nothing, in the short term, that I can do.' I said to him, 'I know there is nothing that you can do.' I was very moved. It was an honest exchange.

I am only just beginning to realise that the repercussions of the experience brought to me by this tiny child will continue as long as I remain open to them. I am often afraid. But I know myself in fear, and of what it is I am afraid. I know that the safety we are being sold is an illusion. It is corrupt. It is the very endeavour to control every aspect of our lives that will cause us to lose it. The greater the degree of protection we seek, the less we will find.

The followers of 'safety' are building their bunkers, are constructing webs of 'safe' rules and regulations, are taking an active part in Civil Defence preparations, are entering into contracts of death with armaments and investments, are destroying the environment desperate to find resources to fuel their fantasies of control. Above all they will not be vulnerable, will not accept that their lives are finite, that they are part of a natural order greater than themselves. They act as if they hate the earth, treating it as a resource, because they cannot

172

come to terms with the fact that they must return to it themselves. They have perfected an economic system to ensure the safety of their children forgetting that all the children of the world are there to inherit it.

We must reclaim the word 'safe', as women reclaim the night. Re-learn how to support each other, to be available, to hear. Reclaim the mysteries of birth and death for the community, become healers, understand the roots of depression and disease at their deepest level, reject those who would solve problems by compounding them, be open, vulnerable, able to celebrate being alive now . . . or there will be no future. I owe this understanding to one, small, severely brain-damaged child.

23
Birth:
The Agony or the Ecstasy?

Caroline Wyndham

Once again, the experience of giving birth provides a focus for exploring a woman's relationship to her own body. Here, Caroline Wyndham, who has had two radically different experiences of birth, tells her story and talks to Hazel Selina, who with other women in Totnes, South Devon, set up a birth centre to help women have a better kind of experience. Together as women, we need not be powerless: the choice of how we bring children into the world can be ours.

My son Leo was born in 1973, the second of my three children. He arrived in this world blue and gasping for life, a piece of wire extending from his head – an electrode, a symbol of our times. His journey to be here was hindered by machines, clouded with drugs, and his eventual entry welcomed by fraught and distressed people, noise, blinding lights and a mother who instead of actively participating in this supreme moment of two lives, lay exhausted by the ordeal of having endured a mechanised hospitalised birth.

I remember his face, before he was rushed away to be resuscitated, distorted with pain and confusion. It did not resemble the 'buddha consciousness' that is the rightful inheritance of all new born beings.

As we lay apart, he with strangers attending him, nothing familiar, nothing known, no maternal smells, soft skin or breast to comfort him, and me with my legs suspended in iron stirrups, a male student doctor with needle and thread sewing together my lacerated skin, I felt cheated and deeply angry; and I wept. For in my attempt to have a natural and un-violent birth for my child, I had failed. After sixteen hours of pleading to be left in peace to allow my baby to arrive in his own time, repeatedly asking them to wheel away their drugs and drips; screaming fearfully when the foetal-heart monitor, to which my baby was connected, ceased to function; crying with relief and anger when they kicked it to life again with a casual 'Oh, it's always conking

174

out dear, don't worry'; I had had enough. With a final surge of emotion I wrenched the heavy metal belt from my throbbing stomach and decided to take no more of their ways, but to follow my own instinctive feelings. My body is mine. They could keep their machines.

To them I was a naughty, rebellious and stupid 'girl'; a number which was not conforming; a troublemaker. Forever branded in my hospital notes for all future personnel to see, 'This woman finds hospital authority difficult to take.'

Three years later Chloë, my third child, was born. With ease and in her own time she slithered from within and lay for the next two hours on my stomach. In that time we gradually came to know each other, by sight, touch and smell, and in gentleness we explored one another. With our hands, her father's and mine, lovingly massaging her body, her tiny head between my breasts, we welcomed her into this world. Slowly she awoke, one eye opened, then the other, a little arm reached out, stretching and retracting, feeling, touching, exploring, her tiny fingers curled around mine. Like the rising of the sun she awoke to life and glowed, warming us with her beauty. In those moments I saw the fragility and strength of all humanity as we start this journey through life.

My two experiences of childbirth are by no means unique. Each day women are being refused the right to choose how they want to give birth. Each year newer, larger and more mechanised maternity units are being constructed causing smaller and more intimate places of confinement to become obsolete; thus denying a woman's need to feel familiar with her surroundings in order to feel relaxed, safe and able to actively participate in her child's birth.

The idea of going into hospital to give birth, suggests that childbirth is seen as an unnatural state of health; an illness. The woman is considered sick; in a state of dis-ease. This totally disregards the possibility that in labour a woman is potentially more aware and receptive than at any other time of her life – in touch with feelings of such a profound nature that to suppress them is an unjustifiable act of aggression.

However women are rebelling. They are heeding those deep, instinctive feelings which are telling them to reject what is offered in the name of childbirth and are beginning to seek alternative ways. They are seeking to restore dignity and peace to women in labour and to reclaim their bodies as their own. They are discovering a strength to challenge the patriarchal structure which enforces controlled and regulated childbirth – which should be the most spontaneous and individual on experiences.

175

There are an increasing number of women who are courageously choosing to give birth in the security of their own homes and to reject the conventional paths to the local labour ward. These women need help and guidance and encouragement which is largely unavailable from within the orthodox system.

In Totnes, South Devon, two women, Hazel Selina and Avis Turner, have created a place which offers such support. The Totnes Birth Centre opened its doors in March 1982. The following is a conversation I had with Hazel, a practitioner of the Metamorphic Technique, about the Centre.

Caroline Wyndham *Hazel, did the centre arise out of your own experiences in childbirth?*
Hazel Selina Yes, my experiences are very similar to yours. I have always felt very strongly about giving birth naturally – the woman being left alone, not interfered with; so that she and the baby can find their own rhythm together.

It was after meeting Joseph Chilton Pearce, author of *Magical Child*, that I decided to actually stop moaning about women's rights in childbirth and the existing system, and do something about it. A part of me felt, 'But what can I do? I'm not qualified.' But another, stronger, part of me said that this was not important, and that if you feel something in your heart, then that should be enough. So I put up some notices around town, inviting women who were interested in having alternative births to come and meet me. Four women arrived. The Birth Centre had begun.

You have been open since March 1982. Has your function changed much since those first weeks?
I think so. At first it provided a place for women to come and just talk about their experiences; their labours; the way they had been treated by doctors in clinics; the problems they were having to face with routine ultrasound scans in hospitals and things of that kind. There was a lot of anger and resentment and frustration coming out. Nobody before had actually listened to them, given them a space to expose those raw areas. It was really a form of therapy which was occurring. Now it seems clearer that we need more structure. So we offer courses and workshops in pre-natal movement, breathing, relaxation, information about diet during pregnancy, discussions about alternative birthing positions and an on-going weekly group. Along with this we are searching for ways to reach more women – women who are hovering on the edge, who need support and care, and just plain medical facts to help them follow their instincts to be

176

active participators in having their babies at home.

Although women who are clear about what they want do not need to come here, these women can and do give very strong support to those less able to take that step. They can help them to overcome the fears which are holding them back.

Women who have experienced home births are busy telling others how beautiful it is and as always, personal experience is our strongest advocate.

We also have a reference library; we run jumble sales to raise funds and we plan to buy a copy of the film *Active Birth* by Janet Balaskas to lend out along with the video of Michel Odent's television programme, which we already show at different events in the area.

What is the reaction of the local doctors to what you are doing?

Suspicion, in a word. We have tried to meet them and explain what we are doing, in the hope that some form of communication could happen. Like just saying: here we are – down the road – this is what we can do for any of your patients who want home deliveries. This would ease the situation and allay the fears of some women who feel that having a home birth would rule out any hospital assistance in an emergency. We have also tried to find sympathetic doctors in local hospitals. Ideally we need a supportive midwife to help bridge that gap. So far this has not happened. But it must happen; it *will* happen. I don't feel worried about it – it's *got* to happen. I suppose it will when enough women wake up and demand their rights.

We all have to stop being 'good little girls' and say: 'My body is mine, and I'm jolly well going to listen to its demands.'

Do you think that we will ever have Alternative Birthing Centres here as exist in America?

You mean where active birth can occur outside of hospital and private homes?

Yes.

It could happen. It's going to take time, though. First we need to make our midwives strong and active again. Confident in their own ability to deliver babies. At present highly trained women are relegated to the position of caring for post-natal, short-term patients, changing vaginal swobs, and checking on new mothers and their babies. Many weeks pass between a home delivery for those women.

In America private medicine is the norm. Here it is very different. We are not used to paying for our medical care. Money is not easily available. But fundamentally the Centre must grow with the needs of the community.

I try in my classes at the Centre to make women aware of the

177

ramifications of a passive, hospitalised birth and what it does psychologically for the child.

It's no good working for peace if we are not bringing peaceful beings into the world.

If Hazel Selina and the women working with her succeed, the seeds they are sowing now will blossom into a loving and caring place where women can come to give birth in peace and with a conscious awareness of the sacredness of all life.

May those seeds fall on fertile earth and find light and warmth and water. They have certainly been planted with love.

24
A New Form of Female Infanticide

Manushi Collective

It is all to easy for technology to be used as the instrument of a sexist culture, especially where women's reproductive functions are concerned. This article, which appeared in a recent issue of Manushi, *a lively feminist magazine published in New Delhi, highlights the collaboration between the manipulation of life pursued by modern medicine, and the traditional patriarchal valuation of sons over daughters – a valuation which is not confined to India.*

'Is it a boy or a girl? It is now possible to find the sex of your child in early pregnancy before it is born, with the aid of latest sophisticated imported electronic equipment. . .' This is how a private clinic in Amritsar advertises its prowess in the *Indian Express* of 27 June 1982. What is the purpose of finding out the sex of a child which has already been conceived? A letter circulated by two doctors in Chandigarh explains:

Most prospective couples in quest of a male child, as the social set-up in India demands, keep on giving birth to a number of female children, which in a way not only enhances the increasing population but also leads to a chain reaction of many social, economic and mental stresses on these families. Amniocentesis and antenatal sex determination has come to our rescue and can help in keeping some check over the accelerating population as well as give relief to the couples requiring a male child. Assessment of the foetus's sex has been made possible by amniocentesis after completion of the sixteenth week and until the twentieth week of pregnancy, when therapeutic abortion is medically feasible and legally permissible. In spite of all precautions, the procedures can be fraught with danger of abortion in 0.1 percent of cases. A charge of Rs 500 only will be levied by the clinic for doing amniocentesis, sexchromatin studies and theatre charges. Sex determination is done in those patients having more than one or two female children.

In other words, scientific techniques are being misused to commit female infanticide before the infant is born. Such tests had been tried at the All India Institute of Medical Sciences in 1974–75, but were stopped when doctors found that women who were carrying female children were having abortions.

The sex ratio (the proportion of females to males in the total population) of India has been declining since the beginning of this century and is now 935 females to 1,000 males. This is due to a higher mortality rate amongst women, and a much higher mortality rate amongst female than among male infants. A girl child is considered a burden on the family. She is discriminated against in matters of nutrition, health, education and employment. After marriage, frequent pregnancies, lack of medical care and the burden of overwork lead to a deterioration in her condition.

In the context of the declining sex ratio, this new method of female infanticide assumes even more dangerous proportions. Unfortunately, even press publicity given to the issue could lead to more people getting to know of the technique and using it to get rid of unwanted girls. Women's organisations and concerned individuals need to treat this as a priority issue and plan a concerted campaign against it.

On 15 July, the All India Democratic Women's Association organised a meeting attended by several women's organisations to protest against these sex determination tests. The meeting passed a resolution condemning the tests as misuse of scientific knowledge to violate ethical principles and human rights while exploiting negative attitudes towards female children. It was observed that the century-old trend of decline in the sex ratio in this country would be accentuated if such attempts are made to annihilate one sex by a form of female infanticide.

The meeting called upon the government to ban the tests, and asked the Indian Medical Council to take disciplinary action against doctors who perform the tests. Four doctors also addressed the meeting.

However, while legal action is often a useful weapon in protest campaigns, a government ban is likely to send the phenomenon underground and proliferate corruption amongst those who are supposed to enforce the ban.

The Manushi Collective
Manushi, CI/202 Lajpat Nagar, New Delhi – 110024

25

Saving Trees, Saving Lives
Third World Women and the Issue of Survival

Anita Anand

It is all too easy for outsiders to import technological expertise into a Third-world context without taking into account the views of over half the population it is meant to serve: the women. On the other hand, as Anita Anand's account demonstrates, women can play an important role in protecting their environment and life-styles against the encroachment of development policies that would sacrifice long-term subsistence for the sake of short-term cash benefits.

In a remote village in Northern India called Reni, nestled in the Garhwal mountains of the Himalayan range, a group of women and children were doing an unusual thing. Hugging trees. They were resorting to Chipko, which means to hug, to prevent trees from being felled. With their arms wrapped around the trees, the women and children cried: 'The forest is our mother's home, we will defend it with all our might.' The women and children stopped about 70 lumberjacks from the forest contractors who were ready to fell the trees.

This event, which happened in 1974, marked the beginning of the now well known Chipko Andolan, or movement, which forced the state government to set up a committee to investigate the concerns of women. The committee reported that about 12,000 kilometres of the sensitive watershed area of the Alkananda Valley were endangered. The government then declared this area out of bounds for felling.

The true birth of the Chipko movement and the women's action, however, goes back to 1970 when the Alkananda Valley suffered an unprecedented flood.[1] The flood washed away five major bridges, 13 suspension bridges, hundreds of head of cattle and several millions of rupees' worth of timber and fuel. The loss gave the local people an increased understanding of the importance of natural resources in their lives. The government response was a reafforestation plan, replacing the indigenous oak with the faster growing and commercially attractive pine. The oak leaves had produced a water-absorbing humus, rich in nutrients. They had also stored the water, releasing it slowly, creating rivers and streams around which local communities had developed over the years. The pine needles, by not decomposing, allowed precipitation to run off. Oak, however, was not a cash crop, so it was felled indiscriminately, to make way for roads, army exercises, landing strips and other services.

Inappropriate Development: Appropriating Resources

Such decisions regarding afforestation and deforestation are examples of inappropriate development planning and implementation. In the Garhwal area, after the Indo-Chinese conflict in 1962, roads and communications facilities were introduced. Since theirs was a marginal economy, local people hoped that some profits of this development would accrue to them. Instead, the ventures enabled forest contractors and speculators to expoit the timber-rich forests for business. Trees were felled for sports equipment, badminton and tennis racquets, for export. Labour was imported into the area. The new water, electricity lines, schools, health-care facilities catered to and could be afforded by army personnel and government officers. Local people's needs, as well as the importance of preserving the environment as a means of livelihood for local people, were never taken into consideration. Besides, once the economy of an area is hooked into catering for a community other than local, development distortions occur. In the Garhwal area, people lived off the forest, meeting their basic needs, and using the surplus for barter and some for cash in nearby towns. With the changes in the 1960s and 70s, men were encouraged to join the army, leave the area. This created additional burdens on women in the area, who not only have to work harder to do their daily chores, but absorb the work of men in their absence. Financial resources invested in the local communities are siphoned off to create infrastructures for an export-dominated economy, based on demand and supply defined by market considerations. This also entails the introduction of new cultural and social trends that could challenge the community to seek new ways to develop and change. However, as the new trends are usually the aftermath of inappropriate development, chances are that the worst of social norms are reinforced or introduced, especially norms regarding male-female roles, interaction between parents and children, and power and control in the community.

Determining Local Needs: Who Decides?

Further examples of insensitivity to people's basic human and survival needs are closely linked to allocation and use of natural resources. Firewood, an important commodity as a source of energy, is vital to thousands of Third-world villages, where women and children spend several hours daily collecting this basic resource for the family. In the Garhwal area, women walk five to ten miles a day to collect firewood for cooking and fodder for cattle. They carry up to 20 lbs in baskets slung over their shoulders, almost bent double under the load.

Yet worldwide, the number of trees being planted to meet this need is abysmally low. Why is this so? Agarwal and Anand suggest that the reason may lie in the sexual division of labour within the family.[2] Men are involved in activities that generate cash, while fulfilling family needs (fuel, water, fodder) is left to women. Introducing techniques to meet these basic family needs would call for a cash investment that men earn, or for community labour, which men mobilise and organise in the third world. Poor women have limited access to the cash earned by their men. Neither do they get to participate in community decision-making. Hence women's needs, however pressing they may be, get neglected.

The role of women in the Chipko movement poses several questions. Are women, inherently, more perceptive and long-sighted about survival needs than men? What are men concerned with? The example of Chipko reveals that leadership in some of the villages has been supportive of the women. In other villages, the husbands and sons have mixed feelings. The men complain that women have become domineering, unfeminine and bold, and one complained that his wife had stopped making him tea![3] The issue is one of control. As Chandi Prasad Bhatt, one of the male leaders of the movement says, 'Control by local people yes, but who among local people: men or women?'

Controlling mechanisms in movements like Chipko are a carry-over from norms in society at large. Male privilege in decision-making cuts across races, classes and cultures. The institutionalisation of patriarchy and heirarchy are rampant and manifest themselves in all levels of society. Role definitions as ascribed to men and women further exacerbate the situation, when self-confidence and worth are being questioned. Expectations of what either sex does best undermine and dehumanise the real potential of both women and men.

A study of the needs and perceptions of women and men could lead us to look at the way both sexes are socialised into accepting what the world means to them. The process of industrialisation has not helped the sexes to re-examine these socialisations. The myth that women run the home, manage the children and act as the emotional and physical sustainers of society and culture are as ludicrous as the ones for men. The men are supposed to be breadwinners, heads of households and to deal with the world of politics, money and the important issues in society. Unless these barriers are broken down and the reality of men's and women's lives acknowledged, little change can be brought about by development.

Technologies of the Real World: Who Uses What?

Biogas plants, plantations of fuelwood, anaerobic latrines and hand pumps are all recognised as 'appropriate technology' that can improve the lives of rural people in the third world. However, success stories are few as people often reject the innovations. Why is this so? Agarwal and Anand suggest that it could be because the specific needs of women, who are most directly affected by these innovations, are not considered.[4] Let's take a look at toilets, and the almost universal failure to introduce them in Third-world villages. Rural sanitation programmes were given considerable importance in India's first five-year development plan in the 1950s. Repeated failure has forced the government to neglect rural sanitation after the second development plan.

The official explanation for this neglect is that these programmes require changes in deep-rooted behavioural factors, which bureaucracies cannot bring about in illiterate people. Rural people are said to be ignorant of the health implications of sanitation and toilets. But the limited sociological literature available shows that the programmes are more accepted by women than men, because of the greater need for privacy women have, forced upon them by society. Designing and implementing sanitation programmes requires asking male decision-makers to invest in programmes that they do not need. Men can squat whenever and wherever they wish. Women, on the other hand, may have to resort to defecating on rooftops, as in many Middle East countries, due to the purdah system. In Bangladesh, scientists at the International Centre on Diarrhoeal Diseases Research reported that women relieve themselves only before sunrise or after sunset: 'When rural women felt the need to defecate during the day, they held it with difficulty until sunset. Sometimes they had to miss lunch so they could hold a bowel movement longer. The missing of lunch occurred several times a month in the case of most of the women. On occasions when they could not hold it back, they defecated hastily in the backyard.'

Various taboos governing women's defecatory behaviour are known to have slowed down the introduction of toilets. In some parts of East Africa, women who have seen the excreta of a male cannot get married; in South Korea, a daughter-in-law is not allowed to sit on the same seat as her father-in-law.

Just as making decisions about the introduction and use of toilets is a male privilege, so is the introduction of community water supply systems. Even though women collect most of the water to maintain the family, they are seldom consulted in the planning and implementation and maintenance of these systems. It was once believed that if communities had access to water supply systems, incidences of diseases would be reduced. This is, however, not the case. Community water taps can supply clean drinking water, but recent research shows that this is not sufficient to reduce infections. Dirty hands and lack of personal hygiene can transmit enough germs to maintain the high incidence of diarrhoea – the Third World's biggest health problem.

Keeping hands clean requires access to adequate quantities of reasonably clean water. If the nearest tap is 100 metres away, there will be little inducement to wash frequently. Surveys show that diarrhoeal diseases are reduced substantially in households that have taps. Some surveys also show that the further the tap is away from the house, the higher is the incidence of diarrhoea. Some alternatives that could be provided to deal with the situation are taps in each household, or men to share in the task of water-carrying from the community tap to the house. It is clear the governments are not committed to this vital need, and men are reluctant to participate in what is perceived as 'women's work'.

In certain villages of Bangladesh, where women are in purdah, they cannot collect water during the day. If the supply of water runs out, a child is asked to fetch the water, or an elderly woman goes, if no males are around. Bangladeshi experts report that households observing the purdah system have limited amounts of water in the home, insufficient even to wash properly after defecation.

Introduction of basic technologies to meet the needs of poor people, where investment opportunities and decisions are made by and controlled by men, will meet with resistance unless the question of sexual equity is dealt with. The social and religious mores, which have created and reinforced stereotypes of the roles of men and women in society, may have to change first.

Sustainability and Progress

A commitment to the preservation of the environment does not necessarily negate the need for progress, if properly defined. Modernisation, as evidenced in the fruits of science and its application in technology, can involve liberating mechanisms, as much as oppressive ones. For too long, development has meant the transfer of large amounts of capital and technological resources from the rich to the poor nations, in an attempt to solve what is perceived as an administrative problem. For too long women have been kept out of the world of science and technology, edged towards home-making, and away from political, social and economic decision-making. For too long technocrats, scientists and economists have assumed that development means economic growth, at the expense of other factors. The political and social ramifications of change, via development, have been glossed over. Some social scientists have argued that equality between classes is a prerequisite for growth. Feminists would argue that no 'real' growth is possible without a re-examination of power relations between the sexes as well. The contribution of feminism to the environmental and development movements is the insistence that all forms of domination must be eradicated and that the living relations of subordination be a central problem for study, reflection and action for change.

The New Society

The Chipko Andolan is one example of how communities define and articulate their needs, dreams and futures. It is a strategy for all communities, governments, as well as the international community. Unless basic human needs are first taken into consideration in the planning and implementation of any development strategy, it is bound to be inappropriate. The concepts of self-reliance and self-sufficiency, which pre-date industrialisation and the conscious movements of development, have relevance for us today. They allow us to raise questions about what we need to survive, how we use our natural and human resources, and what our ultimate goal in life is. They also force us to raise questions about the perceived need for a 'transnational' culture that is growing by leaps and bounds today.

When the Chipko Andolan first gained attention in the early 1970s it was hailed as a movement to save trees. But it was really a movement to save lives. When the women of Reni shouted, 'The forest is our mother and we will defend it with all our might,' they clearly saw the relationship between their resources and their survival. Saving trees was a start for the women of Chipko. Saving the people of Garhwal was the real goal.

26

Time for Women

New Patterns of Work

Sheila Rothwell

A woman's work, runs the old adage, is never done. It has long been difficult for women to make a rigid distinction between 'work' and 'home', being on duty or off. And yet industrialised societies have done just this, their economic balance-sheets ignoring a large part of the contribution women make. The irony is that, with rising unemployment and changing work patterns, the experience of women could well become relevant in formulating new attitudes towards work and breaking down out-dated barriers between our personal lives and our achievements in the 'outside' world. Sheila Rothwell looks into some of the new patterns emerging, their advantages and drawbacks.

Do women have a different time perspective and is this part of their different view of the world? If so, how valuable is this – for themselves and for society? What recognition is there of it? These are profound and difficult questions raising some fundamental philosophical issues. Here I shall attempt to touch on only a few of them in the context of today but, hopefully, it will stimulate further thinking and insights for others.

I

There is a lot of talk at present on 'changing patterns of working time'. This talk is usually generated by discussion of the problems raised by increasing unemployment, particularly in western industrialised countries.[1] Yet when people exclaim that the old pattern of the 8-hour day, 5-day week, 16–65 working life is no longer with us, I always reply that, for half the population, it never has been. For although women have undertaken paid employment in large

189

numbers, and for a much longer period than has been 'officially' recognised, the continuity of this has usually been interrupted by childbearing and domestic responsibilities (even if these interruptions were briefer and less frequent than might have been assumed).[2] Thus, in general, women seem to conform already to what some writers have identified as likely future patterns of working life, containing spells of full-time, part-time, self- or sub-contract employment, and also non-employment. This non-employment period can be interspersed with opportunities for education and training or sabbaticals, more time for family and community-related activity and a more creative use of leisure.[3] Widespread ignorance of this fact relates perhaps to the invisibility and inferiority of women in a patriarchal society, and to the need of capitalism for its 'reserve army' or domestic labour force. It also raises the question of whether making the female life pattern into a *visible* model will encourage trends in the direction of, what I would see as, a much more healthy society, or whether it will mean that, even if men change the pattern of their working lives, they will do so in such a way as to be different from women, or so that the 'status' ascribed to their activities is again superior.

Can we assume a 'functionalist' adjustment to the needs of society and greater convergence between the patterns of men's and women's lives? What evidence is there of change in activities and of attitudes?

II

For men, work has generally been defined as *paid employment*, whereas for women, work has been more consciously divided into 'paid' and 'unpaid' activity. Yet with 40 percent of the workforce now female it is clear that paid employment is the norm for most women at some stage, at least between the ages of 16 and 60. Without their earnings, it has been estimated that 20 to 25 percent more families would be in poverty and dependent on Social Security. That is despite the fact that the majority of women are in low-paid, low-status occupations and are still regarded as a 'marginal' or 'secondary' workforce by employers. This can be seen from attitudes to female 'labour shedding' under the pressure of recession or new technology. The fact that women may leave to have children is used to justify most of the low earning, low training and blocked promotion opportunities experienced by individual women at most levels. This in turn reflects on the attitudes of women, who learn to see themselves as they are seen, and tend to have the organisational characteristics and short-time horizons of the 'stuck'[4] rather than the 'moving'. Analyses of the problems of women in management certainly illustrate the difficulties women experience in looking ahead to the medium-term, in planning their career moves, and in making organisations work for them rather than reacting to the pressures. There is also difficulty in even discussing work versus domestic pressures[5] or the planning of children: the majority still see babies or career as mutually exclusive. Given the way in which young women managers are treated, it is not surprising that many then choose motherhood as a more creative option.

It is also significant, however, that a high proportion (40 percent) of women are working less than full-time. The variations in the patterns of adjustment of working hours are myriad: personally- or formally-negotiated flexi-time; legally defined part-time (less than 8 hours, or 16 hours for first 5 years); job-pairing, one week on and one week off; twilight shift; school shift, not in the holidays; to name but a few of the arrangements.[6] Indeed, on the basis of defining part-time work as anything less than normal working hours, *one in five* people in employment is now a part-time worker. Thus while 80 percent of these are women, more men are also included – so far mainly those over 60 (or over 55), as early retirement becomes more usual.

The scope for extending this to people at the other end of the age-scale has also been realised by the General Electric Company (GEC), and suddenly taken up by government in the form of its 'job-sharing scheme', whereby employers will be paid a subsidy to halve a job and bring in someone off the unemployment register.[7] It is easy to be cynical about the attractions of this scheme for government (it is cheap, reduces the unemployment statistics and helps keep young people's wages down), and to criticise particular features of it (for example, it does not help the unregistered unemployed or those with a family dependent on them, and it reinforces the status of women as a marginal workforce). Nevertheless, the scheme does have its advantages. In practical terms, it could make more jobs available to unemployed women, and it could ease or highlight the problems of lack of part-time benefit, part-time registration and the tightening of benefit eligibility. It could also lead to adjustments of the tax system, and even of travel costs. But, most importantly, it is already forcing employers to look again at the possibilities of job-splitting and making 'less than full-time work' a respectable option for men (managers at least) to discuss.

The 1982 Manpower Services Commission *Review* gives full respectability and significance to the discovery that a quarter of the workforce are now self-employed or part-time.[8] This development has been reinforced by the European Economic Community (EEC) draft directive on part-time work, and the report of the House of Lords Committee set up to examine it, which unequivocally accepted part-time working as important and accepted the moral argument for *equity* (with full-time work) in the terms and conditions of its rewards.[9]

If, therefore, part-time workers are to become equally eligible for pension schemes and other discretionary benefits, and are to be given priority consideration for promotion to full-time vacancies, the debate shifts on to questions of *efficiency*. What are the likely costs of this to companies? Conversely, what is the productivity of part-time as distinct from full-time workers? Employers giving evidence to the Lords Committee were hard put to it to answer this question, although they mentioned some minor administrative difficulties caused by the switch to part-time working. What is true is that many part-timers feel that they are doing a full day's work for half a day's pay.

Trades union hostility to part-time work (and to women workers) as undercutting rates and undermining full-time jobs is certainly valid in these terms. But so far there has been little published research into men's part-time work (or short-time working). Veronica Beechey's studies in the Coventry labour market suggest that the men's work is differently structured, paid and perceived by employers: a possible hint as to future trends?[10]

Discussions about job-sharing and part-time work still, however, tend to focus on low-level jobs: whether this is also related to the low status of anything traditionally done mainly by women is not clear. It also seems to relate to concepts of *commitment*. Managers, while rationalising the impossibility of dividing management jobs in terms of the *continuity* of supervision and involvement that is needed, also imply that a management job by its nature demands high commitment, which is inherently incompatible with part-time working. Yet many of the published examples of job-sharing (in teaching and training, library and social work, community service, etc.) show that it *is* feasible in many occupations in which there is a high managerial/ professional element. Is this another sign of the difficulties of accepting women as managers? Most managers, when challenged, can identify several posts in the organisation that have been 'made into' full-time jobs to fit the male norm, by linking together several tasks or responsibilities that could just as easily have been left separate as part-time jobs. The tendency towards hiring 'consultants' (often recently redundant ex-employees) to fulfil specific tasks may be an alternative approach, and is currently becoming more widespread.

This raises the issues of self-employment or paid work from home which women, like men, have traditionally done in some professions, such as journalism. Home-working in low-level assembly or clerical work has been predominantly female, at scandalously low rates of pay (although on an hourly basis, excluding overheads, above the rate which some could earn in regular employment). Much is now being made of the opportunities in our electronic future of working from home (Alvin Toffler's 'Electronic Cottage'[11]), and increasing numbers of women are working for computer companies on this basis (e.g., for ICL, 'F' International). Yet the difficulties and isolation of work at home may be considerable. There is not much evidence of enthusiasm on the part of employers to stimulate this development, except in respect of their field sales forces (still largely male), despite scope for reduction in overheads.[12]

There are important questions to consider here, however: are women doing enough to take advantage of the opportunities that new technology could, in theory, be giving them to work in new ways from home (and to organise their domestic work)? Or is one of the significant 'meanings' of paid employment that it gets us outside the home and links us with other people and other purposes beyond ourselves and our immediate family? In other words, does paid employment give the 'status' and 'recognition' which we all need?[13] When interviewing women returning to full-time work as to whether they would still go out to work if it were not for financial need, I found that most of them mentioned these other factors: 'I'm more "me", somehow.'[14]

Many women who have responsibility for young children feel they have no choice as to what kinds of working hours they can accept. Indeed, many who are faced with working shifts 'as required' feel forced to give up their jobs completely. On the other hand, a survey into attitudes to patterns of shiftwork of women living in areas of high manufacturing density revealed greater variety than might have been anticipated – for example, a greater willingness to work nights on the part of young women with young children (for whom it was easier to make 'sleeping' than day-care arrangements), and a general hostility to legislative limitation on women's working hours. Significant differences from their men's attitudes were also found.[15]

Most men in employment are also fathers, and it is strange that those who formulate personnel policies are unaware of the fact. 'Do you mean we should let men's wives children use the crèche?' was one company's response to a reminder about equal access for men and women to company benefits and facilities. In fact, if such attitudes were to change, crèches might be as common as canteens, and flexi-time and 'time off' schemes be very much more flexible – just as men's career patterns can be adjusted to 'national service'.

For many people the biggest problem of working shorter hours is the necessity for pro-rata adjustments in income. Society, couples and individuals will have to discuss this further. At present a lot of families need one and a half incomes to survive, so perhaps two people working three-quarters of the time could earn enough – *if* women's earnings were not proportionately lower. Even the Trades Union Congress is now beginning to discuss the possibility of some legal maximum to working hours (as elsewhere in Europe), and some women would be glad if the overtime opportunities and pressures were not available for the men. Many women trade unionists are critical of what they see as men's unnecessary greed in this respect – even when it is the only way of raising low earnings. In the longer run some form of 'social dividend' (as suggested by Keith Roberts[16]) or negative income tax scheme seems essential.

III

For many women their really important work – childbearing, home-making, food producing, etc.[17] – is still largely unpaid. When they have undertaken occupations outside the ome, their aim is often to obtain sufficient cash to support their 'real' work inside the home. The significance of this may alter according to whether there is a partner contributing a proportion of what is needed, but the term 'pin-money' relates only to a patriarchal view of the world (men who use this expression are often unable to answer the question as to what proportion of their own income falls into that category).

Household work is nevertheless *real* work, despite its absence from official statistics of the Gross Domestic Product (largely because of the problems of measuring it; it is currently under research by some economists, mainly in USA and ILO). It is still largely undertaken by women, for the survey evidence of male participation shows this is mainly in the area of decorating, repair and maintenance of the house and garden, rather than in cleaning, cooking and childcare.[18] In other words, domestic jobs demanded of the male are less immediately demanding and therefore have greater flexibility in their timing. Even among 'shared housework' couples, women tend to retain responsibility for the chores that need to be done daily, or cannot easily be postponed until next week, such as shopping, preparing food and childcare. Indeed the shorter time horizon and spatial limitations necessitated by childbearing probably explain in large measure the origin of women's domestic role,[19] which in turn shapes and limits their paid employment roles. Research into time perceptions of different cultural or socio-economic groups have tended to show that subject peoples and working-class communities also appear to have shorter time horizons – necessitated largely by the struggle for survival, and living on a hand-to-mouth, day-to-day basis (although there is still room for interpretation of this sort of research).[20]

Women also play a large part in the 'marginal' economy: in community and local activities which may be partly in the 'gift' or voluntary area (giving time to chat to the elderly, shopping for the sick, looking after someone else's children), partly in that of 'exchange' or 'barter' (my apples for your beans, baby-sitting swaps), or partly in the 'cash', and even 'black', economy (repairing the car, catering for a party, painting the house). To some extent, of course, as more women take up paid employment they participate less in these types of activities, and the 'quality of life' in many localities is noticeably the poorer for it. But the debate is coming more into the open, sparked off perhaps by the government's search for ways of cutting the costs of welfare services and attempts to push them back to the community or the family – i.e. to women. As a result, some are saying, 'Wait a minute! What is this? How am *I* supposed to cope?'

As more men become unemployed, so they too are participating to a greater extent in this marginal area of the economy. Perhaps they do not recognise it, or derive the satisfactions (intrinsic and extrinsic) that such activities can bring, because they still see themselves and are seen as 'unemployed', or even as semi-criminal if they are not 'declaring earnings'. Thus, by its very nature, not enough is known about the 'black economy', despite many attempts to research it.[21] Current estimates are that it is around eight percent, and relatively insignificant in cash terms, but most researchers still add that there is probably even more 'uncovered' marginal earning, by women in particular.

A more useful way of re-perceiving the whole economy might be as one Canadian author[22] has expressed it: not only by *including* the 'domestic' and the 'marginal' economies, but by regarding the former as the main one and all others as derived from it, thus setting the traditional view on its head.

The corollary of reconceptualising working time and the going-out-to-work ethic is for men to play a greater part in household and community work, and for this to be recognised as legitimate. This could ease the feelings of despair and uselessness that currently characterises most enforced unemployment, regardless of the actual financial situation. But would women want this to happen? Is this the last area of activity that has remained the almost exclusive province of women, 'uncolonised' by men? There is some evidence of women delighting in martyring themselves under the dual burden of paid work and domestic work, of being perfectionists in both spheres – or at least of doing very little to adjust the chores more evenly within the family, despite the scope for doing so. Obviously these stresses arise partly from the guilts and fears felt by women in being deviant from their socially-given role, but they are issues that feminists need to face and discuss more openly when considering the sort of soicety they want to move towards. It is often all to easy to turn to the household chores as an excuse for not playing a more powerful role in a community activity or a political party – or to avoid the demands of a more responsible job. In so doing, women may also be denying their own needs for challenge and recognition, which are just as much part of themselves as their needs for giving and home-making. The two most common reactions to fear are 'aggression' and 'flight': if men tend to the former, women often exhibit the latter, with the loss of confidence and depression which may often result.

IV

Leisure time is the third major area of time use and again may be conceptualised in various ways, as mere cessation of normal work, relaxation in order to recover, entertainment and 'fun'; or as creative time giving the opportunity to learn a language, develop art or craft skills, and explore new areas of knowledge.[23] As paid work occupies less time,[24] so the scope for this 'third' type of leisure increases, and larger numbers of women already make use of time in this way, judging from enrolment figures at non-vocational adult education classes. Yet, just at the time when demand is likely to increase, 'the cuts' are reducing the facilities available.

In the use of leisure time (as in other time use), what can be done relates closely to how much time is available, but also to *how* it is spaced – a six-month sabbatical opens up very different possibilities from an extra week's annual holiday, or from a half-time job, or from a one hour reduction in each working day. EEC surveys of employee options on working time reductions have tended to show women favouring the shorter working day, with men preferring the longer holidays and longer hours. This difference is perhaps a result of the women's need of more time for household work rather than for the constructive leisure which many working women deny themselves. Relaxation of the rigidities of time use – in the schedules of organisations, schools and shops – could result in an improved quality of life, as would the generation of a greater choice of new and creative activities with which to fill our increasing quantity of leisure time.[25]

V

In focusing on the short-term time divisions of our daily lives we must not, of course, forget that women also tend to have a very long time horizon, perhaps related to the cycle of birth and death. It is this ability to be aware of patterns of life that makes us so concerned with ecological damage and the nuclear threat.

So where are all these 'time' jottings leading us? To the conclusion that competitive grabbing for whatever employment there is, as much cash as possible, as much expansion as possible along the lines of the traditional 'macho' model of society – what Robertson[26] calls the Hyper Expansionist (HE) Scenario – is undesirable for ourselves and our society? Yes. To the conclusion that women, in their wisdom have got the answer? Yes. Up to a point we are already nearer to achieving what Robertson has called the Sane Humane Ecological (SHE) society. Yet as feminists, we must not forget the need to explore our own ambivalences, uncertainties and shortcomings with respect to the changes that are taking place. Only in this way shall we be able to reflect on and use women's experiences and activities to understand and interpret the *human* condition – not only the basic needs of love and security but also of striving and recognition, of giving, receiving and achieving. It is with such an understanding and interpretation of the human condition that we are able to work towards a more balanced and worthwhile society.

27

Personal, Political and Planetary Play

Lin Simonon

Contemporary western society makes a rigid distinction between work and leisure, the hearth and the outside world, the sphere in which we achieve things and the sphere in which we nurture one another. It is also permeated with an inability to value play as a creative force. Lin Simonon meditates on the dualism which prevents this valuation, and explores ideas for an integration of play with productivity.

The Newtonian, patriarchal, mechanistic view of our world, upon which the Industrial Revolution of the last century was founded, was based upon 'mastery of nature'. This view has been superceded by the recognition, through quantum physics and the development of the science of ecology, that our universe is an interplay of dynamic natural forces, energies which flow, bounce and weave their way through our reality. We now see ourselves as a part of nature, part of a wonderful, intricate, fragile yet resilient web of interconnections. This view is non-linear, non-hierarchical, multi-dimensional, curved, organic and feminine in foundation.

Upon this perception we must now build our lives, our reality. A new dynamic must evolve, since patriarchy, with its highly developed ability to project concepts onto form, has produced an explosive situation which threatens us all. Working in a linear, goal- and work-orientated manner, patriarchy has given rise to highly sophisticated technology: the micro-chip, robotics, and so on. Ironically, there is within all this the potential for a quality of life based around leisure and play, a civilisation based upon humane values. Our present technology has also led us along less wise paths, towards dangerous consequences, primary amongst them splitting the atom that trespasses on the sacredness of life. The decision as to how to use our technology rests with us.

We are now in a painful transition time: marches against unemployment, enforced redundancies, the possiblity of a two-day working week, paranoia about the 'new technology' . . . and an information explosion which is not being adequately disseminated. These are all part of the impetus which has been created by a primarily patriarchal culture.

We must find a balance away from the 'culture of the hunt' towards the 'culture of the hearth'. Our emergent technology must now develop with elegance and truth to nature as a tool to enrich our planet and the quality of our lives. Silicon solar energy, heat pumps, aqua-culture, hydrophonics, wave power, ecological food production, perma-culture, aerodynamics and other gentle uses of the natural energies around us must be looked at. Finally, a new balance of sexual energies must evolve, appropriate to our times and the approach of the twenty-first century. The culture of the hunt has played itself out, the culture of the hearth must now be fostered.

Patriarchy as the culture of the hunt has become oppressive, its values out-worn, irrelevant. This is a system of control and 'order', a linear logic, the culture of categories, analysis, 'either or', the myth of objective truth, materialism, 'achievement', competition, the belief that 'right is might' and 'might is right'.

A new ecology of sexual energies must now come into play: the values of the hearth and the home as a part of the world at large. A womon's place is now in the world, which is, in fact, *our* home.

Whilst patriarchy is the culture of the hunt, matriarchy, or feminism, womonism, is the culture of the hearth, which is about nurturing and cooperation. It is about caring for and giving space to the other. It is about lateral energy structures, not hierarchical power structures. It is about practical synthesis, the practicality of the here and now. It is about our right to be creative without opressing the other. It is about spiritual and emotional values, the intangibles so difficult to quantify, it is giving and taking, inter-play. It is about being with one another and nature. It is about 're-production' rather than 'production' for the sake of production, a science of the hearth; creating a balanced, well-functioning organism – be it the family, the tribe or the earth of which we are a part.

Play is a recognition of the hearth, it is free flowing, an exploration taken within careful confines and practicality. Play is a recognition of an openness to the life forces within us and about us. Often-times tangential. A feminist view of play is surely that this is what life is for. That life is after all for the *living*. Play is for exploring the inter-relationship between all of us and for finding the optimum conditions in which it can take place; in which we all play our individual parts in the spinning and interweaving of our universe. As spacious as the sky, with its foundations upon the earth our home. The past as a dream, the future a fantasy, yet both conditioning the present.

Our children teach us so much about the nature of that approach to life. They are new to it all and just work it out as they go along. They rest comfortably in the now, they choose their playmates intuitively, they are relatively honest to themselves and are honestly dishonest to others. They have a wholeness of vision, before we fragment it into a 'curriculum' in our schools – they have to 'earn their living'.

In our work-orientated patriarchal culture, where are the neighbourhood playgrounds, the community cable TV, the everyday street theatre and other civilised playthings? Why are our children enclosed within institutions called schools for two-thirds of the year and during the daylight hours? Where are the spaces for adults and children to grow and play together? Where is the music on the streets? Where are the spaces for womon and man to find a new ecology of the sexes, to resolve the war, the polarisation, the discord between ourselves? Not on the 9.30 a.m. to Paddington, that is certain.

Our patriarchal world is based upon fear and competition. The newspapers perpetuate it and pornography plays a part in it. The culture demands it. The money system keeps it intact. Necessity makes us all participators in it. Serious work is the order of the day. If we refuse, then the threat is 'the bottom of the pile for you'. Everybody knows that 'No-body wants you when you are down and out'. But if you play the work game well, *then* the capitalist carrot is 'All of ad-land is yours'. Colour supplement paradise with the 'X' ingredient, if you keep your nose to the grindstone.

What a way to live! What a travesty of life this is. When all is said and done, our lives are a mixed blessing. But life *is* still a gift. This is a home-spun truth, but one that lives uneasily with blank tube-train stares, faceless bureaucrats, rampant tower blocks, the early morning rush-hour traffic, a troubled planet and two thirds of the world starving. Under such conditions, there is little incentive to live in the here and now.

Freedom is a myth, we are bounded by physical and personal constraints; it is only within such constraints that human response-ability can function. Play as exploration, is a way of finding new parameters, changing momentarily to suit the need. Play is the natural way to learn. Play is joyful, inventive, flexible, anarchic, finding a space that is inter-determined by mutual trust and the right

200

conditions within which it can take place. Through our play-lives we find new patterns of behaviour, a new culture evolves, new rituals take shape, new symbols come into being. Our play-lives have incredible potential for growth and creativity and the evolution of a new culture. Look at the football pitch, a baseball field, 'macho'-bully games. Enough! let us have cooperative games where there are no winners, no losers: play hard, play fair and no one gets hurt.

Watch womon enacting rituals together, around full moon time, opening out together, trusting and secure together. Loving one another. Laughing with one another. It is the beginnings of the birth of a new culture, a play culture, which includes identification with female values, shaping and refashioning those values through our interplay with one another and the moment.

We have seen enough of masculine values and seen what they have done. They have trapped us into enforced roles, and resulted in men taking themselves too seriously.

Some men are starting to learn the gentle art of play and to lose their rigidity, their need to always be right. Some are actually playing with their children, not forever playing the patriarch game. Some are learning from their children. Some can be seen carrying a child bound next to their hearts, having flexible, circular 'Why?' conversations with little ones. Some are *not* telling children 'not to cry'.

Womon through the ages has had to learn different ways of behaviour. She has had to learn flexibility, tangential ways of working, how to do four things at the same time – real, practical, time-and-motion study. She has had to learn to tune in to children; to learn to play with them; to explain things to them clearly and simply. She has found space to dream the past or the future, to play with ideas. She has had to learn patience, tolerance, cooperation and sometimes to 'leave well alone'. She has had to learn the necessity of expressing emotion in order to stay sane in a rough, old, world. She has learnt compassion for others in their struggles. In her relatively humble role within patriarchy, she has learnt the value of sometimes 'stepping down', managing to 'muddle through'. She knows as an everyday truth that culture can never control nature. She has also learnt other less creative 'truths' in the hot-house atmosphere of the nuclear family. She has learnt the awesome power of the female and how men fear that feminine part of themselves which they do not understand. A knowledge of those intangible everyday home truths is a part of the feminine ability to survive. These and many other things have become a part of the female psyche – your culture.

Both play and feminism are existential. Surely they are related to the way the womon at Greenham conduct themselves – with response-ability, earnestly, creatively, with courage, love and playfulness – as they weave their wool around the sentry boxes. They are the revolution, the evolution, the comedy of survival, their life skills applying themselves: re-evolution, a means consistent with the ends. Re-evolution, the positive beauty in our natures re-affirming itself, the positive interplay yet again of all our unique mortal energies. The personal, practical, political planetary, feminine interplay. A womon's culture, growing in strength to bring peace. A dynamic peace. The wheel turns, we are of age, play is part of our joyful change, our re-creation, our renaissance. Let us play together for a change.

Adult – 'What are you doing?'
Child – 'I don't know, I haven't finished yet.'

28
The Warp and the Weft
The Coming Synthesis of
Eco-Philosophy and Eco-Feminism

Hazel Henderson

We have seen women looking backwards into tradition, forwards into a wiser and better-informed future, and into their own, present lives to come up with inspiration for a better world. Hazel Henderson now puts the growing theory of eco-feminism into the context of cultural change as a whole, taking into account not only changes in values and political structure, but also a profound new direction emerging from within the very science whose mechanistic world-view has up to now underpinned our most disastrous attitudes towards the earth and each other.

Today, our planetary environment is threatened on a scale unprecedented in human history – from the extinction of species and loss of genetic diversity; the build-up of toxic and radioactive wastes; deforestation; desertification; to the massive alteration of the global climate. As this environmental devastation continues and threatens ever more dangerous confrontations between nations over dwindling oil resources, minerals, water and food, we see a retreat to the *laissez-faire* policies of the past: in the US, the politics of the Last Hurrah, the cowboy economics which led to these problems in the first place.

I shall try to explore the paradoxes of today in terms of this global breakdown of the now clearly unsustainable industrial order, with its competitive, expansionist, 'machismo', militaristic, patriarchal nation states. But I shall also try to show the growing evidence of a *breakthrough* occurring, as a new planetary culture is struggling to be born, with ethics and politics more fitted for human survival in the rising Solar Age.

The most fundamental error of the old order is in dealing only with monetary transaction, (never mind whether denominated in dollars, yen, francs, zlotys or roubles). By doing so the old order has created a map of only half the territory, a pale abstraction of production and resource-allocation systems that it calls 'the economy'. Then these one-eyed economists take this narrow, abstract map and try to use it to make social policy. This is the failure of macro-economic management. Economics then compounds this error by heroic levels of data aggregation, dreaming up national averages for such insane abstractions as 'unemployment', 'inflation', 'productivity', 'supply' and 'demand', and manipulating from Washington (or Brussels, Moscow or London) these statistical illusions which do not fit one *real-world case* anywhere! Similarly, a cost-benefit analysis averages out those costs and benefits that it counts, so that it obscures who are the winners and who are the losers: who will bear the costs and who will get the benefits and the profits. I have often speculated on whether there is really any such thing as 'profits' without some equal and unrecorded debit entry, either in some social or environmental ledger, or passed on to future generations. I am still puzzling. Perhaps 'profit' exists when two people exchange good quality information and deeply communicated insight or even wisdom. Perhaps 'profit' is when we really learn how to do more with less and meet our needs (not greeds) with minimal use of resources and disturbance of each other and the ecosystem of which we are a part. Perhaps it is when two species learn to live and co-evolve symbiotically; enjoying each other's entropy as much as 'production'. For production and entropy are two sides of the same coin. Detritus and decay have as much potential as temporarily structured forms. Order and disorder are in the eye of the beholder. When will we learn that there is no such thing as 'waste' – only unappreciated resources? A chicken is just an egg's way of making another egg. Likewise, plants and trees invented people and animals to be their 'waste-disposal units' for excess oxygen and their manufacturers of CO_2 and nutrients. This is Cosmic Economics, Nature's Economics. But humans had better learn it soon. The biggest lesson we have to learn is that we are not in charge of it and cannot 'manage' it or be its 'stewards' – we are its servants and its beneficiaries.

So let us lay to rest the old economic formula: inputs to production are wrongly stated as land, labour and capital. The future formula is that of a minimum-entropy society where the inputs are capital, resources and knowledge and the output is healthy people, healthy bio-regions on a peaceful, healthy, equitable, ecologically-viable planet! All this will require no harder striving than our current striving to destroy ourselves. It will probably be easier! In fact, it must be, since it is our fears which produce the counter-productive striving that underpins all industrial economies and has now led to their mutual checkmate.

Pieces of the new planetary agenda are popping up all over the place – everywhere in the world. Why should we be surprised at this or at the fact that they are in the process of coalescing into a new healthy critical mass? The planet, Gaia,[1] and the universe are now teaching us directly – nudging us along in the direction we must take, reconnecting us with the most fundamental living force: the urge to become all we can be, to evolve and to love it! We have this 'optimal programme' encoded in the proteins of our DNA. We *know* how to be healthy, how to cooperate as well as compete. These are older, deeper programmes than our cultural programming. We are learning once more to tune in to them and in to Nature, our surest teacher.

We do not yet know enough about our lovely, mysterious larger body, the planet Gaia, for us to be pessimistic. So it is unrealistic not to have faith. Today, the idealists and visionaries are truly pragmatic. The 'reality' of the 'realists' has vanished into history! Even economists admit that 'the economy has entered a new and unfamiliar domain'. This is why I subtitled my book *Creating Alternative Futures:The End of Economics*. Reductionist science has become the dogmatic religion of our age. We now have to move beyond both creationism *and* Darwinian evolutionism.[2]

Meanwhile the teeming richness of our whole exquisite biosphere has become our best textbook, as have the uncharted reaches of ourselves. New scientific research and theories (so many of them lovingly collected and offered to us by Marilyn Ferguson in *Brain-Mind Bulletin*[3] and *The Aquarian Conspiracy*[4]) are giving us a new basis for understanding our own power and shared responsibilities. The biologist Rupert Sheldrake writes of the possibility of 'morpho-genetic fields', and of research which can be interpreted to imply that species as a whole can learn from the isolated innovation of any small group.[5] Imagine the new potentialities if learning is proven to be contagious! We would have a new scientific basis for believing in ourselves and in our collective power to pull back from the disastrous brink. To chart a whole new course with new leadership based on 'sapiential authority'[6] wherever it emerges, and shared power and information in networks of autonomous people and communities sharing a similar vision of the human family on our precious little planet. Similarly heady implications are inherent in the Nobel prize-winning chemistry research of Ilya Prigogine, who in 1977 showed how living systems operating far from equilibrium can create more ordered structuring through fluctuations.[7] We need no longer bound our imagination with the dismal deterministic view of a universe winding down like a closed system. In fact, Cartesian science's search for certainty, equilibrium, predictability and control is a good definition of death. We should happily embrace the new view that uncertainty is fundamental, since it also implies that everything can change – for the better – in a twinkling of an eye!

Today, not surprisingly, the rich new yeast of alternative ideas is coming from 'wild card' scientists not intimidated by their peers, from precisely those groups suppressed or subordinated during the industrial era, with its increasing demands for conformity. Every culture is a system of *ex*pressions and *re*pressions of the full spectrum of human ways of being and behaving. Today we see these alternatives emerging from the world's ethnic and indigenous peoples, from subsistence cultures and traditional wisdom; from the world's women and from the rising female principle, whose nurturant energies can be seen in the new breed of gentle-men. They are throwing off the shackles of industrial 'machismo', the need to compete with each other and the fearful need to control, dominate and 'own' not only each other, but women, children, animals, plants and all of Mother Nature. Psychologists know that these unhealthy drives are rooted in the fear of death, the sense of alienation from the natural world, which is produced at the breakdown of the 'bi-cameral' mind[8] and reinforced by western dualistic culture. As Ken Wilber notes in *Up From Eden*,[9] 'Whenever there is *other*, there is fear.' Any separate, egoistic consciousness, to the extent that it feels separated from all life, will fear its individual death as a final extinction, a total loss of meaning that must lead to existential anxiety. This fear has underlain thousands of years of dualism in human cultures. It has shaped western art, literature and scholarship from Aristotle and his either/or logical axiom: the Law of the Excluded Middle (A cannot be equal to not-A). These same fears of death and loss of meaning led to the neurotic notion of scientific objectivity, eventually laid to rest by the physics of Werner Heisenberg and his Uncertainty Principle. We see it in the long saga of patriarchal literature, from the Greek myths of the hero and the hero's journey to the *angst* and alienation from Nature echoed from Hegel, Marx and the Frankfurt School to Hermann Hesse, the existentialists and Sigmund Freud and his followers.

My belief is that this kind of scholarship and mode of experience, together with reductionist Cartesian science is now becoming another cul-de-sac: mental games of infinite regress terminating in a logical double-bind. This may be one more aspect of the dilemma of patriarchy. For this anxiety about 'alienation' is, I venture, a somewhat masculine experience. Since, biologically, humans do come in two asymmetrical bodily forms, it is obviously different to experience life in a male and a female body. Biologically, most women in the world do still vividly experience their embeddedness in Nature, and can harbour few illusions concerning their freedom and separatedness from the cycles of birth and death. Men's experience may give them a sense of having rather more freedom and individualism, and for the past 6,000 years this sense, together with the alienation it brings, has been amplified. All patriarchal culture, scholarship, institutions and history have reflected and amplified male experiencing, and then universalised it as if it were *human* experience. Of course it is not. But until quite recently, women have been relatively silent about their own experience, and *her*-story, which as we know from feminist literature and art is radically different. In precisely this area, women's spirituality affirms and celebrates human embeddedness in Nature and confirms it by researching the early matri-focal cultures and humanity's first great universal religion: that of the Great Mother·Goddess.[10]

Today's eco-feminism is restoring this earlier pre-*history*, and its art and rituals, which celebrate Nature as an order that is, *in principle* not fully knowable precisely because humans are a part of it. Eco-feminism once more views Nature as sacred. It understands the heuristic value of uncertainty, which allows each generation to reformulate its experience, cognition, epistemology and value systems in light of new conditions. Uncertainty is valuable because it keeps us awake and aware, whereas certainty and exactitude allows us to 'hard-programme' our responses to our environment, become rigid or fall asleep mentally. Eco-feminism also values motherhood and the parenting and raising of children and the maintaining of comfortable habitats and cohesive communities as the most highly productive work of society – rather than the most de-valued, as under patriarchal values and economics where these tasks are ignored and unpaid.

Patriarchal scholarship is now arriving at an understanding of many of these more subtle patterns of society, sometimes experientially, as many of the support-systems provided by women break down. In traditional science it is also arriving at the understanding that alienation and the ego-individualistic, dualistic view may have been a trick of the mind. Amazingly these new holistic insights are now being reached through the anomalies and paradigm shifts in science itself.

In such new theories embracing these subtle indeterminacies, the *implicate* order rather than the *explicate*, and the new, open view of a surprising, living, autopoetic, evolving universe emerge.

This new stream of scholarship, together with the enormously rich body of knowledge grounded in ecology can be summed up as *eco-philosophy*, and it represents the simultaneous culmination, compression and transcending of Cartesian forms of representation and intellectual discourse. The separate but parallel stream of scholarship represented by eco-feminism documents precisely the same set of insights, but, as in Oriental modes of cognition and representation, eco-feminism has arrived at them experientially. Thus, up to now, there has been almost no communication between eco-philosophy and eco-feminism, because they have approached the same phenomena from different directions. Eco-feminism has considered the glittering cathedrals of abstract, mathematical, rational patriarchal exposition of this human oneness as a somewhat heroic intellecutal labour about something banal, almost trivial (i.e. 'What's all the fuss and debate about? Doesn't everybody feel that in their bones?'). On the other hand, eco-philosophy senses this disinterest, and assumes that women are just not up to such heroic scientific strivings (after all, the hero's journey *is* a male trip!). Besides, thinks the intellectual, those feminist books are so 'fuzzy' and unreadable. Not to mention threatening, with their celebration of goddesses, trees, orgies, sexuality, witches, spirits, fertility, devas, acceptance of our bodies, our experience of pain, decay, entropy and the endless cycles of birth and death.

I believe that these two separate streams of scholarship and world-views are now beginning to flow together and augur a new cultural synthesis, as well as a more androgynised consciousness, flowering in men and women. The communication is still halting and fraught with old fears, resentments and insecurities. But if we are to prescribe for our almost terminal illness, we must dig deeply for our diagnoses. We can no longer skate around observing surface manifestations, such as those offered by economists: 'unemployment'; 'inflation'; 'declining productivity'; 'the need for national security'; 'stopping communism'; 'restoring the free market'; 'more innovation' and 'supply' to meet 'demand', and all the rest of the psychotic language of alienation, fear and insecurity.

The most enduring tensions in the human psyche have concerned this alienation and fear of death of the ego, and the conflict these feelings generated between the perceived individual will and the requirements of the group or society. These fears have led to what I call the 'Kilroy Was Here' syndrome, where immortality is attempted via leaving one's mark on the environment, be it the urge to create monuments or completely cut down a forest. They have also led to the fundamental conflicts that have preoccupied all political science, social control theories and governance, as well as views of what constitutes 'human nature', its goodness or evil, and what mixes within the spectrum of anarchy and authoritarianism are preferable.

I believe there is a deeper layer underlying this old issue of the individual versus the state, that may shed more light on why matrifocal cultures and religions were overthrown and what led to the rise of patriarchal culture, which is itself now collapsing. Perhaps the deeper and biologically-irreconcilable conflict is that of the individual human *phenotype* versus the species *genotype*. Nature is always profligate with phenotypes, since diversity and range of experimentation require a profusion of these fresh generations of finite forms interacting with every successive set of unique environmental conditions. Only a statistically insignificant number of phenotypes ever produce a genetically useful innovation of form or function that survives and is incorporated into the human gene pool. From the perspective of the genotype (i.e., the species as a whole), the fate of each individual phenotype is irrelevant. Now for *other* species, this ignominious fate may not produce a psychological conflict in the phenotype. At least, we have not sufficiently learned to communicate with other life forms (for example whales, dolphins or chimpanzees) to know one way or the other. But we do know that humans possess this de-stabilised, bi-cameral mind, so that we are aware of being aware of ourselves. We live as phenotypes with will and purposes beyond that of our species genotype, and move beyond pre-human, embedded consciousness which is continuous with the phylogenetic infant experience of oneness with the mother and the world.

I believe that the matri-focal period of human development may have had at its core a value-system tilted toward the genotype, in its celebration of the *processes* of life, its changes, cycles, seasons, subtle forces, as well as the positive value of decay, entropy and death, all of which allows the grand experiment of evolution to unfold. Phenotypes must die if each new generation is to have its chance. But the dying of the body on the material plane of existence is also one more transition, if we have a larger view of ourselves as an integral part of creation: temporarily constituted as a sensory cell of the body of Gaia, but also having a transcendent dimension, as all our spiritual traditions describe. I believe that the early patriarchal revolt against the societies which worshipped the Mother Goddess was partly the agonised scream of the phenotype's newly-individuated, ego-awareness rebelling against the great implacable Goddess/Mother/Earth: the genotype's metaphors for the genotype, that decreed the phenotype's sacrifice and death-sentence. If there is any substance to this hypothesis, it may explain the deeply-buried fear of women, mother and earth and their mythic connection with decay, entropy and death, expressed in mythology and recently examined in male psychology.[11]

We may now be emerging from this period of the revolt of the individuated ego-awareness. The human species learned much in this extraordinary period – too much in this mental/manipulative mode for our own good, as we now face the possibility of accidentally annihilating ourselves. Thus the emerging culture is re-balancing itself by including repressed ways of being based on the heart as well as the mind: feeling, intuition, acceptance of uncertainty, decay as well as growth, and transcendence of ego-death fears and letting go of the need to control and 'own' each other and the world around us. This emerging culture seems also to be re-awakening concern for the genotype and evolution: for example, in the concern over nuclear radiation, mutagenic chemicals and other inter-generational transfers of risk about which economics and political science can say little. Therefore, there seems to be no going back to rugged decentralism, or the frontier, self-sufficient lifestyle of which the survivalists dream, with their shelters, dried food, geiger-counters and guns. Nor can we return to the individualistic, private property-based security promised by the Libertarians, who would repeal government, but do not seem to notice that large industrial corporations would still be there to take over our government overtly.

However, many Libertarian proposals for repealing oppressive, bureaucratic restrictions and laws on personal behaviour of and between consenting adults are very useful, whether in a showdown with the Moral Majority's efforts to control our private sex lives and lifestyle preferences, or the Catholic church's anti-abortion campaigns and their rigid definition of when human life begins which, if enacted, would mean the risk of jail for millions of Americans. But all this too, smacks of the same fears of the old patriarchs who still lead most of the world's nations, corporations, churches, labour unions and other civilian and military institutions. They still send their sons to fight and die for them and seek to 'own' their women and children in male-authoritarian families (now revealed as rife with violence, repression, wife-battering, incest and child abuse). The patriarchs also want to continue dominating the earth, exploiting its forests, minerals and land. They are correct in being fearful of the rising, ecologically-aware, androgynised, planetary culture, because it will overwhelm them and their rearguard actions. Fear underlies the Politics of the Last Hurrah, Reaganomics, and the Moral Majority's attempts to put women back in the kitchen, gay people back in the closet, blacks and hispanics back at the end of the line. Yet the genie will not go back in the bottle. The cultural revolution has already occurred. Politics only ratifies social change after at least a ten-year lag. Even more terrifying for the old patriarchs and their female dupes is the knowledge that the whole culture is 'up for grabs'. For example, it could shift fundamentally in less than a generation *if* women simply took back their reproductive rights, endowed by biology and Nature. All that women would need to do to create a quiet revolution is to resume the old practice of concealing the paternity of their children. As Margaret Mead said, 'Maternity is a biological fact – paternity is a social invention.' Thus, male-dominated families, institutions of inheritance, property rights in wives and children would be undermined. Accumulation of great land-holdings and estates would be less likely. Land trusts and different, more consensual democratised families and social groups might emerge. Children, in whatever group settings they were raised, would have rights as persons, rather than being 'legitimised' by a marriage contract. Indeed, we now have to face up to the fact that, in the US at least, the traditional nuclear family with bread-winning father, home-making mother and two children now only comprises 12 percent of all US families, and that 85 percent of welfare payments to support children in Aid to Dependent Families goes to the ex-wives and children of men who refuse to pay the child-support payments ordered by the courts.[12] Already, the nuclear family is becoming a lost cause.

Only a biological, morphogenetic model of change can encompass and help us see the planetary transformaton now occurring in so many dimensions simultaneously. This change, familiar to biologists as that by which a chrysalis turns into a butterfly, is characterised by acceleration, and by the inability to infer from any of the *existing* states of the system its *future* state. Both eco-philosophy and eco-feminism have shown the capacity to deal with such dimensions of breakdown and breakthrough. Their synthesis, together with insights from ecology and general systems theory, and the perennial philosophy shared by many of the spiritual traditions, may provide the ethics and the value systems for the Solar Age.[13] The logic of the emerging post-Cartesian science will at last transcend 'objectivity' and dualism. It will be based on self-referential, autopoetic logic, where the observers must account for their logical position in the system they seek to describe.[14] This will produce a more honest science where the role and impact of the observer is clearly acknowledged as affecting the phenomena or experiment. It will also provide 'full disclosure' of the personal reasons and motivations of the scientist for studying this phenomenon rather than another, since the first normative decision of any scientist is to decide what to pay attention to, among the infinite sets of data 'out there'. Post-Cartesian science will be a science with reverence, gently descriptive and exploratory without the compulsion to intervene. It will produce a revolution in technology, so that we will think more carefully before intervening, and a problem of production will not always conjure up visions of factories and machines in our minds. Instead, we will scan eco-systems for signs of redundant potential or places where natural ecosystem production can be augmented. This is fundamentally a *heterarchical* view. Hierarchy is an illusion generated by a fixed observer. The synthesis of eco-philosophy and eco-feminism is now being midwifed by both women and men.

Thus in general terms, we are quite aware of the basic principles on which the New World Order must be built:

– the value of all human beings

– the right to satisfaction of basic human needs (physical, psycho-logical and metaphysical) of all human beings

– equality of opportunity for self-development for all human beings

– recognition that these principles and goals must be achieved within ecological tolerances of lands, seas, air, forests and the total carrying capacity of the biosphere.

– recognition that all these principles apply, with equal emphasis, to future generations of humans and their biospheric life-support systems, and thus include the respect for all other life forms and the Earth itself.

Historically, human development can be viewed as many local experiments at creating social orders of many varieties, but usually based on partial concepts: i.e., those social orders, based on the exploitation of nature, worked for some people at the expense of other people. Furthermore, they worked in the short-term but have failed in the long-term. Today, all these experiments of local and partial human development, when seen in a planetary perspective, have been failures in one way or another, based on some form of short-term exploitation (destabilisation).

We now know that such societies are impossible to maintain and that the destabilisations on which they have built themselves are affecting their internal, political stability and the global stability of the planet. Interestingly, these instabilities can all be stated in scientific terms:

1. In classical equilibrium thermodynamics: in terms of the Law of Conservation and the Law of Entropy. That all human societies (and all living systems) take 'negentropy' (available forms of energy and concentrated materials) and transform them into entropic waste at various rates. We can measure and observe these ordering activities and the disorder they create elsewhere, e.g., the structuring of European countries in their colonial periods at the price of the concomitant disordering of their colonies, culturally and with regard to indigenous resources.

2. In terms of biology and the evolutionary principle: 'nothing fails like success.' For example the trade-offs between short-term and long-term stability and structure, or adaptation versus adaptability.

3. In terms of general systems theory: the phenomenon of sub-optimisation, i.e., optimising some systems at the expense of their enfolding systems.

4. In terms of ecology: as violations of the general principle of interconnectedness of ecosystems and the total biosphere. This interconnectedness of all sub-systems on planet Earth is much more fundamental than the interdependence of people, nations, cultures, technologies, etc.

Thus, the aspirations for a new World Order are not only based on ethical and moral principles (important as these emerging planetary values will be for our species' survival). The need for a new World Order can now be *scientifically* demonstrated. We see the principle of interconnectedness emerging out of the very reductionist science which once denied it, and the concomitant ecological reality that redistribution is also a basic principle of nature. Since all ecosystems periodically redistribute energy, materials and structures through biochemical and geophysical processes and cycles, therefore all of the social systems of the human species must also conform to these principles: redistributing these same resources, whether primary energy and materials, or derived 'wealth' (capital, social structures, means of production and political power) as well as continually changing institutions.

213

I can see *six* principles emerging in westernised science itself, which imply human behavioural adaptation of the kind now emerging.

Interconnectedness: planetary cooperation of human societies.

Redistribution: justice, equality, balance, reciprocity.

Change: re-design of institutions, perfecting means of production, changing paradigms and values.

Complementarity: unity *and* diversity, from either/or to both/and.

Heterarchy: as opposed to hierarchy.

Indeterminacy: many viewpoints, compromise, humility, openness, societies capable of *learning*.

Will it be breakdown or breakthrough? Stress is evolution's tool, and today we are being stressed to change and evolve as never before. In this sense, the new resource limits and challenges we face are good news! They are stressing us to grow up – to become all that we can be – to discover 'the possible humans' that we are.

Prayer for Continuation

1

There is a record
I wish to make here.
A life.
And not this life alone
but the thread
which keeps shining
like gold floss woven into cloth
which catches your eyes
and you are won over.

Kyrie Eleison
Baruch a toi
Hosana adonai
Omne padme   Gloria
Nam Myo-Ho
Renge Kyo
Galan
galancillo.
Do you love
this world?

Where is the point I can enter?
Where is the place I can touch?

Let me tell you
I am so serious
and taking aim
like a woman with a bow
eyes looking silently
at each space between the trees
for movement.

2

I cannot begin now.
I do not wish to write these numbers
on this page here.
224 warheads destroy
every Soviet city with a population
over 100,000.
But once I begin writing
the figures do not stop.
A 20 megaton
bomb, a firestorm rages over
3,000 acres.
A 1,000 megaton bomb
destroys
California
Nevada, Utah, Oregon,
Puget Sound.
Destroys.
California.

3

Thirty-seven days from my
fortieth birthday. I have
gone up and down this coast
so many times I could trace
the shape of it for you
with my hands, up
into the high cold trees, down
to warm water and
the sprawling city
where I was
born, 1943.
In that year
while I slept
not entirely wanted
in a still room
behind venetian blinds
somewhere in a foreign language
babies were set on fire.
Their cries did not wake me.

Only I breathed in the dust
of their deaths.

4

It is my love I hold back
hide
not wanting to be seen
scrawl of hand
writing
don't guess
don't guess at my
passion
a wholly wild and raging
love for this world.

5

(Home)
If you look in this block
in the North of California
you will find a house
perhaps a century old
with the original wood shingles
dark from years of sun
and fine old joints, the men
who made them are dead, the attic
made into a bedroom now, the
linoleum added in 1955.
Twenty years ago
I lived there, a student
studying the history of
Western Civilization, reading John Milton,
looking out the attic window
at a cement sidewalk
which was before just a
dirt path
and Spanish, and was before
perhaps, a forest or a
meadow, a field,
belonging to the Ohlone
who have all
even their children

even all traces of who they were
perished.

6

This is the world I was born into.
Very young I learned
my mother and my father
had a terrible sorrow.
And very young
I learned this sorrow from them.

7

The mind is vast
what we know small.
Do you think we are not all
sewn together?
I still argue with her
grit my teeth trying to feel
the pain that riddled her body
the day they told her
she would never walk.
I try to enter her mind
the night she took her own life.

Cells have memory!
I shout to her.
Science gave you
an unnecessary despair.

8

Nor do they argue
nor do they understand
nor do they know
but still it is so.
And there are structures of
unknowing
we call disbelief.

9

Every American city
with a population above
25,000
targeted.
A bomb with the
explosive power
of 20 million tons of TNT.
80 per cent of all cancers.
How is it,
this woman asks,
the brilliant efforts of
American scientists
have been put
to such destructive uses?

10

It is not real, they tell us,
this home we long for
but a dream of a place
that never
existed.
But it is so familiar!
And the longing in us is
ourselves.

11

This is the world I was born into.
I saw the wave and its white curl.
I saw branches coming from trees
like streams from rivers.
And the water poisoned
and the land.
I saw the whale leap out of the water
I saw my child's eyes come out of me
                her first cry.
And the air, the rain acid.

Kyrie Eleison
Baruch a toi

Hosana
Adonai
Do you love the world?

12

Suppose she lay down her bow.
And went into
that place
stepping so slowly
so surely

13

This is what I wanted to tell you.
This is what I wanted to say.
Words come late and dark
near sleep.
She said to me
my head was eating my heart.
And what is good?
What is bad?
The delicacy of transmission.
Old alliances fracture
like the cold branches of a
winter tree.
This is the closest I can get.
The world is washed in space.
It is the words she used
precisely those
and I could not remember them.
Only my conviction.
There was badness and goodness.
One was bad.
The other suffered.
And I wanted to
I wanted to mend her.
She told me the whole story
and I told her what was
good and what was bad,
and this was not what she needed.
You think I am trying
to throw away morality

but I am not.
I am not trying to
throw away caring.
In a dream
I see myself
a handsome man
walking without feeling
into a desert.
I am not like him
yet this dream comes to me
and I feel grief.
Out at the edge of this territory
is a missile.
I know for certain
this weapon is bad.
I do not try to mend her
and this makes me weep
for what she has suffered.

14

(The Enemy)
I wanted you to be good.
I wanted your judgements.
But all your rules became ash.
Your goodness was like an island.
(Your sainthood *was* the sin.)
Now that you have fallen
I cross the water
wrestle with you
charge you to bless me
watch as you
appear and disappear
become me.

15

The mind is vast.
A whale blows.
Shall we pitch ourselves into terror?
Shall we come home?
Enter darkness, weep
know the dimension
of absence, the unreachable deep.

16

How far can they go?
This is my speech
an American speech of whalers
and farmers what my
people did
plain, simple, honed
to the point
how far will they go?
Is there a stopping point?
Everyone knows there is not.

17

What can we make of this?
Two children held hostage together
in a van
for ten months.
What kind of man?
A girl, born three years ago
in California,
a boy who was born in
and survived Vietnam.
How far?
The children were continually beaten
with a rubber hose
and forced into sexual acts
in exchange for being fed.
I am a woman
who reads this story
in a newspaper.

18

(Bone Cancer)
You must not let terror overtake you.
It is a bone breaking in the middle of the night.
It is a misspelled word.
It is everything you thought you knew
becoming unknown, the leaves
stripped from the tree,

all the greenness orange and dry,
it is pain past bearable, you must not.
Down the street in the darkness someone young
is dying. The soil, perhaps, under your feet
is poison, the water you drink.
What is this? Be reasonable. Disaster
is always predicted and look
we exist. Humanity had a day of birth,
slow, unreasoned, surprising. Now,
is it possible, is it possible
could this be?

19

Do we not want
this place
to find it
the body again
hearth, heart.
How is it I can say this
so that you will
see too what I have seen.
After the fires
(after the unspeakable)
there will be no home.
And what of us
will remain in memory?
Nothing?

20

At least we think of them.
The six million.
We long for them.
Want them to be like they were
before
want the music
their mothers and fathers sang
to pass from our lips.
And we ask
How is it they did not know?

21

Do you think it is right
to despair?
No, no, it is not about
right and wrong.
It is the thread
shining.

22

Kyrie Eleison
Baruch a toi adonai
Omne Padme.
New rules
take the place of the old.
Be Here Now
is the lesson.
But I do not want to be.
I am one hundred years away
into the future.
My heart aches wondering.
Will this old tree grow even bigger?
Will its roots threaten the foundation of this house?
Will there be a daughter of a
        daughter of a daughter
        a son? And what is the
look in their eyes? Tell me
what you see there. And
do you like to watch
them as they walk across
fields.

Fields?

Susan Griffin

Notes and References

Chapter 3: Unholy Secrets (pp. 20–33)

1. Graham, S. *et al.*, 'Methodological Problems and Designs of the Tri-State Leukemia Survey', *Annals of the Academy of Science*, 107, pp. 557–569, New York, 1963.

2. Bertell, R., 'Measurable Health Effects of Diagnostic X-ray Exposure', Testimony before the US House of Representatives, Committee on Interstate and Foreign Commerce, Subcommittee on Health and the Environment, 11 July 1978, in *Effect of Radiation on Human Health: Radiation Health Effects of Medical and Diagnostic X-rays, Vol. 2*, US Government Serial No. 95–180, pp. 80–139, 1978.

3. Bertell, R., 'X-ray Exposure and Premature Ageing', *Journal of Surgical Oncology*, 9, pp. 379–391, 1977.

4. *Ibid.*; Bertell, 1978, *op cit.*; Bertell, R., 'Response of R. Bertell to the Critique of Michael Ginevan', *Health Physics Journal*, Vol. 41, No. 2, August 1981.

5. Bertell, 1978, *op cit.*

6. *Ibid.*; Bross, I.D.J. and Natarajan, N., 'Genetic Damage from Diagnostic Radiation', *Journal of the American Medical Association*, 237, (22), p. 2399, 1977.

7. Bertell, 1978, *op cit.*

8. *Op cit.*, ref. 6; Bross, I.D.J. and Natarajan, N., 'Preconception Radiation and Leukaemia', *Journal of Medicine*, 4, pp. 276–281, 1973; Muller, H.J., 'Radiation and Heredity', *American Journal of Public Health*, 54, 1, pp. 42–50, 1964; Bross, I.D.J. and Natarajan, N., 'Cumulative Genetic Damage in Children Exposed to Preconception and Intrauterine Radiation', *Investigative Radiology*, Vol. 15, No. 1, 1980; Shino, P.H. *et al.*, 'Preconception Radiation, Intrauterine Diagnostic Radiation and Childhood Neoplasia', *Journal of the National Cancer Institute*, (US), Vol. 65, No. 4, 1980; Bertell, R., 'The Nuclear Worker and Ionizing Radiation', *American Industrial Hygiene Association Journal*, 40, 5, 1979.

9. Freeman, Leslie J., *Nuclear Witnesses: Insiders Speak Out*, W.W. Norton and Co., pp. 33–35, New York/London, 1981. The Barker Plant was proposed by the New York State Gas and Electric Co. The public hearing was held in Spring 1974.

10. *Ibid.*

11. Stewart, A.M., 'Delayed Effects of A-Bomb Radiation: a Review of

225

Recent Mortality Rates and Risk Estimates for Five-Year Survivors', *Journal of Epidemiology and Community Health*, 36, pp. 80–86, 1982.

12. International Commission on Radiological Protection, *Radiation Standards and Public Health*, Proceedings of a Second Congressional Seminar on Low-Level Radiation, Congressional Research Service, Library of Congress, Washington DC, 10 February 1978. See especially pp. 8–18; ICRP, No. 26, Pergamon Press, 1977, contains information on the history and structure of the organisation.

13. Morgan, Karl Z., 'Cancer and Low Level Radiation', *The Bulletin of the Atomic Scientist*, Vol. 34, September, 1978.

14. United States Department of Energy, 'Announced US Nuclear Tests, July 1945–December 1981', Office of Public Affairs and Nevada Operations Office, NVO-209, Rev. 2, January 1982. See also enclosures.

15. *Ibid.*

16. The Department of Energy will provide update sheets for 1982–83, including kiloton estimates. Las Vegas, Nevada Newspapers also report tests.

17. *Ibid.*

18. US House of Representatives, 'The Forgotten Guinea Pigs: A Report on the Health Effects of Low-Level Radiation Sustained as a Result of the Nuclear Weapon Testing Program Conducted by the United States Government', US Government Printing Office Document, No. 65–7030, August 1980.

19. *Ibid.*

20. *Ibid.* Also Wasserman, H. and Solomon, N., *Killing Our Own*, Delta Publishing Co., 1982.

21. See appendix of International Commission on Radiological Protection, No. 26, Pergamon Press, 1977.

22. Pearson, J.S., *A Sociological Analysis of the Reduction of Hazardous Radiation in Uranium Mines*, United States Department of Health, Education and Welfare, National Institute for Occupational Safety and Health, HEW Pub. No. (NIOSH) 75–171, Salt Lake City, Utah, April 1975. Also Kilgour, A., 'Uranium Mining: Who Pays, Who Profits?', *Our Generation*, Vol. 14, No. 2.

23. United States Department for Health, Education and Welfare, National Institute of Occupational Safety and Health Report, 'The Risk of Lung Cancer Among Underground Miners of Uranium-Bearing Ore', 30 June 1980.

24. Commission of the European Communities, 'Information and Training on Radiation Protection for Trade Union Representatives from Nine Member States of the E.C.', Doc. No. 1975/77e, Luxembourg, June 1977.

25. The bone marrow dose from an ordinary chest X-ray is 1 to 7 millirem, depending on the speed and the shielding. If one assumed the very best equipment, the 500 millirem maximum for the public would be equivalent to 500 chest X-rays for bone marrow exposure.

26. Alvarez, Robert, 'Radiation Exposure Limits', *Bulletin of the Atomic Scientist*, Vol. 36, pp. 58–59, November 1980.

27. Bertell, R. *et al.*, *Umwelteinflusse auf dasÜberleben Unreifer Neugeborener,* Wisconsin, USA, 1963–1975. Arztebundes für Umwelt-und Lebensschutz e.V., Guldenhagen 41, D34 Gottingen, West Germany. (English version under review for publication.)

28. Gervasi, Tom, *Arsenal of Democracy II*, Grove Press Inc., New York, 1981.

29. 'Global Distribution of Commercial Nuclear Generators', *Nuclear News*, August 1979.

30. Kochupillai, N. *et al.*, 'Down's Syndrome and Related Abnormalities in an Area of High Background Radiation in Coastal Kerala', *Nature*, Vol. 262, 1 July 1976; Sternglass, E.J. and Bell, S., 'Fallout and the Decline of Scholastic Aptitude Scores', presented at the Annual Meeting of the American Psychological Association, 3 September, 1979. Published in *Phi Delta Kappan*, pp. 539–545, April 1983.

31. New height and weight charts were issued in the US in 1982 because of the statistically significant increase in weight. Cohn, V., 'A-Plant Involved in Probe of Thyroid Ills', *Washington Post*, 21 February, 1980; Beierwaltes, W.H. *et al.*, 'Radioactive Iodine Concentration in the Fetal Human Thyroid Gland from Fall-Out', *Journal of the American Medical Association*, Vol. 173, pp. 1895–1902, 27 August 1960. Radioactive iodine is used medically to reduce thyroid tissue, lowering the thyroid hormone level in the body. This is related to slowing metabolism rate resulting in weight gain.

32. Based on the research of Ralph Dogherty, Florida State University. In 1938, 0.5 per cent of the male students were functionally sterile. In 1980, 23 per cent were functionally sterile. NB The older infertility rate for males was 1 in 200 or 1 in 250.

33. Female spontaneous abortion rate is hard to document. Loss of embryos is estimated to be as high as 50 per cent. This is a conservative estimate of foetal loss.

Chapter 4: Seveso is Everywhere (pp. 36–45)

1. It has recently come to light that the most toxic synthetic material available in chemical form, '2–4–5–T' with its 'tcf' base (known to be a highly effective chemical defoliant), is being imported into the UK as a pesticide/weedkiller for common use. Much of it is re-exported to Third World countries, but roughly one third is kept in Britain. The Farmers' Union wants to ban it, but the British Government is saying there is absolutely no evidence to show it is dangerous to life.

2. These details come from the District Office of Inspection and Labour Relations.

Chapter 5: The Politics of Women's Health (pp. 46–58)

1. Opinions expressed in this paper are mine, but the ideas have grown out of discussions with women in the Women's Health Movement, particularly

women in The Politics of Health Group, The Women and Science (London) Group, and women on the Health Study Tour to China (1978) and the Health Study Tour to Cuba (1981).

2. Elston, Mary Ann, 'Reclaiming our Bodies: Health Handbooks by and for Women', *Women's Studies International Quarterly*, Vol. 2, p. 117, 1979.

3. Fee, Elizabeth, 'Women and Health Care: A Comparison of Theories', *International Journal of Health Services*, Vol. 5, No. 3, p. 397, 1975.

4. Doyle, Lesley and Elston, Mary Ann, *Medicine and Health*, Open University, Unit 14, Course U221: 'The Changing Experience of Women', 1983.

5. Department of Health and Social Security (The Black Report), *Inequalities in Health*, Report of Research Working Group, DHSS, 1980.

6. 'Women and Health', Report of the Third International Women and Health Conference held in Geneva, June, 1981, *ISIS International*, 20, 1981.

7. 'Genital Mutilation', *ISI International*, 8, 1978.

8. Rakusen, Jill, 'Feminism and the Politics of Health', *Medicine in Society*, Vol. 8, No. 1, p. 17, 1982.

9. Saffron, Lisa, 'A Barrier to Cervical Cancer', *Spare Rib*, p. 14, April, 1982.

10. Wyner, Lesley, 'Under the Doctor: Women and Psychiatric Drugs', 50 Grove Park, London SE5.

11. Doyle, Lesley, *op. cit.*

12. Rakusen, Jill, *op. cit.*

13. *Our Bodies, Ourselves: A Health Handbook by and for Women*, British edition by Angela Phillips and Jill Rakusen, Penguin Books, London, 1978.

Other Useful References

'Health Services in China', a special issue of *China Now*, Society of Anglo-Chinese Understanding, December, 1978.

The Cuba-phile (Health in Cuba), Britain-Cuba Resource Centre, 1982.

The Politics of Health Group Newsletter from POHG, c/o BSSRS, 9 Poland Street, London W1.

Ehrenrich, Barbara and English, Deirdre, (a) *Witches, Midwives and Nurses : a History of Women Healers*, Compendium, London, 1974; (b) *Complaints and Disorders: The Sexual Politics of Sickness*, Feminist Press, New York (1976); (c) *For Her Own Good : 150 Years of the Experts' Advice to Women*, Pluto Press, London, 1979. Three 'classics' of the Women's Health Movement giving a historical perspective to the issues of women's health.

Leeson, Joyce and Gray, Judith, *Women and Medicine*, Tavistock Women's Studies, London, 1978. Includes sections on women as providers of health care, women as users of health services and women organising around health issues.

Doyle, Lesley and Pennell, Imogen, *The Political Economy of Health*, Pluto Press, London, 1979. A good overview of the issues of the politics of health.

Chapter 6: Feminism – Healing the Patriarchal Dis-Ease
(pp. 59–65)

1. Vithoulkas, George, *The Science of Homeopathy,* Grove Press, London, 1980.

2. Shuttle, Penelope, and Redgrove, Peter, *The Wise Wound,* Victor Gollancz, London, 1978. See chapter 6.

3. Special thanks to Mary Daly, *Gyn/Ecology: The Metaethics of Radical Feminism,* The Women's Press, London, 1979, for gyn-ergetic inspiration.

Chapter 7: Feminism and Ecology; Theoretical Connections (pp. 67–72)

1. Briffault, Robert, *The Mothers,* Atheneum, New York, p. 35, 1977.

2. Neslen, Kristie, *The Origin,* Venusian Propaganda, San Francisco, p. 43, 1979.

3. Davis, Elizabeth Gould, *The First Sex,* G.P. Putnam Sons, New York, 1971.

4. Neumann, Erich, *The Great Mother,* Princeton University Press, New Jersey, p. 221, 1974.

Chapter 8: Roots: Black Ghetto Ecology (pp. 73–85)

I want to thank these women for helping me with research: Pat Albright, Suzie Fleming, Solveig Francis, Mary Hawryshkiw, Anne Neale. I am also grateful to Selma James for her analysis, particularly in *Sex, Race and Class* (Falling Wall Press, Bristol, UK, 1975) and *The Power of Women and the Subversion of the Community* (Falling Wall Press, 1972). This essay reflects years of organising experience shared by women in The Wages for Housework campaign.

1. King, Martin Luther, Jr., *Why We Can't Wait,* p. 24, Mentor Books, The New American Library, New York, 1964.

2. *Ibid.,* p. 137.

3. 'Pay Women Not the Military', *Wages for Housework Campaign Journal,*
p. 6, Spring 1982.

4. Chowka, Peter Barry, 'Cancer Research: the $20 Billion Failure', *East West Journal,* p. 37, March 1981.

5. Northrup, Christiane, MD., 'Examining Cancer: A Doctor's Diagnosis', *East West Journal,* p. 52, March 1983.

6. Chowka, Peter Barry, 'Separate and Unequal', *East West Journal,* p. 66, July 1981.

7. *Ibid.,* p. 67.

8. Passwater, Dr Richard, A., *Cancer and its Nutritional Therapies,* pp. 48–49, Keats Publishing, Connecticut, 1978.

9. Chowka, Peter Barry, 'Separate and Unequal', *East West Journal*, p. 66, July 1981.

10. Orth, Maureen, 'The Hot Political Issues of the 80s', *Vogue*, p. 291, April 1981.

11. Hall, Eve, *Forum 80*, p. 4, 17 July 1980.

12. Jones, Maggie, *Forum 80*, p. 7, 15 July 1980.

13. Steady, Filomina, 'In Sickness and in Health', *Unicef News*, p. 14, 104, No. 2, 1980, Unicef Information Division, New York.

14. Chowka, Peter Barry, 'Separate and Unequal', *East West Journal*, p. 66, July 1981.

15. *Ibid.*, p.68.

16. Northrup, Christiane, MD., *op. cit*, p. 52.

17. Theodores, Martin and Showstack, Randy, *Whole Life Times*, No. 16, p.13, Jan-Feb 1982.

18. Chowka, Peter Barry, 'Cancer Research: the $20 Billion Failure', *East West Journal*, p. 37, March 1981.

19. 'Pay Women Not the Military', *op. cit.*, (information provided by Campaign Against the Arms Trade).

20. Power of Women Collective, 'The Home in the Hospital', in *All Work and No Pay*, edited by Wendy Edmund and Suzie Fleming, p. 88, Falling Wall Press, Bristol, 1975.

21. *Ibid.*, p. 85.

22. *Ibid.*, p. 73.

23. *Ibid.*, p. 75.

24. Kushi, Michio, *Natural Healing Through Macrobiotics*, edited by Edward Esko with Marc van Cauwenberghe, MD., p. 43, Japan Publications, Tokyo, 1979.

25. Domencich, Mrs Loretta, 'The Welfare System is an Indian-Giver', *Welfare Mothers Speak Out*, p. 59, Milwaukee County Welfare Rights Organisation, W.W. Norton & Co. Inc., New York, 1972.

26. Downer, Mrs Cassie B., 'Guaranteed Adequate Income Now', *ibid.*, p. 135.

27. Milwaukee County Welfare Rights Organisation, Welfare Mothers Speak Out, pp. 31–39, W.W. Norton & Co. Inc., New York 1972.

28. Sanders, Mrs Beulah, *ibid.*, p. 124.

29. Prescod-Roberts, Margaret and Steele, Norma, *Black Women: Bringing It All Back Home*, pp. 45–48, Falling Wall Press, Bristol, 1980.

Chapter 10: Thought for Food (pp. 91–100)

1. Yudkin, John, *Pure White and Deadly*, Davis-Poynter, London, 1972.

2. Wright, Hannah, *Swallow it Whole: The New Statesman's Survival Guide to the Food Industry*, New Statesman Report, No. 4, London, 1981.

3. George, Susan, *How the Other Half Dies*, Penguin, London, 1976.

4. Schustan, Claudio, 'The Challenge of Feeding People', *Social Science and Medicine*, Vol. 13C, No. 2, 1979.

5. Moore Lappé, Frances, and Collins, Joseph, *World Hunger: Ten Myths*, Institute for Food and Development Policy, US, 1978.

6. *Science for People*, Vol. 34, from British Society for Social Responsibility in Science, 9 Poland Street, London W1.

7. *Food and Profit*, The Politics of Health Group, Pamphlet no. 1, from BSSRS (address as above).

8. Leghorn, Lisa, and Parker, Katherine, *Woman's Worth*, Routledge & Kegan Paul, London and Boston, 1981.

9. See Chetley, Andy, 'The Baby Killer Scandal', for War on Want, 467 Caledonian Road, London N1, 1979.

10. See also Melrose, Dianna, 'The Great Health Robbery', Oxfam, 274 Banbury Road, Oxford, 1981.

Further Reading:

Doyal, Lesley, *The Political Economy of Health*, Pluto, London, 1981.
Tudge, Colin, *The Famine Business*, Pelican, London 1977.
Ledogar, Robert J., *Hungry for Profits*, IDOC/North America, New York, USA, 1975.

Chapter 11: The Power to Feed Ourselves (pp. 101–106)

1. See e.g. Godelier, Maurice, 'Perspectives in Marxist Anthropology', translated from the French by Robert Brain, *Cambridge Studies in Social Anthropology*, 8, pp. 105–6, Cambridge University Press, Cambridge, 1977. The concepts here apparently originate with Claude Lévi-Strauss, with his 'absolute priority of patrilineal institutions over matrilineal institutions', and permeate more conventional as well as Marxist approaches. Lévi-Strauss, Claude, *The Elementary Structures of Kinship*, translated from the French by James Harle Bell, John Richard von Sturmer and Rodney Needham, p. 116, Eyre and Spottiswoode, London, 1969.

2. See Douglas, Mary, 'Is Matriliny Doomed in Africa', in Mary Douglas and Phyllis M. Kaberry (eds) *Man in Africa*, Tavistock Publications, London, 1969.

3. Achola, A. Pala, *African Women in Rural Development: Research Trends and Priorities*, Overseas Liaison Committee Paper, No. 12, American Council on Education, Washington DC, 1976.

4. de Wilde, John C., *Experiences with Agricultural Development in Tropical Africa, Vol. 1: The Synthesis*, p. 142, published for the International Bank for Reconstruction and Development, John Hopkins University Press, Baltimore, 1976.

5. de Wilde, *op cit.*, pp. 140–141.

6. Kinsey, Bill H., *Rural Development in Malawi: a Review of the Lilongwe Land Development Programme*, p. 1, African Rural Development Study Background Paper, IBRD, (mimeo), Washington DC, 1974.

7. Hanger, Jane and Morris, Jon, 'Women and the Household Economy',

in Robert Chambers and Jon Morris (eds), *Mwea: an Irrigated Rice Settlement in Kenya*, pp. 210–211, *Afrika Studien*, 83, Institute für Wirtschaftsforschung, Weltforum, Munchen, 1973.

8. *Ibid., passim.*

9. *Ibid.*, pp. 124–25.

10. Brain, James L., 'Less than Second-class', in Nancy J. Hafkin and Edna G. Bay (eds), *Women in Africa: Studies in Social and Economic Change*, pp. 275, 279, Stanford University Press, Stanford, California, 1976.

11. Société Africaine d'Etudes de Développement (SAED), *Etude sur les Besoins des Femmes dans les Villages de l'A.V.V. et Proposition d'un Programme d'Intervention,* p. 32, Ouagadougou, translation by the author. Autorité des Aménagements des Vallées des Volta, Ministère du Développement Rural, 1977.

12. *Ibid.*, p. 6.

13. See Haswell, Margaret, *Economics of Development in Village India,* chapter I, Routledge and Kegan Paul, London, 1967. Also Hunter, Guy, *The Administration of Agricultural Development: Lessons from India,* p. 20, Oxford University Press, 1970.

14. Farmer, B.H., *Pioneer Peasant Colonisation in Ceylon*, pp. 207, 290, Oxford University Press, 1957.

15. Swift, M.G., 'Capital, Saving and Credit in a Malay Peasant Economy', in Raymond Firth and E.S. Yamey (eds) *Capital, Saving and Credit in Peasant Societies: Studies from Asia, Oceania, the Caribbean and Latin America*, pp. 147–8, George Allen and Unwin, London, 1964.

16. Frank, André Gunder, *Capitalism and Underdevelopment in Latin America: Historical Studies of Chile and Brazil*, p. 28, Monthly Review Press, New York, 1969.

17. Garrett, Patricia M., *Some Structural Constraints on the Agricultural Activities of Women: the Chilean Hacienda*, Research Paper No. 70, p. 28, Land Tenure Centre, Madison, Wisc., 1976.

18. *Ibid.*, pp. 1, 36.

Further Reading:

Rogers, Barbara, *The Domestication of Women: Discrimination in Developing Societies*, Tavistock Press, London, 1981. This covers in more detail the ideas in this article.

Chapter 16: Gaea: The Earth as Our Spiritual Heritage (pp. 131–135)

1. I have spelled Gaea with an 'e', since this is quite simply a more powerful spelling for women than 'Gaia'.

1. Individual spellings of key words such as these (see also Chapter 27) have been retained at the request of the authors.

2. I have used the word 'masculist' rather than 'masculinist', as it denotes more directly the notion of supporting male supremacy and the values attendant thereon.

3. Ross, A., *Pagan Celtic Britain*, Routledge and Kegan Paul, London, 1967; Boston, Mass., 1967.

4. Howard-Gordon, Frances, *Glastonbury: Maker of Myths*, Gothic Image, Glastonbury, 1982.

5. Rudd, E. (ed), *Dragons*, W.H. Allen, London, 1980.

6. Lee, C., *Further Thoughts on Feminism*, Lamia Publications, BM-Liberation, London WC1N 3XX.

7. This spelling of our name identifies our autonomous existence according to our gyn-ecology.

Chapter 18: All of One Flesh: (pp. 141–151)

1. I shall call these creatures 'animals' here although I would rather call them non-human animals because, of course, we are all animals.

2. Singer, Peter, *Animal Liberation: A New Ethics for our Treatment of Animals*, Avon Books, New York, 1977.

3. Bryant, John, *Fettered Kingdoms: An Examination of a Changing Ethic*, Ferne House, Wansbrook, Chard, Somerset, 1982.

4. The Vegetarian Society has now advised that 'a new Council . . . has been elected to serve 1982–83. This new Council has already reversed the earlier decision and we can now accept advertisements from groups and magazines such as yours . . . I, the editor, have been asked by the General Secretary to point out to you that we have already lost at least one member because of this.' Letter from Bronwen Humphreys, Editor *The Vegetarian*, dated 18 January, 1983.

5. Shafts, *A Paper for Women and the Working Classes*, 1892 (available from the Fawcett Library, London.)

6. Vyvyan, John, *In Pity and In Anger*, Michael Joseph, London, 1969.

7. Adams, Carol, 'The Oedible Complex: Feminism and Vegetarianism', *The Lesbian Reader*, Amazon Press, 1975.

8. Salt, Henry, *Animals' Rights*, Society for Animal Rights Inc., Clarks Summit, Pennsylvania, 1980.

9. Singer, *op. cit.*

10. Duffy, Maureen, 'Why Animal Lovers Become Hunt Saboteurs', *The Times*, 12 April 1978.

11. Neslen, Kristie, *The Origin*, Venusian Propaganda, San Francisco, 1979.

12. Mauras, Gisele, 'About Feminism and Animal Liberation', *Sequel*, No. 27 London Sept/Oct 1982.

13. Schleifer, Harriet, Reviews: *Pornography: Men Possessing Women* by Andrea Dworkin, *Ordeal* by Linda Lovelace in *Agenda*, magazine of the Animal Rights Network, P.O. Box 5234, Westport, Ct. 06881, USA.

14. Photographic centrefold (uncredited) *Zig Zag*, No. 129, August 1982, 118 Talbot Rd, London W11, UK.

15. Vyvyan, *op. cit.*

16. Brophy, Brigid, 'The Rights of Animals'. This is from a slightly up-

dated version of an essay first published in *The Sunday Times* in 1965, and subsequently included in *Don't Never Forget*, Jonathan Cape, London, 1966.

17. Miller, Jane, *A Calf is Born*, Dent, London, 1981.

18. Neslen, *op. cit.*

Chapter 20: Invisible Casualties (pp. 155–159)

1. Marwick, Arthur, *Women at Work*, Fontana, London, 1978.

Chapter 21: Alternative Technology (pp. 160–165)

1. Slocum, Sally, 'Woman the Gatherer: Male Bias in Anthropology' (1971) quoted in Judy Smith, 'Women and Appropriate Technology – Something Old, Something New, Something Borrowed, Something Due', Women and Technology Project, 3155, 4th E Missoula, MT 59801, USA, October, 1980.

2. Wallsgrove, Ruth, 'The Masculine Face of Science', *Alice through the Microscope: The Power of Science over Women's Lives*, Brighton Women and Science Group, Virago, London, 1980.

3. 'Introductory Booklet', Girls into Science and Technology Project (GIST), Manchester Polytechnic, 9A Didsbury Park, Didsbury, Manchester, 1981.

4. Zimmerman, Jan, 'Technology and the Future of Women: Haven't we Met Somewhere Before?', *Women's Studies International Quarterly*, Vol. 4, No. 3, 1981.

5. Griffin, Susan, *Woman and Nature – The Roaring inside Her*, Harper & Row, New York, 1978.

6. Reuther, Rosemary Radford, *New Woman/New Earth: Sexist Ideologies and Human Liberation*, The Seabury Press, New York, 1975.

7. Dickson, David, *Alternative Technology and the politics of Technical Change*, Fontana, London, 1974.

8. Dickson, *op. cit.*

9. Elliot, Ruth, 'Women and AT', *Undercurrents*, 17, Aug/Sept, 1976.

10. Smith, Judy, 'Women and Appropriate Technology – Something Old, Something New, Something Borrowed, Something Due', Women and Technology Project. See above ref 1 for details.

11. McCormack, Margaret, 'A Feminist Perspective', *Social Policy*, Dec, 1977.

12. Smith, *op. cit.*

13. Fee, Elizabeth, 'A Feminist Critique of Scientific Objectivity', *Science for the People*, Vol. 14, No. 4, July/Aug, 1982.

Other Sources:

'Women and Technology: Deciding What's Appropriate', Conference Proceedings, Women's Resource Centre, Missoula, Montana USA, 1979.

Undercurrents, No. 29 Aug/Sep 1979 on 'Women and Energy' and No. 46 June/July 1981 on 'Women in Coops'.

Women's Studies International Quarterly, Vol. 4, No. 3, 1981, a special issue on 'Women, Technology and Innovation'.

Scarlet Women, No. 14, Jan 1982 on 'Women and New Technology'.

'Taking Hold of Technology', CoMann, Gee, Bush, American Association of University Women, Washington USA, 1982.

Chapter 25: Saving Trees, Saving Lives (pp. 182–188)

1. Agarwal, Anil, 'Gandhi's Ghost Saves the Himalayan Trees', *New Scientist*, 14 August 1975.

2. Agarwal, Anil and Anand, Anita, 'Ask the Women Who Do the Work', *New Scientist*, 4 November 1982.

3. Joshi, Gopa, 'Men Propose, Women Oppose the Destruction of Forests', *Center for Science & Environment*, 1982.

4. Agarwal, Anil and Anand, Anita, 'Ask the Women Who Do the Work', *New Scientist*, 4 November 1982.

Chapter 26: Time for Women: (pp. 189–197)

1. Teriet, B, 'Technical Progress and the Arrangement of Working Time', *Labour and Society*, Vol. 7, No. 2, April/June, 1982.

2. Greenhalgh, C. and Stewart, M., 'The Training and Experiences Dividend', *Employment Gazette*, August, 1982.

3. Handy, C. in 'The Redistribution of Work', Turning Point Paper, No. 1.

4. Kanter, R., *Men and Women of the Corporation*, Basic Books, New York, 1972.

5. Cooper, G. and Davidson, M., *High Pressure : Working Lives of Women Managers*, Fontana, London, 1982.

6. Rothwell, S., 'Women and Working Time', *Equal Opportunities International*, Vol. 1, No. 1, 1981; Rothwell, S., 'Work Paid and Unpaid', *Resurgence*, Spring, 1981.

7. Syrett, M., 'How to Make Job Sharing Work', *Personnel Management*, October 1982; Dungate, M. 'Will Two Into One Go?', *Initiatives*, August 1982; Goodhart, P., 'Stand on Your Own Four Feet', *Bow Group*, 1982.

8. Manpower Services Commission, *Manpower Review, 1982*, Manpower Services Commission, 1982.

9. House of Lords Select Committee on the European Communities, 'Voluntary Part-time Work', *House of Lords Paper*, 216, HMSO, 1982.

10. Beechey, V., 'Part-time Work in Coventry', publication forthcoming.

11. Toffler, A., *The Third Wave*, Collins, London, 1980.

12. Bird, E., *Information Technology in the Office*, Equal Opportunities Commission, 1980; Tenne, R., 'Training for the Electronic Office', *Employment Gazette*, June, 1981.

13. Jahoda, M., 'The Psychological Meaning of Unemployment', *New*

Society, 6 September 1979.

14. Yohalem, A., ed, *Women Returning to Work : Policies & Progress in Five Countries*, Marion Boyars, London, 1981.

15. Marsh, A., *Women and Shiftwork*, OPCS, HMSO, 1979.

16. Roberts, K., 'Employment and Automation: Towards a National Dividend Scheme', *Computer Bulletin*, June, 1981.

17. Novarra, V., *Women's Work, Men's Work*, Marion Boyars, London, 1980.

18. Oakley, A., *Sociology of Housework*, Martin Robertson, London, 1974; Davidoff, L., 'Rationalisation of Housework' in D. Leonard and S. Allen, *Dependence and Exploitation in Work and Marriage*, Longman, London, 1976.

19. Scharf, B., 'Sexual Satisfaction and Social Satisfaction', *British Journal of Sociology*, Vol. 28, No. 4, December, 1977.

20. Green, H., 'Temporal Attitudes in Four Negro Sub-cultures', in Fraser, Haber and Muller, *The Study of Time*, Springer Verlag, W. Germany, 1972; Jackson, A.P., 'Time Perspective and Personality', Henley (unpublished thesis).

21. Gershuny, J., 'The Informal Economy', *Futures*, February, 1979; Alden, J., 'A Comparative Analysis of Moonlighting in Britain and the USA', *Industrial Relations Journal*, Spring, 1982; Clark, G., 'Recent Developments in Working Patterns', Manpower Services Commission, *op. cit*, pp. 20–21.

22. Dyson, W., *Towards a New Work and Income Orientation*, Varnier Institute of the Family, Ottawa, 1976.

23. Mason, S. and Martin, B., *Leisure and Work: the Choices for 1991 and 2001*, Leisure Consultants, 1982.

24. Williams, B., 'Technology, Economic Growth and Unemployment', *Policy Studies*, January, 1982.

25. Owen, J., *Working Hours*, Lexington Books, New York, 1979.

26. Robertson, James, *The Sane Alternative*, J. Robertson, London, 1978.

Chapter 27: Personal, Political and Planetary Play (pp. 198–202)

*To the author 'woman' has the connotation of 'men with wombs', whereas 'womon' is a word without such a connotation – although making a connection with the moon. The author has asked that the distinctive spelling of this, and other, key words be retained.

Neville, Richard, *Play Power*, Paladin Books, London, 1971.

Orlick, Terry, *The Co-operative Sports and Games Book*, Pantheon, New York, 1978, Writers and Readers' Cooperative, London, 1979.

Griffin, Susan, *Pornography and Silence*, The Women's Press, London, 1981.

Gearheart, Sally, *The Wanderground, Stories of the Hill Women*, Persephone Press, Watertown, Mass., 1978.

Ward, Colin, *The Child in the City*, Architectural Press, London, 1978.

Arguelles, Miriam and Jose, *The Feminine, Spacious as the Sky*, Shambala Publications, Colorado, USA, 1977.

Meeker, Joseph, *The Comedy of Survival*, Scribners, New York, 1980.

Pedler, Kit, *The Quest for Gaia: a Book of Changes*, Souvenir Press, London, 1979.

Daly, Mary, *Gyn/Ecology*, The Women's Press, London, 1978.

Chapter 28: the Warp and the Weft (pp. 203–214)

1. For the origin of the Gaia hypothesis, see: Lovelock, James, *Gaia: A New Look at Life on Earth*, Oxford University Press, Oxford, 1979.

2. For example: Jantsch, Erich, *The Self-Organising Universe*, Pergamon, New York, 1980.

3. *Brain-Mind Bulletin*, PO Box 42111, Los Angeles, California, 90042, USA.

4. Ferguson, Marilyn, *The Aquarian Conspiracy*, Tarcher, Los Angeles, 1980; Routledge & Kegan Paul, London, 1981.

5. Sheldrake, Rupert, *A New Science of Life*, Tarcher, Los Angeles, 1980; Blond and Briggs, London, 1981.

6. A term coined by Robert Theobold to denote a leadership of wisdom which is recognised and operates by attraction and loyalty.

7. Prigogine, Ilya, *From Being to Becoming*, W.H. Freeman, San Francisco, 1981.

8. Jaynes, Julian, *The Origin of Consciousness in the Breakdown of the Bi-Cameral Mind*, Houghton Mifflin, Boston, 1976.

9. Wilber, Ken, *Up from Eden*, Doubleday, New York, 1981; Routledge & Kegan Paul, London, 1983.

10. A comprehensive guide to this literature is contained in Charlene Spretnak, ed, *The Politics of Women's Spirituality*, Doubleday, New York, 1981.

11. See, for example, Lederer, Wolfgang, *The Fear of Women*, Harcourt Brace, New York, 1968.

12. 'Catching up with Parents Who Don't Pay Child Support', *Christian Science Monitor*, 18 February 1982.

13. Henderson, Hazel, *The Politics of the Solar Age*, Chapter 13, Doubleday, New York, 1981.

14. See for example Maturana, H., and Varela, F., 'Autopoiesis and Cognition', *Boston University Studies in Philosophy of Science*, Reidel, Dordrecht, Holland, 1980.

Suggested Further Reading Relating to Eco-feminism:

Barfoot, Joan, *Gaining Ground*, The Women's Press, London, 1978 (fiction).

Brighton Women and Science Group, *Alice Through the Microscope: The Power of Science over Women's Lives*, Virago, London, 1980.

Caldicott, Dr. Helen, *Nuclear Madness*, Bantam Books, New York, 1980.

Carson, Rachel, *Silent Spring*, Penguin Books, Middlesex, 1965.

Colegrave, Sukie, *The Spirit of the Valley*, Virago, London, 1979.

Daly, Mary, *Gyn/Ecology: The Metaethics of Radical Feminism*, The Women's Press, London, 1978.

Dillard, Annie, *Pilgrim at Tinker Creek*, Harpers Magazine Press, New York, 1974.

Feminism and Nonviolence Study Group, *Piecing it Together: Feminism and Nonviolence*, available direct from the group at 2 College Close, Buckleigh, Westwood Ho, Devon EX39 1BL, UK.

Gearheart, Sally Miller, *The Wanderground: Stories of the Hill Women*, Persephone Press, Watertown, Mass., 1978 (fiction).

Gilman, Charlotte Perkins, *Herland*, The Women's Press, London, 1979 (fiction).

Griffin, Susan, *Woman and Nature, The Roaring Inside Her*, Harper & Row, New York, 1978; *Pornography and Silence*, The Women's Press, London, 1981; *Made from this Earth*, The Women's Press, London, 1982.

Gyorgy, Anna, *No Nukes: Everyone's Guide to Nuclear Power*, Southend Press, Boston, Mass., 1979.

Hall, Nor, *The Moon and the Virgin*, The Women's Press, London, 1980.

Henderson, Hazel, *Creating Alternative Futures: The End of Economics*, Berkley Publishing Corporation, New York, 1978; *The Politics of the Solar Age*, Doubleday, New York, 1981.

Jones, Lynne (ed), *Keeping the Peace*, The Women's Press, London, 1983.

Koen, Susan and Swain, Nina, *Ain't Nowhere We Can Run: Handbook for Women on the Nuclear Mentality*, WAND, Box 801, Norwich, VT., 05055, USA, 1980.

Leghorn, Lisa, and Parker, Katherine, *Woman's Worth: Sexual Economics and the World of Women*, Routledge and Kegan Paul, London, 1981.

Lessing, Doris, *Shikasta*, Jonathan Cape Ltd, London, 1979 (fiction).

Luke, Helen M, *The Way of Women Ancient and Modern*, Apple Farm Press, Michigan, US.

McAllister, Pam, *Reweaving the Web of Life: Feminism and Nonviolence*, New Society Publishers, Philadelphia, 1982.

Merchant, Carolyn, *The Death of Nature: Women, Ecology and the Scientific Revolution*, Wildwood House, London, 1982.

Murphy, Yolanda and Robert F, *Women of the Forest*, Columbia University Press, New York, 1974.

Neslen, Kristie, *The Origin: An investigation into ancient matriarchal societies, the patriarchal takeover and its effect on society today, and the building of a just and egalitarian post-patriarchal society*, Venusian Propaganda, San Francisco, 1979.

Piercy, Marge, *Woman on the Edge of Time*, The Women's Press, London, 1979 (fiction).

Reuther, Rosemary Radford, *New Woman/New Earth: Sexist Ideologies and Human Liberation*, The Seabury Press, New York, 1975.

Shuttle, Penelope and Redgrove, Peter, *The Wise Wound*, Victor Gollancz Ltd, London, 1978.

Sigmund, Elizabeth, *Rage Against the Dying*, Pluto Press, London, 1980.

Singer, Peter, *Animal Liberation: A New Ethics for our Treatment of Animals*, Avon Books, New York, 1977.

Spretnak, Charlene, *The Politics of Women's Spirituality*, Doubleday, New York, 1981.

Thompson, Dorothy ed, *Over Our Dead Bodies: Women Against the Bomb*, Virago, London, 1983.

Ulanov, Ann Bedford, *The Feminine: in Jungian Psychology and Christian Theology*, Northwestern University Press, Evanston, 1971.

Wittig, Monique, *Les Guerrillères*, The Women's Press, London, 1977 (fiction).

Notes on the Contributors

Anita Anand was born in West Bengal, India in 1949. She has academic and work experience in India and the United States. Her academic work is in Education and Political Science. Anita has lived in the US since 1973, going to school and working in several areas. She has designed and taught courses at the university level, evaluated rural development programmes, and organised food and tenants' cooperatives. Currently she is living in Washington DC and working as a public policy analyst with the United Methodist Church. She travels, takes photographs, does workshops, writes, and thinks a lot.

Ngahuia Te Awekotuku was raised among the Te Arawa people. She recently completed a PhD in the United States, and is currently employed by the University of Waikato.

Norma Benney was born in New Zealand. At present she is living in London, putting gynergies into co-editing a lesbian/feminist magazine *Sequel*, and writing and campaigning for animal rights.

Rosalie Bertell is a member of the Order of Grey Nuns, and worked on the Tri-State Leukemia Survey at the Roswell Park National Cancer Research Institute in Buffalo, New York, until her involvement with the nuclear issue led to her resignation. A skilled scientist specialising in biometrics (the application of mathematics to living systems) she has continued her controversial work under the auspices of the Ministry of Concern for Public Health in Toronto, Canada, travelling the world to gather data and disseminate information both among specialists (she recently set up a new journal called *International Perspectives in Public Health*) and the anti-nuclear movement at large.

Wilmette Brown was an organiser in the civil rights, Black power and peace movements in the US during the 1960s. She taught secondary school in Zambia in the early 70s. She is co-founder of Black Women for Wages for Housework and joint coordinator of the King's Cross

240

Women's Centre in London (at 71 Tonbridge Street, WC1, Tel: 837 7509). Wilmette is a lesbian woman. In November 1982, she participated in the twelve-day occupation of the Church of the Holy Cross in London, with the English Collective of Prostitutes. She is the author of *Black Women and the Peace Movement*, and welcomes opportunities for speaking and discussion around these issues.

Liz Butterworth has lived in East Anglia for over ten years, and is now regional contact for *Women for Life on Earth* in the area. The rapid development of the women's movement in East Anglia has coincided, she says, with the increasingly obvious military presence there. 'When I started talking with other women at a gut level, I saw that we couldn't stop at one aspect of the problem. We started airing our feelings about a whole host of things, feelings which until then had been hard to talk about because they didn't fit with the establishment view. Looking at the food question was a very personal way of putting my own feelings about my body, after nine years of having babies, into the context of the horrific things happening in the world outside.'

Jean Freer has been politically active campaigning and organising since the early sixties. A lesbian, she founded the Feminist Archive, a women's reference library and museum based in Bath, UK. She has written two books, *Further Thoughts on Feminism or What is to be Done* (as Carol Lee) and *Toward a Reclaimed Tarot*, as well as helping to produce a collection of poetry, *Under Wide Waters*, as a member of Bath Feminist Writers. Her commitment to peace and women's liberation inevitably focussed her attention on ethical questions. A priestess of the goddess Diana, Jean has recently initiated a grove of witches who are reclaiming womyn's wisdom and power as healers and seers.

Hazel Henderson describes herself as 'an independent futurist' and says she has always been a political activist. Her latest book is *The Politics of the Solar Age* (Doubleday, New York, 1981). She recently created a weekly television series called 'Creating Alternative Futures' which was aired from the University of Florida in Gainesville, USA, where she lives.

Frances Howard-Gordon is a freelance journalist and active campaigner for women's rights, living and working in Glastonbury, Somerset, UK. 'Translating *Seveso is Everywhere* has been an incredible experience for me. Though I knew about the incident and the amorality that is generally practised by big business, I had never before felt so totally and personally involved. It has made me even

241

more aware that it is the strength, wisdom and passionate non-violent caring for life of women that will stop the governments and multi-nationals from eroding our lives and threatening the future of our children.'

Ynestra King is on the faculty of the Goddard College Institute for Social Ecology. She has worked as a professional community organiser and been politically active for over ten years, most recently in the women's and anti-nuclear movements. She is at present writing a book on feminism and ecology, *Feminism and the Re-enchantment of the World*, which further develops the ideas and vision out of which Women and Life on Earth originally germinated.

Penelope Leach trained as a social worker at LSE after a history degree at Cambridge. 'We were supposed to provide families with answers but I had only questions. Home Office research into Juvenile Crime showed that nobody had any answers: borstal and probation produced identical non-effects. Back at LSE I did a PhD in social psychology, learned how to ask questions and, thanks to the Medical Research Council, spent the next years asking how human infants actually develop and how they and their parents affect each other.

'Research data was only for the "experts". Other parents (we had a daughter by now) weren't being told what is, or what is not, known about children and parenting. So I wrote *Babyhood* and then *Baby and Child*.

'But just giving out information and opinions isn't enough. We had a son as well by now and I was involved in PPA, with STOPP and a lot of self-help and community groups. They were, and still are, working against social attitudes which ignore the needs of human beings and of people-who-are-parenting. I wrote *Who Cares?* in two furious months and it was published as Mrs Thatcher took office. The fight for a society for people rather than people for society is still on.'

Lesley Merryfinch was born and brought up in the West of Scotland and worked as coordinator of the Campaign Against Arms Trade, before going to work for Amnesty International. She came into the peace movement in 1971 through anti-Vietnam War activities in Paris and in 1976 she discovered to her great joy the women's liberation movement. Since 1977 she has been part of a feminism and non-violence study group. She is a lesbian, aged 32 and she loves playing and listening to the cello.

Jill Raymond has followed her vocation as a weaver since 1970. She first used homœopathic treatment for hepatitis, in the winter of 1980, since her orthodox GP's attitude only added to her despair and illness rather than inspiring any kind of healing. The writing of her article was made possible through the sharing and respect she and Jan Wilson initially experienced together in their consciousness-raising women's group.

Barbara Rogers is a writer and political activist whose work has been mostly in international issues, especially the Third World and the role of women there. She has also worked extensively in South Africa. Her interests have extended to British politics, and she is now a Labour Councillor in the London Borough of Islington. She has written a book for the Women's Press, *52%: Getting Women's Power Into Politics*, calling for a complete change in the way political parties formulate issues, if they are to be relevant to women and win women's support.

Sheila Rothwell is Director of the Centre for Employment Policy Studies at Henley – The Management College. She has researched and lectured in industrial relations and personnel management at London School of Economics, and was Assistant Secretary (Negotiations) of the National Union of Bank Employees, and then Assistant Chief Executive of the Equal Opportunities Commission. Her current interests include collective bargaining and worker participation; future trends in employment and unemployment; women's career patterns; technological change and skill re-deployment.

Hazel Selina works as a Metamorphic Technique practitioner and lives in Devon with her husband Peter and two girls, Lauri and Zoe.

Lin Simonon has been working with the Hackney Play Association and the Hackney Borough Council creating parks designed with the help and the imagination of the local people. 'My feminism is about being a womon in a world of men, of predominantly male values, where children are not a part of our culture, but are compartmentalised into schools. As a womon who has chosen not to have children I need contact with children to learn from them. My work, oftentimes my play, is about co-designing playspaces, learning places with children.'

Manami Suzuki is a member of the still embryonic Japanese Green Movement. She has been active in the anti-nuclear campaign, working with Friends of the Earth, Greenpeace and Gensuikin, the Japan Congress against A and H bombs. Manami also works as a journalist and translator, and is interested in issues ranging from Japanese exploitation of Third World countries and the nuclear-free Pacific campaign, to food and holistic health.

Christine Thomas has a long involvement with the environmental and alternative technology movements. She has recently been working with the Alternative Technology Group at the Open University, and during this time became involved in starting the NATTA (Network for Alternative Technology and Technology Assessment) Women and Technology Group. Currently she is struggling to pursue these interests while caring for her first baby.

Jan Wilson is a mother of two and a single parent. Her experiences as a young widow have made her very aware of a woman's place in society. She has been studying homœopathic medicine since September 1981. Both feminism and homœopathy have enabled her to unlock many old patterns.

Nancy Worcester has been involved in the women's movement since the late 60s. 'Groups particularly important to me have included the North Kensington Socialist Feminist Group (early 70s), the Women and Science – London Group, and the Politics of Health Group, especially its Women's Health Information Centre Collective. Professionally, my background is in nutrition, but in 1976 I gave up my rats and test tubes for people and changed to work in adult education as a course organiser and tutor of nutrition, health, and women's studies courses.'

Margaret Wright was born in Benwell, Newcastle-upon-Tyne, and has lived most of her life on Tyneside. She joined the Ecology Party in 1978 and is active in the Green Movement, which led to her involvement with Hexham Peace Camp and Ouston Peace Camp in 1982. She has recently moved to be by the Bridge in St Ives, in Cambs, UK. Some of her poetry has been published in *Walking on the Water*, Virago, 1983.

Caroline Wyndham is a photographer and journalist and a founder member of Women for Life on Earth. An active campaigner in the Women's Peace Movement, she is currently working as a trainer in nonviolent direct action. She lives with her three children in South Devon.

Marta Zabaleta is an Argentinian, 45 years old, and an economist specialising in development. Both she and her Chilean husband are exiles, living in the UK since 1976. Both have spent time in prison – in Argentina and Chile, respectively. She has spent her entire life

244

struggling against poverty and injustice with the help and support of people from many different ideologies from all over the world. Her only concern is to help to construct a society which encompasses the hopes and ideals for which many of her friends in Argentina and Chile have given their lives. She is presently working on a book about ideology, consciousness and political mobilisation for women in Argentina.

About Women for Life on Earth

Women for Life on Earth is a network whose primary purpose is to provide a means of linking together and support for women working in different ways towards similar goals. We support each other in non-violent direct action, such as our march from Cardiff to Greenham Common U.S. Air Base in 1981 which resulted in the Women's Peace Camp at Greenham Common, and has inspired the setting up of many more peace camps in Britain, Europe, and the US.

We put women in touch with each other locally, nationally, and internationally, and publish a quarterly magazine as a means of sharing news, ideas, and creative expression relating to the Earth and the issues that affect us. We also have speakers, videos and educational material available for rallies, conferences, and local meetings. The proceeds of this book go to support this work.

Subscription details from: 2 St. Edmunds Cottages, Bove Town, Glastonbury, Somerset BA6 3JD, UK.